JERUSALEM EM

JERUSALEM EMBATTLED

A Diary of the City under Siege
March 25th, 1948 to July 18th, 1948

HARRY LEVIN

CASSELL

Cassell
Wellington House
125 Strand
London WC2R 0BB

PO Box 605
Herndon
VA 20172

First published by Victor Gollancz Ltd, 1950

This edition published by Cassell, 1997

British library Cataloguing-in-Publication Data
A catalogue record for this book is available from the British Library.

ISBN 0 304 33765 X

Printed and bound in Great Britain by Biddles Limited, Guildford and King's Lynn

TO THE MEMORY OF

TANCHIK

AND TO HIS COMRADES OF THE PALMACH

JERUSALEM UNDER SIEGE 1948

On 15 May 1948, following the departure of all British troops from Jerusalem, three Arab armies - those of Egypt, Iraq and the Arab Legion from Transjordan - together with Syrian troops, surrounded Jerusalem, bombarded the City, and sought to capture it. In four weeks, 170 Jewish civilians were killed and 1,000 were injured by Arab shellfire. A truce was signed on 11 June 1948. On 7 July, at the end of the truce, Israeli forces captured Ein Kerem from the Egyptian forces holding it.

'During the last few weeks we have succeed in substantially increasing our effective strength on land and in the air in all parts of the country. It is absolutely essential that Jewish Jerusalem shall continue to stand fas during these days of trial. Notwithstanding, the end of the fighting in the Old City, strenuous efforts to relieve Jerusalem and it surroundings are in hand and being pressed.. Be strong and of good courage'.

**DAVID BEN GURION,
MESSAGE TO JERUSALE
30 MAY 1948**

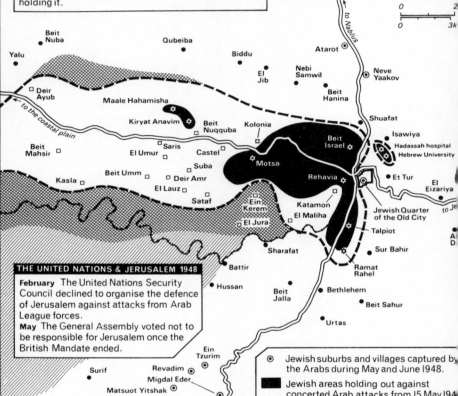

0   2
0   3k

to Nablus

Beit Nuba
Yalu
Qubeiba
Biddu
Atarot
Neve Yaakov
El Jib
Nebi Samwil
Deir Ayub
to the coastal plain
Maale Hahamisha
Kiryat Anavim
Beit Nuqquba
Kolonia
Beit Hanina
Shuafat
Isawiya
Hadassah hospital
Hebrew University
Beit Mahsir
Saris
El Umur
Castel
Suba
Deir Amr
El Lauz
Sataf
Beit Umm
Kasla
Motsa
Beit Israel
Rehavia
Et Tur
El Eizariya
to Je
Ein Kerem
Katamon
El Maliha
Jewish Quarter of the Old City
El Jura
Sharafat
Talpiot
Sur Bahir
Battir
Ramat Rahel
A D
Hussan
Beit Jalla
Bethlehem
Beit Sahur
Urtas

THE UNITED NATIONS & JERUSALEM 1948

February The United Nations Security Council declined to organise the defence of Jerusalem against attacks from Arab League forces.

May The General Assembly voted not to be responsible for Jerusalem once the British Mandate ended.

Ein Tzurim
Surif
Revadim
Migdal Eder
Matsuot Yitshak
Kfar Etzion
to Hebron
Beit Ummar

On 1 August the Israeli Government declared west Jerusalem to be occupied territory and appointed a Military Governor, Dov Joseph. On 17 September, following the assassination of the UN mediator, Count Bernadotte, by Jewish terrorists, the Israeli Government forcibly disbanded the terrorists, and in February 1949 declared west Jerusalem an intregal part of Israel.

⊙ Jewish suburbs and villages captured by the Arabs during May and June 1948.

■ Jewish areas holding out against concerted Arab attacks from 15 May 194 and completely cut off from the coast.

□ Arab suburbs and villages captured by Israeli forces, May to June 1948, and abandoned by their Arab inhabitants.

- - Front line between the Israeli and Arab forces at the first cease-fire.

▨ Captured by Israeli forces between the first and second cease-fires.

▨ Captured by Israeli forces, October 194

● Arab villages occupied by Transjordan i 1948, and forming part of Jordan until 196

© Martin Gilbert 1977

INTRODUCTION

THE STORY OF JERUSALEM is 2,900 years old. There was a city here 1,000 years earlier. But the real story of Jerusalem begins with David, King of Judah.

Labouring to win peace for his people, David at last united the tribes of Judah and Israel. But biting into his flank between the northern territory and the southern lay the old, battle-beaten fortress of the Jebusites, Urusalim, the last post held by the enemies of Israel. In an action of superb skill and courage, David conquered it. He made it his capital, and called it Jerusalem.

Belonging neither to the tribes of the north nor to those of the south, it was acceptable to both as the centre of their new unity. Its main value lay in its location. High up on a broad, naked ridge of Judea, it was difficult to attack. In itself the city was not much to boast of. It was primitive, lonely, poor in water or other resources, its shallow soil strewn with boulders. It possessed none of the natural conditions of a great city. But it could shelter David's throne and army and the religious treasures of his people. It was elevated and secluded, giving a wide view earthward and heavenward, a place where men might rise above earth-bound trammels and restraints. It could be the seed-bed of a new beginning for the united nation, and for the fulfilment of the worship of the One God His people had been the first to recognize.

The kingdom grew, and with it corruption and intrigue. The turbulent tribes set up rivals to Jerusalem. To emphasise their claims to independence, they created also gods of their own. Endless wars were waged, but their end was only to strengthen the bond between the secular life of the Hebrew people and their religious beliefs, and the centrality of Jerusalem. Over the generations the victories of Jerusalem over Bethel and its other rivals were both the triumph of true religion over false, and decisive stages in the development of national unity. The gathering of all Israel in Jerusalem on the great pilgrimage festivals not only consolidated the Temple as the heart of the faith of Israel; it also reaffirmed the unity of the Jewish nation.

But never was it given to the Jews to live in tranquillity in Jerusalem for long. In the clash and conflicts of empire, hegemony over this strategic land and its capital city passed from Power to Power. Down the vista of perpetual shifts and changes and realignments of those centuries runs the trail of storm and conquest of Jerusalem. Folly or malaise within frequently aided in its destruction. But seldom did it fall except after bitter siege and before overwhelming force. And always it rose again.

In little more than four centuries from the time of David, Jerusalem was sacked in turn by Egypt, Philistia, Arabia, Syria, Egypt again, and Babylon. The destruction by Babylon was complete. After a siege of eighteen months, Nebuchadnezzar's general "burnt the house of the Lord and the King's house and all the houses of Jerusalem. . . . The rest of the people that were left in the city did Nebuzaradan the captain of the guard carry away."

Outwardly the Hebrews were a decimated, disinherited, exiled nation. Nothing seemed left. But they carried with them their faith and devotion and the new spirit that had already reached consciousness in them, the spirit of the Holy Scriptures and the words of the prophets. They carried Jerusalem with them, and it was of Zion and Jerusalem that their poets dreamed and sang:

> *"If I forget thee, O Jerusalem,*
> *Let my right hand forget her cunning.*
> *Let my tongue cleave to the roof of my mouth,*
> *If I remember thee not. . . ."*

Fifty years after the razing of Jerusalem, Babylon was delivered into the hands of Cyrus, King of the Medes and Persians, who set the exiles free. They returned, and achieved the seemingly impossible. In the face of hardship and suffering, they restored the Temple, reconstituted themselves a people, and established the Second Jewish Commonwealth.

Persia passed, its power broken by Alexander the Great, and Jerusalem fell under the sway of the Greeks. Soon Alexander too, passed, and Jerusalem oscillated between Egypt and hellenised Syria, the contenders for succession to Alexander's Asian empire. Syria sought to force its hellenism on Judea, finally decreeing that Judaism be suppressed. Like the flare-up of a fire, the nation leapt into rebellion. For four years handfuls of tattered rebels under the Maccabees waged savage war against the great hosts of Syria, and routed them. Their first task was to cleanse the Temple and re-dedicate it to God. Then they passionately went on with the struggle. For twenty years they fought, until their triumph was complete. The last of the Syrians was driven from the land, and Judea and Jerusalem were independent.

In the eighty years that followed, the new splendour faded in the dusk of tragic conflict from within. The Roman eagle had been hovering over the East. Frustrated and in despair, the Pharisees, concerned only with the study of the Holy Law and its fulfilment, appealed for help to Rome. And Rome took over.

In 139 B.C.E. Rome passed a decree recognizing the independence of Judea; seventy-six years later it wiped Jerusalem off the map. Arbitrary and extortionate, Rome had soon roused against itself the flames of revolt. It quelled them swiftly and brutally. But revolt sprang out again and again. The hand of Rome grew heavier. Its armies pillaged the land and looted the Temple. Torn and bleeding, Judea resisted more stubbornly, and Rome retaliated more savagely.

By 66 C.E. it was full-scale war. Jerusalem was hermetically besieged. No valour could save it now. Yet starving, subjected to every kind of horror, the Jews held the might of Rome at bay until 70 C.E., fighting to their last inch of ground, until they could fight no more. Hundreds of thousands of them perished. The city was razed to the ground. Survivors were scattered as slaves through the Roman Empire.

The independence of Judea had long before this been suppressed. Jews remained in the land even after the dispersion and sixty-two years later even dared again to revolt against Rome. What marked the year 70 C.E. as the end of an epoch in Jewish history and the beginning of a revolution in the life of the Jews was the destruction of Jerusalem and the Temple.

Amidst the mounting tension and conflict with Rome, a young prophet arose, Joshua, who came to be known as Jesus of Nazareth and whose life and death were so profoundly to alter the history of the world. For the great number of his fellow Jews, writhing in the talons of Rome, his public ministry and tragic death passed unnoticed. But when the final dispersion of the Jews took place, a new religion had begun to arise out of the movement he set afoot. As it spread its sway, its centre receded from the place of its birth and established itself in other lands. In the currency of Western speech, Jerusalem and Zion came to have an ideal meaning. But for Judaism and the Jewish people Jerusalem remained obdurately concrete, the one and only centre; and from it they never looked away.

Into the Diaspora the Jews took with them the sacred covenant with their faith and the profound social and political ideas it inspired, and with the land and city in which that faith evolved and in which they grew to nationhood. Their vow never to forget

Jerusalem was implicit in the whole philosophy of Jewish life. "Remembering Zion" was woven not only into their daily liturgy, but also into the texture of their daily life, into its exalted moments and trivial, into its personal joys and sorrows, from birth to death. And working out their destiny through the bitter centuries of the Exile, belief in the divine promise of eventual Return gave them the steadfastness with which they have clung to their faith and national consciousness and endured unparalleled persecution.

On the site of Jerusalem the Romans built a city of their own, Ælia Capitolina. Then Rome declined and Jerusalem passed to the Eastern or Greek Empire. Its population now was predominantly Christian, although Jews had meanwhile returned. In 614 the Persians conquered it, but the Greek Emperor regained it thirteen years later. Then came a tide of conquest out of the deserts of Arabia. Mohammed had appeared. After a four-month siege in 634, Jerusalem surrendered to Caliph Omar. The Caliphs held it till 1077, and the city became a secondary sanctuary for Islam.

In 1099 the Western world surged back in the Crusades, and with them a horrifying wave of massacre of Moslems and Jews. Jerusalem became the capital of a Latin Kingdom. Eighty-eight years later Saladin reconquered it. By agreement with the Sultan in the thirteenth century, a Crusading Emperor held it again for a brief period. Then again the East swarmed back, and Jerusalem passed successively under the Tartars, Egyptians, Mamelukes and, finally, the Ottoman Turks, whose dominion lasted until our own time.

Throughout the centuries there were Jews who broke the shackles of the Exile and made pilgrimages to Jerusalem. Except for short periods there was always, after the Romans, a Jewish community there. Pseudo-Messiahs arose and prepared to lead the people back. But the first practical steps in the Jewish Return took place in the early 1880's. The old Jewish idea of waiting for the Messiah had begun to be reinterpreted. Gropingly, the movement of resurrection grew and the trickle of Jews returning to Palestine grew with it. In 1896 a modern Jewish prophet, Theodor Herzl, arose, and a year later the Zionist Movement opened a new era in Jewish history. Its purpose was the practical and political organization of the Jewish return to Palestine and Zion. The time had come for the national contact, spiritually, mentally, emotionally and, through hardier souls, even physically maintained for nearly 2,000 years, to be fulfilled.

Even earlier, in 1860, a new city had been started by Jews in Jerusalem outside the Walls. By 1873 Jews formed the majority of the population of the city.

When Allenby captured Jerusalem from the Turks in 1917 the Zionist Movement had become a force. Two years later, for the first time since Rome destroyed it, Jerusalem became the physical capital of the land, under the administration of a British Mandatory Government. The building up of the Jewish National Home was internationally recognised. To millions of Jews throughout the world, "Next year in Jerusalem" of their liturgy became pregnant with immediate meaning.

On May 15, 1947, the Mandate was wound up. On the same day the independent State of Israel was proclaimed. The Third Jewish Commonwealth had come into being. Its provisional capital was established in Tel Aviv. For Jerusalem lay besieged.

This diary tells the story of that siege. It is told as I, a Jew, experienced it. It is coloured inevitably by my attitude, for that is part of the vivid and tenacious "remembering Zion" of my people.

It is necessarily incomplete, as the narrative is a personal one. Every man, woman and child lived through his own experiences. These are mine, as they were recorded at the time. Nothing has been added to them, and nothing changed.

H. L.

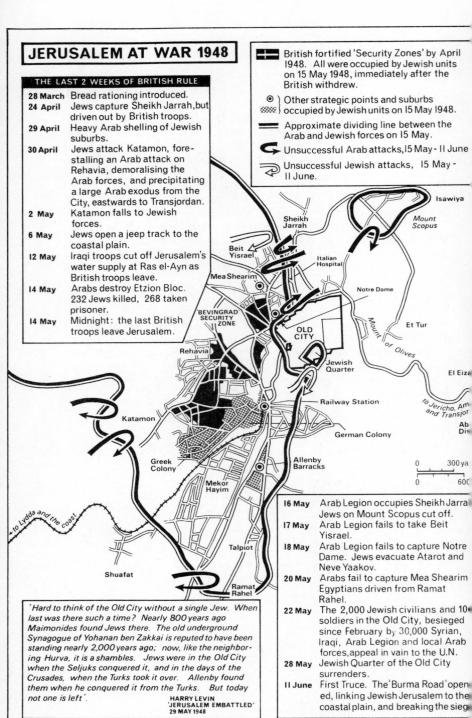

JERUSALEM AT WAR 1948

THE LAST 2 WEEKS OF BRITISH RULE

28 March	Bread rationing introduced.
24 April	Jews capture Sheikh Jarrah, but driven out by British troops.
29 April	Heavy Arab shelling of Jewish suburbs.
30 April	Jews attack Katamon, forestalling an Arab attack on Rehavia, demoralising the Arab forces, and precipitating a large Arab exodus from the City, eastwards to Transjordan.
2 May	Katamon falls to Jewish forces.
6 May	Jews open a jeep track to the coastal plain.
12 May	Iraqi troops cut off Jerusalem's water supply at Ras el-Ayn as British troops leave.
14 May	Arabs destroy Etzion Bloc. 232 Jews killed, 268 taken prisoner.
14 May	Midnight: the last British troops leave Jerusalem.

British fortified 'Security Zones' by April 1948. All were occupied by Jewish units on 15 May 1948, immediately after the British withdrew.

Other strategic points and suburbs occupied by Jewish units on 15 May 1948.

Approximate dividing line between the Arab and Jewish forces on 15 May.

Unsuccessful Arab attacks, 15 May – 11 June

Unsuccessful Jewish attacks, 15 May – 11 June.

Isawiya

Mount Scopus

Sheikh Jarrah

Beit Yisrael

Italian Hospital

Mea Shearim

Notre Dame

Et Tur

'BEVINGRAD' SECURITY ZONE

OLD CITY

Mount of Olives

Rehavia

El Eiza

Jewish Quarter

to Jericho, Am and Transjor

Railway Station

Katamon

Ab Dis

German Colony

0   300 ya

0   60

Greek Colony

Mekor Hayim

Allenby Barracks

to Lydda and the coast

16 May	Arab Legion occupies Sheikh Jarra. Jews on Mount Scopus cut off.
17 May	Arab Legion fails to take Beit Yisrael.
18 May	Arab Legion fails to capture Notre Dame. Jews evacuate Atarot and Neve Yaakov.
20 May	Arabs fail to capture Mea Shearim Egyptians driven from Ramat Rahel.
22 May	The 2,000 Jewish civilians and 10 soldiers in the Old City, besieged since February by 30,000 Syrian, Iraqi, Arab Legion and local Arab forces, appeal in vain to the U.N.
28 May	Jewish Quarter of the Old City surrenders.
11 June	First Truce. The 'Burma Road' opened, linking Jewish Jerusalem to the coastal plain, and breaking the sieg

Talpiot

Shuafat

Ramat Rahel

'Hard to think of the Old City without a single Jew. When last was there such a time? Nearly 800 years ago Maimonides found Jews there. The old underground Synagogue of Yohanan ben Zakkai is reputed to have been standing nearly 2,000 years ago; now, like the neighboring Hurva, it is a shambles. Jews were in the Old City when the Seljuks conquered it, and in the days of the Crusades, when the Turks took it over. Allenby found them when he conquered it from the Turks. But today not one is left'.

HARRY LEVIN
'JERUSALEM EMBATTLED'
29 MAY 1948

25 March, 1948

THE STARS WERE GOING out when Ruth and I left the Tel-Aviv hotel. The clock said 5.15. Shooting was sporadic now, after the savage night. Double-barrelled mortar blasts and the spasms of machine-guns diminished and renewed themselves since early evening like the unwinding of an endless chain. From our balcony we watched the red-and-purple tracer bullets knifing their way upwards and flares splashing fiery globes of light into the sky. The sounds of a dance party floated across from a nearby flat. Lorries filled with young Jews rushed through the street below, heading for the Jaffa border, about half a mile away. The white night was filling our room when we turned in at midnight and the little clock ticking peacefully on the table shone dimly.

The early evening scenes kept flickering in my mind. The weight of the Arab assault was unexpectedly heavy. Cinemas and cafés near the border emptied quickly. From the poor, crowded quarters, Jews fled blindly, like ants streaming from an over-turned ant-heap. Men and women straining under mattresses and bulging suit-cases; frightened children, still in their trumpery Purim fancy-dresses, little Esthers, Mordechais, Bedouin chiefs, tears coursing down their painted cheeks. Tel-Aviv this is, I had to remind myself, not some ghetto in Europe.

Don met us, as arranged, at 5.30 this morning. Tel-Aviv, eager, vital, tumultuous, fascinates him. What New York is to the world, he says, Tel-Aviv is to the Jews. For me a little of Tel-Aviv goes a long way, though I like to renew that little often. Don had to get back to Jerusalem, to University and Haganah. "And Tamara," Ruth teased him.

Don has grown a dark moustache and Vandyck beard, and looks like a grandee. He was wearing the lumber jacket that I saw him in the night he returned from the sapper job in Jerusalem. There was a dark stain on it then, Mati's blood. Mati, a

Yemenite, was one of his team mates. An incongruous team, that sapper group: long-striding, amiable Americans, like Don, and the small, swarthy Oriental Jews, sons of porters or petty crafts-men from Yemen, Kurdistan, Iraq. The Americans even-tempered and easy-going; the Orientals fiery, with an animal streak about their sharp white teeth and ruthless tempers. Yet they work well together. The Americans provide the covering fire. Their mates, sacks of explosives slung over their shoulders, creep up to the objectives and set the charges. That night the Arabs were keeping close guard and two of the *hablanim* (saboteurs) were killed. Don helped to carry in Mati's body.

The city's bulk was still dark against the dawn when we arrived at the starting-point. There were 26 buses drawn up in a line; battered-looking and dingy in their khaki war-paint. All steel-plated against attack, peep-holes with flaps on the insides and adjustable visors over the wind-screens. *Zilla Hayafa* (Beau-tiful Zilla) was painted on the cabin door of one. A huge, beak-like iron shovel to clear away road obstructions protruded from another. The driver of our bus was a small, cheery fellow whom Ruth knew from Jerusalem. Everyone called him Siomka because his Russian surname is unpronounceable.

The last to board our bus was a frowsy, bearded man with a lot of small packages. Before him came an elderly German Jew. He was very timid, kept wiping his glasses gently, and tried to make himself as small as possible. The seats and racks had been removed and we were tightly squeezed together on three narrow, backless, lateral benches running the length of the bus. Seven or eight young men stood in the aisles. Don was placed in another bus.

A young man in khaki shorts looked in.

"Not enough women here," he said. A few minutes later he returned with two girls. They seated themselves on the floor in the narrow aisle behind the driver. One carried a box wrapped in newspaper, handling it gently.

"Cakes," she said, smiling, to the driver.

"Uhu, such cakes!" Siomka commented.

Six fellows and a girl formed our Haganah escort. All were wholly or partly in khaki, but wore no insignia. A tall dark lad they called Boaz was in charge. He had the head of a Greek god and eyes that sparkled. The girl of the party was plump and blue-eyed and moved her shapely shoulders with smooth indolence. She threw Boaz long glances which he answered.

A small saloon car scouted on ahead of the convoy. We drove through the narrow-meshed back streets of the city. Daytime sounds were stealing on the stillness of the early morning. From somewhere in his shiny gaberdine, the bearded Jew pulled out a prayer-book and mumbled from the "Prayers to be said when Starting on a Journey." Nobody paid much attention to him. Only an old woman, who sat motionless like a swaddled lump of flesh, uttered a quavering "Amen" whenever she thought he reached the end of a verse.

We wound along twisting paths to avoid the Jaffa outskirts. Soon the edge of the orange belt spread before us like a sea of green. The look of it and the smell of the blossoms filled me with elation.

To avoid Arab Yazour, where a Jewish patrol car and its ten occupants were wiped out yesterday, we turned off along the narrow tracks between the orange groves. The milky languorousness of the early morning sky was changing to the provocative blue of a bright Mediterranean day. The sun sifted its way through the closely-growing trees, gilding the shiny young leaves and diapering the yellow earth with dark patterns. A pleasant, smiling land, this Sharon, and the white blossoms and pigeons and humming bees made our steel-plated buses, creaking beneath their weighted clumsiness, look monstrously unreal.

At 8 we pulled in to Rehovoth. By the regular Tel–Aviv–Jerusalem highway, only 40 miles, we should have been in Jerusalem by now. Here we heard that last night's food convoy to Jerusalem was attacked and partly destroyed in the Judean hills. I spoke to the sergeant of a British police armoured car that drew up in the main street. He was polite and very neutral, and claimed to know nothing. But as I walked away one of his mates called out loudly: "Hope they bloody well get smashed up too."

Beyond the township we stopped again and some heavy sacks were handed in to Boaz. "Here it comes, girls," he grinned, and began pulling out the dismantled parts of sub-machine guns and pistols, and hand-grenades and ammunition. The women hid them about their bodies. Ruth had a revolver under an armpit and a sten-gun barrel under her skirt. The old woman who looked like a swaddled lump of flesh called out in Yiddish:

"Aren't you going to give me something?"

"All right, Granny. Here's a piece for you too."

Gingerly the old woman laid hands on the sten-gun magazine, hesitated for a second, then slipped it into her bosom. She closed her eyes and shuddered as the cold metal touched her flesh, then wriggled in discomfort. We moved on.

The search several minutes later was a desultory affair. Two British soldiers fumbled casually under the benches and ran their fingers over the pockets of the younger men. The women, most of them now very pregnant-looking, stared stonily at them. Flustered by the stares, the soldiers left off suddenly.

"Nothing 'ere," we heard one of them report outside. The second added:

"Least as 'ow nothing we could find."

Before Akir, the doors and peep-holes were shut. The only light found its way through the 2 foot by 3 inch slit beneath the wind-screen visor. The escort called for the gun parts. The old woman writhed. Hers had wriggled down and was inaccessible. She whispered in a desperate tone:

"But it's there. I can feel it. It's cold. It hurts."

All was silent in Akir. One of our escort, a freckled lad with serene voice and a worried brow, told us of his convoy trip through Akir a week ago when four people were killed by a mine. More mines exploded harmlessly between other buses. He was in one of these; it was his third lucky escape. After this trip he was returning for a time to his University studies. Whenever the door was opened to let in light, and the rest of us looked out hungrily, he would read from a paper-bound copy of Farrington's *Greek Science*.

We bumped and tossed along a rough track, the relics of a Roman road. At 11 we stopped near Hulda and all of us tumbled out. Boaz turned to the plump girl of his escort with a twinkle:

"Samson's country, the Vale of Sorek. Recognize it, Delilah?"

It is 3 o'clock now and we are still here. I am writing this seated on the ground, leaning against a boulder. Young grain, dotted with anemones, sways over the undulating plain. Our convoy passengers lie sprawled about the fields. Most, perhaps 400 in all, are Haganah men. Their sten-guns or rifles are slung carelessly over their shoulders, like banjos or water-bottles. You wouldn't say they are an army. They look like a big party of care-free youngsters out hiking. Some fresh-faced girls among them, wearing the same khaki, and as untidily. There must be officers, too, but you cannot tell from their uniforms or bearing who they are.

From where I sit I can see far across this open, easy Shephela. Its low limestone hills and loamy soil are very different from the sandy, orange lands. Northward, only a mile or two away, runs the main Jerusalem highway. For us now it might be on the moon. British armoured cars are said to patrol it, but the Arab bands control it. Eastward, the contours rise gradually towards the Mountains of Judea, as though the land were lifting its skirts and climbing languidly from the level coast to the plateau. Like a grey-blue wall, framed in dreamy edge-lines, the Judean slopes guard the way to Jerusalem.

Boaz has been pointing out the historic associations of the landscape with an air of passing on something he witnessed yesterday.

"See where our scout is posted on that hillock? Samson probably posted some of his scouts about there when he went raiding with his 'Foxes.' . . . Over there David met Goliath. . . . Saul and Jonathan drove the Philistines that way. . . . The Pharaohs came up along there in their invasion. . . . The Arabs call that gap Wadi el Afranj, the Vale of the Franks, after the Crusaders. . . ."

Battles were always rolling across this Shephela. Inevitable, when you see how it divides the mountains from the plain, a bulwark for the plainsmen against the mountains, and an outpost of the mountain folk against the plainsmen and foreign invaders. Must have been a comfortable land for an invader to fight in; no natural barriers, rich villages to plunder, natives who adapted themselves easily to conquerors. An easy-going lot, those Shephela folk; loved games, women, good food, lots of gods. Up in the mountains the Israelites were rugged and uncompromising, clung to one God, and hated the plainsmen.

A beautiful afternoon. The sky is soft and friendly-looking. It needs an effort to recall that a few miles away, among the mountains, Arab bands are lying in wait. The wide vale before me is completely tranquil. But here, too, you feel that men are watching, waiting among the dips and spurs.

The cars of our convoy, dozing in the sun, lie strung out along the track. The convoy leaders are consulting in a little circle off the road. A few minutes ago a motor-cyclist drew up alongside them and handed in a message. The fragile, silvery Haganah plane that has been with us on and off since Rehovoth has disappeared toward the mountains. Now we know the reason for our delay: a stretch of the highway among the mountains was blocked by the food lorries wrecked last night. Haganah units are clearing the road and engaging the Arab positions near the wreckage. Upon the outcome depends whether we go on or return to Tel-Aviv.

Later

Expecting to move any minute. A line of 51 food trucks, the drivers' cabin steel-plated, have driven out from Hulda and joined our convoy. They are the balance of yesterday's food convoy; 13 others were destroyed. Many of the drivers are middle-aged men, hard-bitten farmers driving their settlements' produce to town. Max of Ein Geb among them; told me that he set out from Ein Geb before dawn yesterday with 4 tons of butter, cheese and vegetables. His convoy was attacked near Beisan, and again at Wadi Ara. They got into the gorge of the Judean mountains after 8 p.m.

"We'd have smashed through there, too," he said, "but the first trucks were blown up by land-mines and barred the road for the rest of us. I was turning to go back when I saw through my peep-hole that the truck behind was ablaze. Like the gleam of a lamp that smoked a bit. Then the gleam grew. In the firelight I could see its sides dripping with egg yolks. Funny how you notice things like that in all the excitement. I could hear the Arabs whooping with joy. They shot the driver as he tried to escape. The fire spread and the dripping eggs looked like molten flames. Shots were pouring into my truck too, but I managed to turn it. Then our armoured car came along and shovelled the burning truck into the ditch, and I drove down. Our escort fired back all the time, but if it weren't for the Haganah men who came from Kiriath Anavim I don't know how many of us would have got away. About 2 in the morning, after we got on to the level road near Hulda, some British armoured cars came along to help. Nicely timed!"

The other drivers were also telling about the battle. Soon they stopped being serious and started chaffing one another. One said:

"I was crawling in the ditch with the shots whizzing over me and suddenly I nearly fainted from fright. There was a great black bear just ready to spring on me. He had a huge head of wild hair and his belly was so big that his paws hardly reached the ground. And what d'you think it was? It was Tuvia!"

Someone asked: "Where's Nathan?"

"Oh, he's counting his bananas," came a reply. They told how Nathan refused to abandon his lorry-load of bananas even when ordered to do so by the convoy commander, and eventually got it towed to safety.

Nathan came strolling up, a slight, bespectacled, solemn-looking man.

"*Nu*, Nathan, all the bananas safe?" Tuvia asked.

"Yes," said Nathan without the shadow of a smile.

5.30, and we are about to move.

Night

After 11, and I am utterly exhausted. But I must put this down while the memory of it, the way things happened and the way they looked, are still so fresh. About 80 vehicles in the convoy when we left. We creaked and lurched over a path that Samson may have trodden but was never intended for motor traffic. At one point every car had to be towed across a *wadi* (dry river-bed) by tractor. At the level road near Bab-el-Wad we stopped to allow the slower-moving food lorries to catch up. The plain looked very peaceful in the half-light. The armoured cars raced up and down the 2-mile line of the convoy, the men in charge calling out final orders to the drivers. Then the doors and peep-holes were shut. In several minutes we entered the Bab-el-Wad bottleneck, enemy territory.

It was dark and breathless inside the bus. The boys stood with their arms cocked near the peep-holes. Everybody silent, but you felt the tenseness. The fat old woman, snoring slightly, was dozing against her neighbour. Up and up we went through the winding hills. The grating of the bus gears as they shifted seemed louder than usual. In my mind I saw the road I know so well—the old hills, some covered with cypresses and pine groves, others, parted centuries ago from every shred of verdure; the gullies and hollow sunless clefts deep among the hills through which we used to hike in the peaceful days. All that was most distinctive in this land, her wars and worships, her heroes and sages and ideals, came from the mountains, most of all from these mountains of Judea. "Her gods are gods of the hills."

The bus was shuddering up an incline when a dull crackling rang out. In a minute it came sweeping down on us from all sides. The first shots sounded surprisingly like pebbles against our steel sides. We could hear others striking the rocks and spattering the road. The boys coolly fired back through the peep-holes. The driver got up speed, but the shooting ran along with us. The first tenseness subsided. Seemed nothing to it either way. They were not penetrating our steel plating, and I doubted if we were penetrating their cover of rock and darkness. Then above the din came a series of hoots from the bus ahead. "His tyres are punctured," exclaimed our driver. We slackened speed, manœuvring to the side to cover its flank. A slight tilt showed that our outside wheels were over the brink of the ditch. Through the emergency door on the inner side our second driver wriggled out, slipping beneath the other bus.

Our stationary targets drew devastating fire. The escorts' guns blazed back. No longer the sound of pebbles. The bus quaked beneath the impact. The ratatat, whistling and thuds merged into an unbroken uproar. Through the peep-hole openings above our guns I glimpsed criss-cross flashes streaking through the darkness. Above the clangour we heard a shot hit our engine. Then two more pierced our roof. One of them struck the back wall of our bus; the other hit the paper-covered package which one of the girls had described as cakes (a wireless transmitter). For those of us who were not handling guns the only thing was to sit quiet and sweat. Some crouched on the floor wherever there was an inch of space. Most bent low where they sat. During a brief lull I heard the bearded man murmuring psalms. The fat old woman breathed fast and heavily. Nobody tried to speak, but several people cried out when the shots penetrated. One man sitting in the rear gave a shout of terror, then moaned for an instant. But it was only fear.

Suddenly, a low cry from the freckled student, who was standing near me. His hand rose slowly, then he slumped down on top of a man crouching on the floor. The girl of the escort pushed her way forward, torch in hand. She was very business-like now. She took out a battle-dressing from its pouch and gave crisp directions. He had been hit in the side of the head, a chance shot through the peep-hole. In a few minutes he died. In a glimpse of the torch-light I saw that the worried look on his brow had passed. It was serene now, as his voice had been. The blood oozed down the side of his shirt, and into his trouser pocket.

Farrington's *Greek Science* peeped out, smudged with blood.

An urgent knocking on the emergency door. The driver opened it slowly while one of the escort held it covered; the second driver clambered in and said the other bus was all right now. Just then another bullet crashed through our roof and grazed Boaz's leg. The roof seemed to be our most vulnerable part; I wondered why more shots weren't penetrating. Boaz ignored his leg, keeping his eyes on his gun-sight. We heard the bus beside us moving off. We moved after it, our engine gurgling irregularly.

Twenty minutes later we pulled up outside Kiriath Anavim. It was very quiet, as though the world had stopped breathing. The night was studded with stars. From Jerusalem a searchlight pierced the darkness; its white, preying fingers poked and flitted among the hills. Don came looking for us. He was unhurt, but in his bus the driver was wounded. The convoy officers went from bus to bus to see how each had fared. There were 5 dead and 9 wounded, but no vehicle abandoned. We drove on, still without lights. Before Castel and Kolonia the escort again removed their safety catches, but nothing happened. After 15 minutes our driver raised the wind-screen visor. Jerusalem lay darkly outlined against the sky. Fireflies were shining out across the road.

We drove into Jaffa Road, our headlights on. It was ghostly quiet. In the shadows, a few silent figures. Two police armoured cars came in sight. Our lamps illumined them against the blackness of the night. Beside the dark silence on either side, the squat panoply of steel, guns in the turrets, made an ominous pattern. The armoured cars slid by almost noiselessly, as though treading on tiptoe. Further up Jaffa Road was light and movement. Seeing our convoy, people cheered and waved wildly. Our journey ended behind the Egged bus terminus, finishing quietly, like the anti-climax of a play.

26 March

W E WOKE UP LATE, feeling low, Ruth pale and very quiet. We felt as if we had been away for months, but it was only a week. The cuttings announcing Tanchik's death, which took us to Mark and Leah in Tel-Aviv, were still where I had left them on my desk. Beside them lay the list of guests invited to our marriage party, that didn't take place. Outside, the skies were grey.

Enough has happened this week in Jerusalem, too. While we were being attacked by one Arab band yesterday, another smashed up a Haganah convoy to Ataroth, killing 14. In the city there has been a run on the food-shops. The attack on Wednesday's food convoy sent everybody in Jerusalem frantically buying up all they could. Some shopkeepers closed their doors, but angry shoppers nearly tore them down. Michael says it looks bad. I did not tell him that I knew there were food supplies in Jerusalem, at the beginning of March, for only three weeks.

Knoller, whose parents in Tel-Aviv gave me a little food parcel for him, is among the dead in the Ataroth convoy. The parents themselves have only just arrived from Holland, their last European haven after fleeing the Nazis from country to country.

In this morning's *Post* an Englishwoman who came by the Ataroth road in an Arab bus describes the scene after the ambush. As British soldiers removed each body, the Arabs, over a thousand of them, acclaimed it with bursts of shouting, then broke into a kind of war dance around the wrecked cars.

How long can we hold Ataroth and the other settlement outposts? The Arab plan is to disrupt all Jewish lines of communication, destroy the outposts, besiege Jewish Jerusalem, and starve it into submission—the pattern of all the ancient conquests. Strategically, they are well placed. Hundreds of Arab towns and villages stand between us and the other Jewish centres. They hold the hills surrounding the city. Jerusalem is an island in a hostile Arab sea. And our only life-line, with Tel-Aviv, lies half-paralysed by their attacks. Jamal Husseini warned U.N. that the partition line will be "a line of blood and fire." It's true already in Jerusalem. And under U.N.O.'s plan precisely Jerusalem is supposed to be neither Jewish nor Arab, but international.

The streets are slushy after the snow. Before lunch I was telling Michael and Judy about the last snowfall a few years ago and how fantastically it transformed the medieval architecture of the city. The heavy grey clouds suddenly became tinged with green and opal. One cloud floated low like a great hovering bird and the flakes began swirling down, a rain of white feathers. Jerusalem looked as unreal then as a Christmas card, only more beautiful.

Ruth came in, very agitated.

"We're about to starve and you talk about green and opal clouds."

She was out shopping and found the shops almost empty. We have little foodstuffs put away. Sudden police curfews and martial law have taught most people to keep emergency reserves. But Ruth has not yet acquired the habit in the month she has been back from England. The B.'s, who arrived from New York in November, are in a similar position. And Judy's condition calls for good food and plenty. Michael and Ruth are now out for-aging together.

It is a strange, long, grey afternoon, with the rain beating down steadily. Unusual for this time of the year. I am feeling dreary and tired. In a few minutes I must leave for the "news-room." Look forward to resuming the broadcasts.

27 *March*

SHABBATH (SABBATH), and we are trying to relax. But there's a brooding restlessness everywhere. M. came round. Her cheerfulness is manifestly assumed.

"There are few people to whom one can say what is in one's heart," she remarked, "and there are many things in one's heart. For the sake of morale you refrain from saying anything that smacks of gloom."

Her University work is daily becoming more difficult. Nobody goes up to Mount Scopus because Arab snipers are covering the road at Sheikh Jarrah. Most students and many of the staff are full-time in Haganah, anyway. Some departments are trying to keep going in private houses in town.

Glad to get back to my broadcasting last night. I try to keep to the policy we laid down; to give the facts as honestly as we can and let the fair-minded Englishman judge for himself. The average Englishman in Palestine doesn't like us and doesn't believe us. One reason is that we have plugged him with too much propaganda. Bring any Jew in touch with a Gentile and at once he becomes a high-powered salesman.

Nothing changed in the tiny, blacked-out "news-room." Still only two tables and three chairs for the five of us, and the second typewriter hangs together by a miracle. News sources as skimpy as ever.

As 9 o'clock drew near, the atmosphere became hectic, as usual. Hava was loudly remonstrating that we'll be late. I, finishing a feature piece on our convoy from Tel-Aviv. Somebody from the Hebrew section popping in to see if we have any news that they haven't. Outside, shots flying about. Inside, typewriters clattering and the telephone buzzing endlessly. Ted looking in to see if everything is running smoothly. Minna arriving chewing hungrily at a sandwich and mumbling, "What? Not ready yet?"

At one minute past 9 we dashed out. The guards said shots were tearing up our street and we had better duck and run close to the wall. At 5 past 9 we tumbled into the waiting car beyond the barricade. Five minutes later we were knocking at the door of Asher's fifth-floor flat, which is our transmission station. The technician started whistling into the mike our 8-bar signature tune from *Hatikvah*. At 9.15 listeners heard: "This is *Kol Hamegen Haivri*, the Broadcasting Service of the Haganah, calling on a wave-length of 35 to 38 metres or 7 to 7·5 megacycles. Here is our English transmission." Afterwards I heard that we were jammed in the middle of the programme, and that at the end an English voice mimicked Minna with "Try more baby food, do!" Somebody doesn't like our underground service.

Night

Grim news from the Etzion road: 250 Haganah men and drivers trapped, and with them most of the armoured cars and plated lorries that could be mustered in Jerusalem. They left before dawn in a hazardous attempt to bring supplies to the besieged Etzion settlements. The road runs entirely through Arab territory and the settlements have been cut off for months. The column got through without mishap. But returning it found the way barred by road-blocks and Arabs lying in ambush everywhere along the road. The leading armoured car smashed through seven blocks, but collapsed at the eighth. Falling back, the uncrippled lorries ran into new blocks that cut their retreat. They fought their way into Nebi Daniyal, an abandoned Arab village near the road, and took cover in some houses, which they barricaded with their trucks. That's where they are now, fighting it out.

British Army reports estimate about 4,000 Arabs in action and say four Jewish planes are bombing them. We haven't any bombers; they must be light planes dropping grenades. A Haganah relief party from Jerusalem had to turn back this afternoon because of the heavily-mined road. An Army unit from Bethlehem also turned back.

At Haganah *Mateh* (H.Q.) to-night they were going about tight-lipped. The last wireless message from Nebi Daniyal says the party are in good spirits, but without food and water, and running short of ammunition.

28 March

No DAY HAS BEEN like this. The suspense weighs on the city like something physical. Many people have relatives or friends who may be among the 250: and everyone realizes that this combat unit and these vehicles form a notable part of our fighting resources in Jerusalem: in to-day's conditions, almost irreplaceable.

While chafing for news from the Etzion road we learned of yesterday's convoy disaster on the road to Yehiam in Galilee. British troops found the bodies of 42 Haganah men with the wreckage of 5 armour-plated buses. Ruth is worried sick. The convoy's point of departure was Naharia, where her family lives; many must have been Naharia men.

A bright sunny day, but I doubt if people notice it. Time drags. Every hour I look into Y.'s room at the *Mateh*. His expression shows that there is no fresh news. They are still holding out. But later he quietly mentions other reports coming in: attack on Neve Yaakov; a six-hour attack on Sejera in Lower Galilee; a clash with British troops in the Old City when our men resisted confiscation of their arms after a search; 11 Jewish casualties, 7 British.

Machine-gunning and sniping all over the new city. This is not "disturbances" any more. It is war. Beneath the present gloom everybody, I think, senses the forebodings of still harsher days to come. The coil is tightening. East, west, north, and now the Etzion road southward—all our outlets are being stopped.

Night
A beating, but what a relief! The Government, through the Christian Arab Mayor of Bethlehem, finally negotiated a truce. The 30-hour battle at Nebi Daniyal stopped at 5 this afternoon. We have 13 dead and 50 wounded. A British report says 135

Arabs killed and the Bethlehem hospitals full of Arab wounded.

At 7, I watched British armoured cars off-load the party—dead tired, filthy, but in good spirits—at the Jewish Agency courtyard. Parents, wives and friends crowded on them. There were some moving scenes, exclamations breaking down in embraces and gestures. I wondered how many thought they would see their families again. Some let loose a flood of recountings of fear and elation. Others, silent, just stood close to their relatives and friends. Max of Ein Geb was there. Three such experiences in four days. What a life for a man who merely set out to bring the farm produce to town!

The vehicles had to be abandoned to the Arabs. But the Army also left the arms to the Arabs as loot. The *Mateh* and officers of the unit are very bitter about it. They say the arrangement was that the Army would hand back the arms to them in Jerusalem.

Walking home to-night, I tried to fathom what lies ahead. This time it is going to be a real show-down. Many people are saying that, but I wonder if they realize how horribly we are going to be battered. I believe that finally we shall come out on top. We must, or it will be the end of us. A Haganah officer put it this way to some new recruits a few weeks ago: "If you can't face death, you can run; but remember, if you run you can't just run a mile. You must run a thousand miles."

For the first time I felt a whiff of personal insecurity. It flashed across my mind—strangely enough now, when the Etzion convoy has been rescued, yet not when I was in the thick of it on Thursday—that I may not come out of all this alive.

When I got home Ruth told me that Vita M. was killed a few hours ago, just outside her house around the corner.

29 March

RUTH WAS OUT EARLY, shopping, and returned despondent.
Four hours of tramping and cajoling yielded only 9 tins—nothing
of it very substantial—2 packets of candles, and some dried fruit.
The only things in plenty are tea, expensive canned fruit, and
Australian asparagus soup that nobody seems to want. We
decided to lay in asparagus soup in a big way.

There is talk of rationing of essentials. But what stocks can
there be on hand and how will even essentials get through from
Tel-Aviv?

Michael appeared after lunch, also disconsolate. His shopping
experience was similar to Ruth's. Outside the Workers' Restaurant, where he lunched, a notice was posted up: "No bread
to-day." There was a run on cake-shops. A doctor's certificate
entitles Judy to a glass of milk a day and 4 eggs a week, but they
are irregular. So much concern about food—I never thought
such a time would come in Jerusalem.

Walked down Jaffa Road at 6.30. The main street, and yet in
utter darkness, with hardly a soul about. Had supper at the
Palestine Restaurant: thin potato soup, one sausage and mash,
and a cake of *matza* in place of bread. I shared a table with a man
who has been trying desperately to return to Tel-Aviv. Hundreds
of people gather hopefully outside the Egged bus station every
day, but there has been no down traffic for over a week.

This afternoon Wilhelm H. called about our party, postponed
from when Tanchik was killed. Seems crazy, having a party now.
He says he can get things "of the best, and," he adds, "the last,
even on the black market." I believed it when he told me the
prices. His suggestions were out of an epicure's catalogue. H. is
a waiter by training and a waiter by instinct, but built for the
lordly measure. Despite my drastic slashing of his party design,
he left beaming in happy anticipation. As he stepped away a

fresh wave of shooting crackled out from Katamon. It was like
waking up from a dream.

Max was here when I got home to-night. The effects of his
ordeal still showed in his twitching hands and endless smoking.
He bemoaned the loss of his armour-plated truck. Only a handful
of them are left now in Jerusalem. He told us about Nebi Daniyal.
The Arabs fired all the time, sometimes in great blanket amounts
and sometimes single shots. They were not in lines or any kind
of formation, but just covered the countryside like a great army
of beetles. From one flank or another they were always making
sorties, shouting "*Aleyhoum!*" ("At them!") and yelping their
shrill, vibrating war howl.

"We waited till they were close, then gave them all we had. It
went on like that all day and night and again next day. While
fighting, we lived on our nerves. But when there was a bit of
quiet the minutes dragged horribly. I'll never forget the night,
the whistling bullets, the crackling fire as some of our trucks
were set alight, the howls that made your spine grow cold, the
light of the moon; and our crowd, tense, hungry, thirsty, but
full of spirit, exchanging quips and talking airily of the absurd
things they would do when they got out of this. You felt it was a
nightmare from which it wasn't possible you could come out
alive."

He said the troops that relieved them were very stiff at first,
but a few loosened up afterwards. One officer said to Max: "You
put up a great show." He was in Bethlehem during the fighting,
he said, and the Easter bells were drowned by the echo of the
Nebi Daniyal fighting.

30 March

ONE OF THE QUIETEST days for weeks. Some odd sniping from St. Simeon Monastery (now a fortified Iraqi stronghold) and from the Moslem Cemetery in Manillah Road. But yesterday was very lively. Haganah ambushed Arab traffic on the outpost roads. In the city, the endless sound of rifle fire.

More Haganah calling-up posters on the hoardings to-day. Now it is the 26–35 age group, men and unmarried women; some for part-time Haganah, others for civilian services. The *Yeshiva* (Talmudic College) students of the 17–25 age groups are still keeping aloof, as though all this has nothing to do with them. One Rabbi said to T.:

"What is a *Yeshiva* boy? He is one of those of whom Gedeon said: 'Whoever is fearful and afraid.' He is frail and filled with dread. The mere act of living is full of endless hardship for him. And you want to teach him to use firearms!"

Yet, oddly, it's just some of these ultra-pious youths who have been drawn to the terrorists, especially to the Stern Group. A fascinating subject for study, the twisted passage of these physically timid, other-worldly pietists to terrorism. Once I met one at Rabbi F.'s. A typical *Yeshiva* youth, bony body, round shoulders, and melancholy eyes in a taut, hypersensitive face. He spoke very little at the Rabbi's, but walking down the street with me he began holding forth in that quick, assertive way of talking that seems common to many terrorists. He attacked the Jewish leaders nearly as venomously as the British. He still attended *Yeshiva*, but not regularly. I asked him how he reconciled terrorist methods with his pietism.

"Do you think I like these methods?" he exclaimed angrily. "I despise physical force. That's the tragedy. Man has been created not to kill his neighbour, but to continue the Creator's work in harmony with his neighbour. But he hasn't been created, either, to be subjugated and tyrannized. If these British oppress us for their purposes, we must fight them by their own methods. Force against force, iron against iron, brains against brains, blood against blood. That's the great commandment, moral, human, and divine, too. As long as the British are here, that's the only way we shall rescue what remains of our people. And only when we live here freely, like any normal nation, can we do our share in creating justice and brotherhood and peace in the world, which is the spirit of the Torah and the tradition of the Prophets."

I didn't try to discuss it. It would have been like opening discussion with a flood.

31 March

BREAD RATIONING HAS begun: 200 grams per day per person—that is, about four normal slices. With so little else, how long can we continue on that? No new supplies since our convoy last Thursday, six days, and Haganah reports speak of heavy massing of Arabs around Bab-el-Wad. If Government knows about the new Arab bands, it is too well-bred to betray its knowledge. The 100,000 Jews of Jerusalem need a bare minimum of 60 truckloads of food a day. Not one has come in for a week. Everyone talking about food.

To-night we tried out a reserve transmitting station, also in a private flat (my tobacconist's; some time or other you meet everyone in Haganah). There was a new technician on duty. I saw him peering through the window from behind a curtain. He laughed at my questioning; said it must be habit. He was a wireless operator in the underground in Yugoslavia during the Nazi occupation. The Nazis were always on their tracks in detection cars disguised as mail or delivery vans. He was wounded once while fleeing.

Little likelihood of our being caught here. Since the Ben-Yehuda Street explosion, the Jews have barricaded the main streets, and British police and soldiers cruise around in them as little as possible.

Got a second continuity announcer this evening, Esther C., a London girl who came out as English mistress to a girls' school. Already full-time in Haganah, but volunteered for this additional duty. Quiet and unassuming; looks as if she has plenty of character.

Back at home I found Michael and Judy's room full of young people, most of them American ex-G.I. students. Yesterday the doctor confirmed that Judy is pregnant and ordered her to keep to bed for another six weeks. The crowd came to divert her. They played records, danced, drank American blackberry liqueur and chatted loudly. I noticed again what a grave face Judy has, in a gentle, remote way, and her dark, languid eyes and soft speech strengthen that impression.

Tried working on the History to-day. The infernal crackling of shots made it seem preposterously unreal. Remembered the story of Hegel wrapped in his writing within hearing of the Battle of Jena, and when he stopped for dinner, asking his servant who had made the noise. But knowing how Hegel took it didn't help me. When the shots weren't disturbing them, my thoughts just kept congealing.

1 April

Seething indignation at United States' action at U.N.O. It has asked for a new session of the Assembly to reconsider the vote for partition on the ground that it cannot be enforced. The Arabs are jubilant. And we are suspended between enemies trying to crush us and friends who desert us. Shertok's defiance to-day is absolutely sustained here: "We have passed the threshold of statehood. We refuse to be thrown back."

Heavy fighting has flared up on the road. Started with an attack on a food convoy yesterday. The convoy returned to Hulda. But Haganah hit back hard. Haganah reports 17 of its men and 72 Arabs killed until this morning. The battle continued all day, with a lull this evening.

Ruth and I decided to eat out as often as possible; in any case, to open only one tin a day. Restaurants crowded and their food deteriorating. But there's no other way. Shopping in a new district to-day, Ruth got some dried beans, lentils, and 4 tins of vegetables; also more tinned asparagus soup. Green-grocers had minute rations of potatoes and onions. All prices have soared. . . .

Night

Our party to-night was grand. In these days of tension and dreaded anticipation, it was like emerging for a spell from a dark, dank forest into sunlight. All the troubles of recent years and the long periods of curfew have made most people forget what it is to come together for diversion. Duty prevented some friends from coming; others didn't care to be out after dark. P.: "Shots in the dark seem much more deadly than in daytime." I missed Wilhelm H. He came to tell me that his substitute for guard duty to-night was wounded by a sniper. He gave the provisions a last look-over, pronounced them adequate, told me about the party he arranged for a German Baron on the night of a Berlin Reichstag fire, and left with a bow and a sad look.

People rubbed their eyes. It did seem an anachronism: all those delicacies when bread is rationed and the food-shops are empty. But someone must have "the last," and thanks to Wilhelm H. we did. There was probably more laughter than in all of Jerusalem in the past month, and in spite of the new bitterness over U.N.O. Didn't have to press many people to "have another," and the loosening influence released talk of things not much heard of these days, from music and water research in the Negev, to Ben-Gurion's passion for the Greek philosophers, and Henry Moore. S., who always greets me with a gloomy, "Well, what's going to happen now?" came up and said, "Did I ever tell you that I was at school with Goering?" and the brandy glowed bright red on his sunken cheeks. Suddenly, I thought of Tanchik in his muddy grave up in Galilee and the other new graves all up and down the country. . . .

There was talk, of course, also about the situation, but it was only when Michael C. brought George Fielding Eliot, the American military analyst, that it became a principal topic. He is a burly, ponderous fellow, emphatic in his opinions. Has seen the High Commissioner and the G.O.C., and spent some time with Haganah and with the Arabs. Doesn't think much of the Arabs as fighters. He says Haganah have "almost too much guts," but too little equipment. As for the Jewish sectors of Jerusalem, "they are a strategic monstrosity and quite indefensible," he declared with complete finality. After a while the little group around him broke away, feeling low. I trundled them towards the drinks.

2 April

AM LESS AND LESS inclined to believe that the solution will come through U.N.O. We shall have to work it out ourselves, though God knows at what cost. But when one remembers the price we have paid through the centuries just for the right to live, whatever the cost, now it will be cheap.

Yesterday, partition was to have been implemented. Instead, the General Assembly is "to consider further the problem of Palestine." Just a year ago Britain proposed an identical resolution (only without the word "further"), and was shocked when partition was adopted. Now intrigue at Lake Success has done its work.

In Tel-Aviv to-day Ben-Gurion announced that the Jews will continue to set up their State in accordance with U.N.'s original decision.

At the P.I.O. Press conference Stubbs was asked about the Army's search for Haganah arms in the Old City. He said the British are responsible for security (the record: 935 Jews and 1,700 known Arab dead in four months!) and the presence of Haganah there is "a menace to peace." Asked why the rest of the Old City was not searched when everybody knows that Abdul Khader Husseini's H.Q. are there and armed Arabs walk about openly, he replied, "The fact that other people go around armed is no reason for not searching the Jewish section." The presence of Abdul Khader Husseini is "unlawful, and he should not be there." He looked hurt when we laughed.

Earlier to-day, at the Jewish Agency Press conference, Eytan said that the Government has been pressing the Jews for months to evacuate the Old City; at least, that they be disarmed. The more defenceless, apparently, the safer: 1,700 Jews in the Old City and about 30,000 Arabs, besides bands of Syrians and Iraqis.

Three restaurants cleaned out when Ruth and I got to town

for lunch. At the fourth we had a sausage and potato salad. Didn't enquire what kind of sausage. At the next table a man was saying that he came upon a queue last week where they were selling rabbit, but he thought it was cat.

A cable to me from London took 2 days to reach Jerusalem and 6 days for delivery from G.P.O., about half a mile away. Government services are collapsing even before the fixed dates. Officially, incoming surface mails will be suspended on April 15; but no letters have reached me for over a week. We keep on posting mail, but I doubt if it is cleared. Some mail boxes are too crammed to squeeze in another letter. Most phones are out of order and it's useless reporting the faults. (So far, mine seems to have dispensation.) The Law Courts haven't been functioning since the Arabs started sniping into the Compound over a month ago. Staff and lawyers refuse to attend until Government ensures security or moves the Courts.

The Press has reproduced from an Australian paper excerpts of a letter from Rex Keating, Deputy Director of the P.B.S. (who is still here). He wrote it as far back as February. Says: "It's an awful thing to take part in the disintegration of a country; to have to watch the collapse, one by one, of the props of civilization—postal services, communications, public works, medical services, and, above all, security. And we don't seem to give a damn, officially. It makes you ashamed to be an Englishman. . . . At the moment I proclaim loudly that I'm Irish, thank God."

No news from the road, and no convoy. More people are trying to grow their own vegetables; articles in the Press about hydroponics, growing vegetables in water without soil. Michael came back to-day with packets of cabbage, carrot and lettuce seed which he will try planting in wooden boxes.

Bertie called with his platoon commander, a Hungarian fellow he calls Emery. Beside his friend's hawk face and sinewy body, Bertie's round green-blue eyes and baby smile make him look a caricature of a soldier. Yet Michael tells me Bertie had a remarkable war record in the Pacific. Everyone in his Haganah unit has been railing at him because of "his Truman."

3 April

SHABBATH AGAIN, AND spring in the air. Sporadic firing during the night, and in my sleep, towards dawn, I dimly heard a loud explosion. But when we got up the world glittered serenely in the cool, fresh sunlight, and an exhilarating breeze swept over the hills. No one with life in his body could stay in on such a day. We decided to go for a walk. I thought it would also help Ruth shake off her growing restlessness.

Question was, walk where? Examining the possibilities, we realized how hermetically the Jewish sectors are sealed in by the Arabs. Walk out straight in any direction and you invite death in less than a mile. Strange, in fact, that I haven't yet been killed almost anywhere I move. Only concealment by the buildings shields one from the snipers.

Am galled by this feeling, especially this morning. If I stroll out along roads or paths I have taken a thousand times I walk to certain death. Not to danger or resistance or battle. Just to death. If I arm myself openly to meet the enemy, it is I who will be arrested by police or soldiers roving around in armoured cars. Government will sit in judgment on me for illegal possession of arms. Their Honours will preach to me about "undivided authority of the Government . . . which alone is responsible for security," etc. They would certainly sentence me for contempt as well were I to say it seemed to me that *I* should be sitting in judgment on Government.

We walked out all the same, mostly in the lee of the built-up area. But at the edge of Rehavia, where the brow of a hill protects the Mar Salabe dip, we touched the fringe of open country. Snug and verdant earth. Peach and late almond blossoms pushed out their airy clouds of pink and white; crocuses, anemonies and daisies in the fields. It was all right so long as you kept your eyes to the earth. The trouble was in the air. The moment you raised your head and looked up to the hills you felt a heaviness, an affliction, hanging over you. Every so often came the echo of shooting; from Mekor Haim in the south, sounds of a regular battle.

These times are breaking down the social barriers. Neighbours are becoming friendly and helpful, and people are forced out of their normal channels. Met M. F. and his wife, who used to live in Katamon in a quiet, roomy house standing in a charming garden. Since February they are in Mekor Baruch, lucky to get a room with use of kitchen. They share the flat with a bus-driver. M. is a German Jewish intellectual, as rigid as you would expect of a German lawyer backed by four generations of other German lawyers. He must feel that life is singularly harsh to throw him into the bosom of a large, noisy Polish family. Yet he sounds philosophical about it. His wife and the bus-driver's have even begun exchanging recipes, for the time when there's something to cook. He is getting to know new people. On duty one night at a road-block, he discovered that he and his partner had met before; the other used to manage a hotel in Trieste, at which M. once stayed.

New stone and iron check-posts have sprung up in the Jewish quarters. Not only against Arabs; also against the possibility of another outrage by British deserters like the Ben-Yehuda Street explosion. Talk is that they may try to get through again in a Jewish-style, closed-in bus.

Guards at the check-posts are a mixed bunch. Saw Professor M. in that role the other day. "One of my boyhood ambitions come true," he said. "I always wanted to be a traffic cop." He said that most of the British troops take the check in good part. One officer even pointed out how a barrier might be improved.

A guard who held me up once was an elderly, bearded man with side-locks. Very earnest and resolute, and new at his job. He stood in the middle of the road, earlocks swinging in the breeze and eyes tightly screwed up in the glare of the headlamp. My driver hadn't his identity card yet. The guard shut one eye,

stared at him with the other with a look that said, "You won't
fool me, young man," and started questioning him.

"Are you a Jew?"

"Obviously."

"Where are you going?"

"I'm driving him"—nodding towards me—"on duty."

The old man pondered a minute, tried to think of the next
question: Then:

"Are you *b'seder* (O.K.)?"

"Yes; I'm *b'seder*."

"Then pass."

The guards don't carry arms. But near each post a few young
men, arms hidden about them, lounge on the pavement. In
other places the armed men or girls are out of sight, in an
adjacent building.

Night

Splendid news. Palmach has captured Castel, that sniper's
citadel on the road to Tel-Aviv. Syrians and Iraqis held it (some
of the 8,000 foreign Arab fighters who have infiltrated into the
country). A big step towards freeing the road. Everybody very
cheerful about it. Our boys wormed their way up the slopes
during dark and stormed it before dawn, a typical Palmach job.

No Haganah arrangements yet for correspondents to cover its
operations in Jerusalem. The Commander seems just not interested in the foreign Press. The Arab Commander shows more
perspicacity. He takes the Press into his confidence even if only
to tell them whimsicalities.

4 April

LAST NIGHT THE High Commissioner broadcast the U.N.O. resolution calling for a truce. He added his own plea and said it was everyone's duty to sustain the influence of United Nations. Coming from the head of the Government which has openly flaunted U.N.O.'s original Palestine resolution, that is rich.

Nobody is hopeful about a truce. The Jews will stop fighting the minute the Arabs do; they have no stomach for it. But why should the Arabs stop, as long as their attacks go on weakening the U.N. stand on partition?

As head of the Government, Sir Alan Cunningham is heartily detested by the Jews; but not as a man. They sense a certain goodwill and chivalry about him, though he lacks the strength to make them felt against these odds. We know that he is personally critical of Bevin's policy and has tried to mitigate it; that he urged Whitehall to relax its stubborn immigration policy. A quota of 4,000 immigrants from Europe a month that he advocated, instead of the rigid White Paper figure of 2,500, for all that it would not have altered the ultimate solution, what a difference it would have made to the Jews and to their relations with Britain! And how easily it could have been effected after the Anglo-American Commission's recommendations! Last year Cunningham offered his resignation. It was not accepted; but influence passed gradually out of his hands. The Chief Secretary, Sir Henry Gurney, unsympathetic and completely Bevin's boy, seems to be the real power in the Government now. I wonder if Sir Alan knows everything being done in the name of his Government?

Still no sign of a food convoy. The fuel position also critical; there has been no kerosene since February. People are using D.D.T. and Flit as fuel. But Castel in our hands has eased the

anxiety a bit. Much talk that a big Haganah clearing-up operation is imminent on the road. Ruth went out shopping again
among the sordid little streets behind the market and came back
with a tin of Postum (450 mils—9s.) and some dried beans; also
some tins of asparagus soup. Got a ration of margarine, 1½ oz.
per person. Greengrocers are now selling *malvia*, the wild pseudo-
spinach that Oriental women have been picking in the fields.
P.B.S. even suggests recipes for its preparations. But that is also
running short, because no one ventures beyond the built-up
sectors. H.'s young son was beaten up the other day by some
Oriental boys when he went picking it; they said it was only for
poor people.

J. R. of Melbourne dropped in this morning. Just knocked at
my door and walked in. He is *en route* to England. How he got
here from Tel-Aviv? Easy, he said. By British police armoured
car, strictly unofficial, £30 each way. (Peace-time taxi fare: 14s.
return per person.) Some British police are in the business in
Jerusalem, too. Fares to the dangerous areas vary from £5
upwards. A few enterprising Jews act as intermediaries.

Ruth is trying to get transferred from Haganah poster-
drawing to the map-drawing unit. The trouble at present is her
hours; she is busy when I am free. Except for hurried meal hours,
the only time we have together is from 10 at night. And it isn't
a month since we were married!

Shooting and explosions all over town to-day. A mortar shell
shattered a balcony a few doors from us; another pulled down
the telephone wires and dug a crater in the middle of the road
100 yards away. Very early this morning British guns opened up
on the Jewish Quarter of the Old City. The Jews say it was completely unprovoked, and claim it is part of Government's campaign to force them to evacuate the Old City. Government says
it was retaliation for a land-mine which they accuse Jews of
laying near a British Army post.

P.B.S. Orchestra Concert to-night, the first in Jerusalem for
months. What a joy! The programme—mostly Handel, Bach,
Beethoven—must have been chosen with an eye to the times.

Preferred Bach this evening, so serenely joyous and effortless in his creation, and almost childlike in his adoration.

Don was with the Bs. when we got home. A short, dark girl from Detroit, named Frances, was also there. She's a sharp-shooter, transferred to Jerusalem with the last convoy. In Detroit she was a stenographer. Got her training in a settlement in Galilee, the only girl in her group of 35 trainees. I asked her if it wasn't awkward for her as the only girl. "I forgot I was a girl there," she laughed. "I was just another sniper in training."

One of the boys in the Etzion food convoy last Sunday brought Don a letter from Tamara. Sitting on the bed in Judy's room, he read parts of it to us. He had read it so many times that it was beginning to wear in the creases. I made a note of some passages:

"We are living in the adjoining derelict Arab village. To-day we moved from 'Casablanca' to 'Hotel Royal' in the 'Street of Idleness,' which used to be occupied by students of philosophy. The lower part of our building housed the cattle, and the upper part the Arab family. We are 11 girls in it. Ours is the only room that boasts a proper table and we have covered it with a dish-cloth. The roof leaks, but not too badly. The 'recreation room' has two long boards on trestles. There are some newspapers of various dates. By the time I've finished a four-week old paper I don't feel like reading one of five weeks ago. But we've a nice little library. The walls are decorated with reproductions of Picasso, Van Gogh and pin-up boys. Each girl has her personal mouse and in summer will no doubt have her very own bugs.

"We have our showers at Kfar Etzion, a fairly long walk. We train hard, but find time also for other things, especially talk. Twice a week we have lectures on various subjects. On Friday evenings we have *mesiboth* (group talks) and discussions on all kinds of topics. . . .

"Baruch lives at the 'Einstein Institute' in 'Relativity Street' with some of the other physics students. They have written to Einstein about their most recent discoveries. They observe red 'meteorites' and have established certain standards of time measure. For instance, it takes exactly 22 minutes to wake up

Shaul; a fortnight is an unlimited period verging on the Infinite. . . .

"It seems years since we tasted sweets, and chocolate is something we only dream of. Just now our dreams are also concerned with roast beef, eggs, tomatoes, cocoa. (The food has become worse in the past few weeks.) And a real bed with white sheets cannot really exist. . . ."

5 *April*

THE ARABS HAVE rejected U.N.'s truce appeal.

Church dignitaries abroad are again expressing anxiety about the safety of Jerusalem and the Holy Places; so are statesmen. The smoothness of some of it is beginning to sound offensive. The Jewish Agency has warned U.N. of elaborate Arab plans to isolate the city and establish military control over it; it declares that the Jews have counter-plans to resist. It suggests the transfer to Jerusalem of the 10,000 Scandinavian troops now on occupation duties in Germany. Not likely! Perhaps U.N.O. might be shaken into action if the Holy Places *were* damaged. Or are Holy Places only another chequer-piece on the Middle Eastern board?

Nobody about when I got home this afternoon. I went into Judy's room to offer her a cup of tea; found her lying there pale and dejected, staring through the window at the high pine trees. I told her of the success yesterday at Mishmar Haemek, where they beat off the heaviest Arab attack made yet against any settlement. Firing broke out from Katamon while we spoke; sounded very close. I didn't mention to Judy the man shot dead by snipers this morning a few streets away. Judy said anxiously that she hoped Michael wasn't on his way home. Michael spends most of his time now with Haganah's economic warfare group; his particular job seems to be concerned with reports on shipments of petroleum supplies to the Arabs.

The theft of Government property is becoming a joke. Everybody is doing it with impunity—Arabs, Etzel, Stern Group. In the past week Army supplies—arms, money, film equipment, office furniture and engineering gear—have been stolen. The greatest loot is cars. A list of cars stolen every day has become a regular feature of the P.B.S. news bulletin; anything on wheels will do, from armoured cars to Post Office vans.

No convoy yet, but a ration of 2 lb. of *matza* per person. It is

marked "Iron Ration," and the public is advised to put it away.
Smoked my last pipeful of tobacco to-night; no more to be had.
Cigarettes also vanishing.

On my way home from broadcasting I had to step in to T.'s.
They were waiting for Dalia, who had been out since midday.
Only 16, so she is still in an auxiliary unit. She came in after 10
and you felt everyone breathe more freely. She said casually that
they had been out in the hills, and that the commander was an
idiot. Her young brother tried to question her, but she brushed
him aside.

"I've got to go to school to-morrow, and haven't done my
homework yet."

I felt gloomy most of the day, and hungry. Have seen hardly
anything of Ruth these last few days.

It's springtime, and the world, somewhere, is soft and glad.
Days of promise, and days of death.

6 April

A FOOD CONVOY AT LAST! Excitement everywhere as the news flashed through the city. People ask if the supplies will be distributed at once. More likely to be stored.

Heavy clashes on the road preceded the convoy's arrival. It started when Haganah units went out during the night to force open the way. The battle swayed through the hills towards Jerusalem; before dawn the Arabs tried to storm Castel and Motza, but were driven back. The convoy slipped through during a lull in the morning's fighting. Between here and Bab-el-Wad the Arabs have a score of villages to act as bases. If we had 10 Jewish rural settlements protecting it, instead of only 3, the road would never have been closed.

Met Dick P. this afternoon at the Atara Café (they still serve coffee, with saccharine, but no cakes). He is certain the Arabs are going to throw all they have into sealing the road. He was bursting with something; finally, lowering his voice, he told me what it was. He believes he has discovered one of the masks under which Etzel is operating as a secret cell in the Hotel and Café Employees' Association. In this way, they place their men in ideal listening-posts, as waiters. A good story, if true. A likeable and amusing fellow, Dick, and one of the few British correspondents sympathetic to the Jews. But he seems to regard terrorism as a kind of romantic game, like a grown-up version of Red Indians. If he were a Jew, he says, he would join them.

Leo R. was also at Atara. He is still police graphologist, but there is no work for him to do. Police H.Q. are quietly collapsing, he says. Behind the façade of normality, a creeping paralysis. Letters and reports are received, registered, passed around, but rarely dealt with. Court cases are seldom concluded; everyone concerned knows that some reason or other will be produced for adjourning them.

Everything went wrong this evening. Little news for the bulletin; I got to the mike four minutes late; the engineer was hoarse and I had to whistle the signature tune myself, doing it horribly (besides adding a bar that shouldn't have been there). Finally, I was told that we were jammed again. The service car failed to call, so I had to walk home. Twice I took cover from shots. At home I found Ruth anxious and irritable. The pseudo-spinach croquettes she made for supper were dried up and tasted unmistakably like what they are, insipid weed; but at least it is green. (I must dry some and try it as pipe tobacco.)

Can hear Michael pottering around their second room, surveying it as a projected nursery. Can't see him finding room for a baby *and* all the ingenious hobby sets, tools, paint boxes and masses of assorted stationery he brought over from the States.

7 April

At U.N.O. America has "informally suggested" a Palestine trusteeship, to be held by 57 nations—"until Jews and Arabs agree on a form of Government"! Is it merely lack of sense of reality, or poltroonery? Increasingly one feels cheated when one thinks of U.N.

In Tel-Aviv, where the World Zionist Council is meeting, a newspaper reminds it of Mazzini's words to the Italians 100 years ago: "Act like men who have the enemy at the gates and at the same time like men who are working for eternity." That sense of destiny runs, I think, through the whole community.

Castel battle in its fifth day. Abdul Khader Husseini, Arab Jerusalem Area Commander, is himself leading the attack and has massed men from far afield. Urgent calls for reinforcements from our force, outnumbered and exhausted, have gone unheeded. Are we *so* badly off?

Arab shooting in and around the city grows heavier. Mekor Haim plastered all night and day, but holds firm. The British colonel at the nearby Allenby Barracks, a friendly fellow who would like to help them if he were allowed, calls our men there "suicide squad." Says he can't see how only a few hundred can hold out against those odds. If he only knew! I don't think we have more there than a few score.

Haganah's attacks to-day were directed mainly against Arab traffic, especially on their reinforcement routes. Picked striking units weave unseen through Arab territory, mine roads or ambush the convoys, then move swiftly out again before the Arabs can cut them off.

Hardly a day goes by that I do not hear of the death of someone I know. On Sunday I heard that Aliza S. was killed on patrol duty. When they brought her father the news, he said, "I shall not complain, for so it must have been decreed. Our daughter was given to us for nineteen years less one week." To-day we learned of the death of Erwin S., an old friend of Ruth's; he was ambushed near the railway station, pulled out of his car, and killed.

One has the feeling that everything is being speeded up in Jerusalem, as though someone had stepped on the accelerator. Also that we are far worse off in men and equipment than most people guess. Haganah has never been strong here; too many strata in the population and too little coherence among them. Yet most business houses and institutions already seem half-crippled by reduction of staffs.

Saw the log of yesterday's Palmach action that cleared the way for the food convoy; I made these extracts:

0238 hours. All designated enemy strong-points and bridges in our hands.

0400 hours. Convoy reached Kiriath Anavim. 150 armed Arabs resisted at Dir Muhsein. Joined by 80 from Abu Shushe. Two-hour battle. We occupied Dir Muhsein.

0600 hours. Near Kolonia Arabs constructed five road blocks and dug three ditches across highways.

0715 hours. Enemy pressure forced us withdraw from Suba quarries. Convoy left Kiriath Anavim under heavy covering fire from us. Stiff fighting at Castel.

0850 hours. Convoy has come up against the road blocks near Kolonia. Our armoured vehicles have engaged the enemy lying in ambush.

0930 hours. Advance party pierced the road blocks and bridged ditches.

1010 hours. Convoy arrived in Jerusalem. No casualties.

1400 hours. Arabs attacking with large reinforcements. Our forces withdraw from all strong-points around Castel, but hold Castel. Large Arab forces with five armoured cars attacked our occupying force at Dir Muhsein. Held our ground, then counter-attacked. Arabs retreated.

1450 hours. British officers ordered us to leave Dir Muhsein or would blast us out.

1800 hours. Order from Haganah Command to leave Dir Muhsein and inform British we are complying with their order to avoid clash with them, but if Arabs return we will attack again.

There was no service car this evening to take us to the transmitter, and only 8 minutes to go. I stopped a small private car—few and far between these days—and produced my Haganah card. The driver nodded, the two women with him got out and began walking, and we jumped in.

Michael, finding house-work and cooking (what there is to cook) too much for him, has at last discovered a maid for three mornings a week. She hails from Germany, very superior; asks to be addressed as Miss M.

Don was in this evening. I like him and enjoy his company. Has a great gusto for life and the friendliest smile, and looks as though he can not have an enemy in the world. His ideas wander rather muddily sometimes, but are sincere, often provocative. The other Americans don't quite understand why he is here; his Jewish interests are very tenuous. He says it was a toss-up between Princeton and Jerusalem, and he knew Princeton and didn't know Jerusalem. Says he misses the beat of New York sometimes, but is glad to be here.

8 April

WE HAVE LOST CASTEL; a heavy blow. I heard it first from Avri, slouching half-dead from his battered car near the *Mateh* early this morning. It fell at 2.30 a.m., changing hands three or four times in hand-to-hand fighting. About 600 Arabs attacked in the final stages. We had one success: Abdul Khader Husseini was killed; also a British Army deserter, in the forefront of the command. The Arabs are celebrating their victory. From a rooftop at midday we caught glimpses of their beflagged processions near Jaffa Gate and heard the echo of their shouting. They haven't announced Abdul Khader's death yet.

Fighting all day along the road. A convoy that left Jerusalem at dawn for Tel-Aviv was turned back before the edge of the city. The passengers must be desperate; some have been waiting for over a month to get home to Tel-Aviv.

The explosions we heard during the night were 18 evacuated Jewish houses being blown up by Arabs near Sheikh Jarrah. Once, Arab neighbours there beat off a band that came to set up snipers' posts against the Jews. Only over their dead bodies would they allow such a thing, they said; that was last December, a long, long time ago.

Met S. buying clothes this afternoon before returning to England. Other Englishmen are doing the same. All not engaged in essential work have again been urged to leave. For those British civilians who have "deep roots" here—churchmen, for instance —the Government has planned four zones, supplied with food, fuel and wireless communication. S. says the women are the least anxious to leave. Compensation for British officials (from the country's taxes) exceeds their own expectations. Many are getting last-minute retroactive promotions, which also means still higher compensation. S. confirms that some Government heads are systematically throwing their departments out of gear; others allowing theirs to disintegrate. A few are bitter at having their work of years pulled to pieces, but are powerless to check it.

S. spoke sadly of the position. I have known him since he arrived almost straight from Oxford, 15 years ago. A decent fellow, though that hint of frost in his blue eyes, even when he smiles, is something to which I have never become accustomed. "Here's one Englishman who isn't going to take sides," he said when he came. I think he tried to abide by that; yet he wasn't shy of freely criticizing Jews, Arabs and British alike. Once, however, after ridiculing the Jewish political party system ("factionalism gone grotesque"), he added, "Anyway, people who can create the *kibbutz* and love the soil the way the Jews do might still teach the world a few things." He said to-day that most civilian Englishmen here think the Arab states will march on Palestine after 15 May and haven't much faith in Jewish ability to withstand them. "They see the chinks more than armour," he said. He doesn't share that opinion; believes we'll come through, but with a thin margin. Says the G.O.C. also holds that view.

Ruth was filled with excitement when I met her for lunch. She and Rivka R. went painting this morning. People must have thought them brainless. One passerby did remark, "Nothing better to do in times like these!" They chose a protected spot in the lee of a large building. Ruth's picture is well conceived, with fine sense of colour and vivid depth. She's gifted, but paints with so much passion that it leaves her exhausted for hours. She kept brimming over all through lunch, talking even faster than usual. How she loves life and the world, and what a concentrated, intense vision she has of it! When she is happy it's hard to be gloomy in her company. But these days she is looking thin and pale; am very concerned about her. To-morrow she starts on her new *tafkid* (duty) in the map-drawing section.

Great discovery! Dr. B. across the road has agreed to serve us lunches (for the present). Having lost his Arab and British patients, he and his wife started a private *pension*; and had the foresight three months ago to lay in large supplies.

Our kerosene down to half a tin. Cooking only by electricity now, but the current is burning at low pressure and is cut off altogether two nights and two half-mornings a week. The Electric Corporation warns us of greater cuts, as Government will not help it replenish fuel stocks for its generators. Some people are cooking on wood fires. No candles to be had anywhere.

9 April

WE ARE BACK IN CASTEL: a grim fight, from midnight to dawn. Our losses not yet released, but known to be heavy. While Palmach attacked, other units warded off reinforcements streaming from three directions. With the Arabs in flight (and our men in pursuit) a passenger convoy cut through from Jerusalem to Tel-Aviv. But nothing came up from Tel-Aviv.

Last night Etzel captured Deir Yassin. Appalling accounts are circulating of their indiscriminate killing of men, women and children. The entire purpose of the operation is questionable. Deir Yassin was one of the few peaceable Arab villages around Jerusalem. When an Arab band tried to make its base there last month the villagers themselves repulsed them, at the cost of the life of the *mukhtar's* (headman's) son. And now this hideous act! And to round off their brutality, they proceeded to parade their prisoners through the streets. At 2 o'clock this afternoon I saw three trucks driving slowly up and down King George Avenue bearing men, women and children, their hands above their heads, guarded by Jews armed with sten-guns and rifles. The *mukhtar* of Deir Yassin, his womenfolk and children were in the truck. In front was a young boy, a look of anguished horror bitten into his face, his arms frozen upright. The *mukhtar* himself stared blindly ahead. A few street urchins cheered, but the bystanders around me looked revolted. This afternoon, Haganah forced Etzel to give them all up and handed them over to the Government.

For the broadcast this evening I found a stop on all detail about Deir Yassin. The Commander had a cold, furious look in his eyes. It seems that Haganah is also involved. During the attack Etzel found itself in difficulties and called on Haganah to help extricate their wounded. That was in the earlier stage, before the butchery. Had he followed his inclinations, the

Commander would even then, I fancy, have left Etzel to get out of its mess as best it could. He called their subsequent action "an orgy of slaughter" and "deliberate murder," and said that, on completing their handiwork, they "ran away." He will issue a statement about it to-morrow. The Arabs will raise a terrible outcry, and the Government will help them. But Jewish opinion, too, will be outraged. Into what shame and mischief Etzel is leading us!

10 April

DEIR YASSIN IS THE one topic. Full details are still unknown and Haganah is allowing no one to go there. It has taken over the place and ordered Etzel out. At a Press conference at a secret venue last night, Etzel tried to justify their action. They claimed that an armed band had occupied the village and was preparing to attack Jerusalem. They declared that they had warned the villagers to leave before launching their attack. They stressed that Haganah also had a part in it, but awarded the full credit to themselves and to the Stern Group that participated with them. For all the lack of detail, it is clear that this was not a straight military operation. It may have started that way, but it ended as a massacre. I saw de Reynier, of the Red Cross Delegation, who visited the place yesterday. He would not talk, merely tightened his lips and said, "Horrible, horrible."

I spoke with two I. and H. who went there with the Red Cross as Haganah photographers. I. was too shaken to say anything. H. told me he saw a large pile of burned and half-burned bodies in a pit; another pile of children's bodies, about 16 of them. In a room of one house were the bodies of a woman and a child; in a second room the bodies of two villagers and two uniformed Syrians. The Arab Executive say 254 people were killed.

None of the barbarities the Arabs have committed in the past months can excuse this foul thing done by Jews. Most Jews I have spoken with are horrified. Some still refuse to believe it. Yet there are others—cultured, kindly people, like the R.'s—who condone it, say the Arabs started, and this is the only kind of reply they understand.

David (the Haganah Commander) still had no statement to-night for the broadcast. He purses his thin lips, his pale blue eyes grow colder, and he says: "Not a word yet. That's all." During our transmission an English voice cut in: "What about Deir Yassin, you murderers!" We shall hear plenty about it.

Castel is firmly in our hands, though the Arabs are maintaining their attack.

From various parts of the north comes good news. At Mishmar Haemek our counter-attack swept through four Arab villages and is gaining momentum. Kaukji sent out truce feelers there, via the British, but Haganah rejected them. On the Syrian frontier, settlers drove back a Syrian band across the border. In Tiberias, Haganah retaliated sharply when Arabs broke the uneasy local truce. In Haifa, also, the Arabs have taken a blow. But all over the Middle East their Press and radio continue to proclaim dazzling victories: they conquered Mishmar, for instance, in 90 minutes; and go on to predict the conquest, at that rate, of all of Jewish Palestine, with Jerusalem, in just one month.

Could not close my eyes last night for the shooting, which crackled simultaneously from all parts of the city. Got up and read Josephus' account of the battle for Jerusalem in far-off days; the bloody furrow the Romans ploughed west of the city—where the road runs now to Tel-Aviv; then south—where the Etzion settlements stand to-day; then at last up to the walls of the city itself. The siege (which, I note, started on this calendar date, 10 April); the devastating internal dissensions. Jews butchering each other in the dirty, high-walled city hardly a mile square; the ghastly famine. The might of Rome savagely pounding, pounding away; the Jews resisting like maddened lions for six months, until they were utterly done for. A handful of men, they defied the mistress of the world with "a courage which has never been equalled."

I fell asleep before daybreak, during a lull. Woke up this morning to the sound of renewed firing, which continued all day. On the surface, people are taking it calmly. Michael was horrified to see families, with children, taking their *Shabbath* morning stroll in Rehavia (can't go further southward) while snipers' bullets were crackling out only a few hundred yards away. Even the little children now run around calmly collecting the cartridge cases. But underneath, people's nerves are getting on edge.

Rations this week: 2 oz. of margarine, $\frac{1}{4}$ lb. of potatoes and, by some miracle, $\frac{1}{2}$ lb. of meat. No water in the taps to-day; the water pipe-line from Ras-el-Ain, which runs by the side of the Tel-Aviv road, was damaged by a mine.

Called on the Edward J.'s this afternoon. We sat in the dining-room; their front-room, with half the rest of the house, is occupied by Haganah. Sometimes there are as many as 40 men; they sleep on chairs, couches and the floor. Most of the houses on the boundaries of Rehavia are like that. At the J.'s, hand grenades which they fill explode occasionally, and one of the boys will put his head into the dining-room and say to the J.'s with a grin, "It's quite all right. That was ours." One lad—Mussa, they called him—was eagerly talking Communism to Edward the other day when he was suddenly called away on a *peula* (operation). He said he would continue the discussion on his return. Next day they told Edward that Mussa was dead.

11 April

My birthday to-day and Ruth decided we would cele-
brate. Not very gay. The big surprise was a cake she made (out
of some of our flour reserve, egg powder, milk powder, and
saccharine). I took the evening off from the wireless and we
went to Marcus Café, then on to a cinema. The coffee was un-
drinkable, the biscuit they offered us in lieu of cake, leathery.
The film was a poor revival—there have been no new ones for
nearly a month. Walking home through King George Avenue,
we passed by the thick stone and cement wall that Haganah has
put up against snipers (about 600 feet long and 8 feet high).
Through its peep-holes we saw the Old City darkly silhouetted
on its hills and the great company of spires and domes within
and all around it.

At home we opened a tin of *paté* and finished half a bottle of
wine. Ruth, who is in a permanent condition of half-empty
stomach these days, was soon tipsy, and drew funny pictures on
the margins of the newspaper. She has sobered down now, and is
enlarging a Haganah map that must be ready in the morning:
section of an Arab area, showing every path and every surface
detail (down to low stone hedges) that might provide cover.
From Katamon and other parts we hear the ratatat of Brens and
heavy machine-guns and can see flares and tracer bullets around
Yemin Moshe.

The daily shooting and death has become a habit. One's
emotions are no longer deeply stirred by it. When I hear of
someone killed whom I knew, I am upset by it for a shorter
spell each time. But sometimes, as to-day, something insidious
nags at me. Not fear or worry or any private misery; but a feeling
that all this is a prelude to a new condition made up of castas-
trophe and glory, like a sky grimly darkening all around while the
colour of a new day glitters faintly on the horizon. I shall see the

catastrophe all right, but am not sure I'll be there for the glory.

In London *The Times* foresees Palestine being laid waste; the *Economist* says the fighting is too advanced to be stopped; Bevin warns the world of the chaos which no one is doing more than he to promote. In Tel-Aviv the World Zionist General Council confirmed the Zionist programme: a Jewish State according to the U.N.O. Resolution and Jewish-Arab co-operation; in the international sphere, support of United Nations, and alignment with neither West nor East. At Rehavia Secondary School to-day they awarded graduation certificates to the senior boys, who marched out in military formation after the ceremony and will be on duty to-night as men of the Haganah.

12 April

At last got the chance I've been waiting for, to eye-witness a Palmach operation: capture of Kolonia. Just about getting into bed last night when Avri phoned: "Here it is," he said. "Meet me in half an hour." We drove to Kiriath Anavim, just he and I in his car, and an armoured carload of men ahead of us. We drove without lights, but there was moon and starlight enough to show up the winding road.

It was a queer sensation, travelling like this along the road towards Tel-Aviv in an open car, Arab villages in the valleys and among the brooding hills. Everything dark, and wonderfully peaceful. Only frogs croaked in the *wadis* and a pariah dog barked half-heartedly somewhere in the distance. The air was fresh and brisk. Avri told me that most of the Kolonia villagers had left during the fighting around Castel. It was occupied now by an armed band that was attacking Castel and traffic on the road.

Advance base was among the trees at Kiriath Anavim. The boys were lolling on the ground, oiling weapons, chatting and laughing among themselves. A few girls among them, distributing sandwiches and tea. I got a brief and incidental welcome. Avri handed me a pair of rubber-soled shoes, like those the others were wearing, and a steel helmet. Zero hour was at midnight. They were to move across country, armoured cars and ambulances following along the road. Officers, maps in hand, made the rounds, checked on the preparations, issued final clipped instructions. That was the only way to tell the officers; nothing they wore distinguished them. "Any questions?" There were none.

We set out in two columns, one marching in the *wadi*, the other along a ridge. I went in the first, and was placed towards the rear. Scouts went ahead and behind us, and more, unseen by us, were on the hilltops. Everyone wore green camouflaged

Explosion in Ben Yehuda Street

Barricade against sniper fire on Mamilla Street

uniforms. They carried a medley of weapons, sten-guns, rifles, machine-guns and hand-grenades; a few carried "walkie-talkies." They moved like wraiths down the *wadi*. Their bodies hardly swung; every line and sag was part of an effortless motion. Their feet seemed to gloss over the earth. They were young, mere boys, but their sureness gave them years. Watching them by the dimmed light among the trees before we left, I saw what kids they were, hardly out of school. Some probably claimed to be 17 or 18, but looked 15 or 16, students, young clerks, apprentice craftsmen, or lads from the settlements. Here they seemed to belong to a world a million miles away from all of that, and even further away from the studies of Rehavia and the cafés of Tel-Aviv.

The hills around there aren't high, but are constant; and bare, except for occasional clumps of olives. We advanced in the direction of Jerusalem, only 20 minutes by car from Kiriath Anavim, but very remote it seemed from these winding *wadis*. Peering towards the city up on its height, it struck one again how much the fighting for Jerusalem to-day bears the stamp of the past. Pure Bible, this is. Tactics, strongpoints, lines of communication, all follow the ancient patterns. Only the weapons and characters are different. Joshua's men, the tribes of the Judges' days, Syrians, Greeks, Maccabees, Romans; and after them, Crusaders, and Allenby's forces in World War I—all marched before us along these *wadis* at dead of night. Even Kolonia's name is the relic of a colony of Roman Legionnaires. And what, except centuries of time, distinguishes Palmach from Gideon's picked 300, or the Maccabees?

No one talked. The rocks were like ghosts in the thin moonlight. One skull-headed boulder seemed to move as I looked at it. Some shots rang out; they came from a distance, but their echo lingered among the hills. In under an hour we came to a halt, Kolonia before us. I couldn't see it, for it sprawled down the forward slopes of the hill, and I was at the rear. But a few houses on the summit were darkly outlined against the sky. The other unit had swung round and would attack from the further flank.

Our men tightened their belts and waited. At the order they advanced, moving across the slope to approach from the given angle.

Suddenly the village seemed to erupt. Our mortars started it, and at once came a bedlam of answering fire. We saw the summer-lightning flashes of their guns and the shots passing overhead. They fired wildly, to all points of the compass—except to where our men had dropped and were crawling forward almost as fast as they had walked. All the time, the hissing rain of machine-guns poured down on the village. Suddenly, an explosion that seemed to rip open the hillside; shrieks of terror. Our shock troops and sappers had reached the houses. So had the advance party of the other unit. More explosions. The Arabs were firing with all they had, raggedly, as though in a panic.

Hardly any orders were given; it might all have been rehearsed a score of times, this party sped here, that one there, each knew its job. Afterwards I heard of one fellow in our detachment, a newcomer from Austria on his first operation, who lost his nerve and clung to a rock, groaning as though he had been shot. They hit him hard, and he moved on again. . . . Arab resistance, feeble from the start, soon crumbled. When our men got to them, many of the houses were empty. Others continued to spit fire, but not for long. I saw grim resistance from one house. More of our men came up and attacked it from three sides. Maybe the machine-gun ended its resistance, maybe the hand-grenades flung through the windows.

In half an hour it was over. Most of the Arabs had fled into the darkness. I counted 14 dead, but there were more; two of their officers killed, one looked like an Englishman. Our casualties were one dead, three wounded. I wondered at the swiftness of it all. Were our men so good, or the Arabs so poor?

From house to house they went looking for Arabs who might be hiding. They found some bodies and plenty of ammunition. One fellow, big-boned and narrow-faced, passed me clutching a chicken by the legs. "Join us for breakfast," he shouted as he dashed past. That was the longest sentence addressed to me since we set out from Kiriath Anavim.

When I left, sappers were blowing up the houses. One after another the solid stone buildings, some built in elaborate city style, exploded and crashed. Within sight of Jerusalem I still heard the explosions rolling through the hills; and in between, somewhere in the lonely distance, still rose the half-hearted barking of the village dog.

13 April

A BLACK DAY FOR Jerusalem. Doctors, nurses, hospital patients—people immune in all wars—University scientists and staff, 130 in all, have been ambushed at Sheikh Jarrah. To-night we know of 50 dead, 20 injured, and many more missing or unidentified. For 7 hours, four vehicles of the convoy to Mount Scopus were trapped under merciless fire. Then, only then, the Army decided to rescue the survivors: there were eight.

A feeling of frightful outrage weighs everyone down. People stop each other only to ask for news. How many are involved? Who are they? What is the Army doing? And Haganah? The anger is almost greater at the Government than at the Arabs. For within whistling distance of Sheikh Jarrah are troops, police, tanks, all the instruments of authority and law. Two hundred yards away, at the Mufti's House, is an Army post put there to guard this very road. And it pleased them to wait until all but eight were dead. The gloom grew heavier with the lengthening day as one heard the echoes of continued shooting and saw the rising smoke. Everyone went around with hard, set faces; voices were lowered, and there weren't even rumours.

Electric mines damaged the first cars, pinning them down. Then from the hills all around the fire poured down. More and more Arabs joined in the attack. The Haganah escort, from its armoured car, could only keep them from closing in. Haganah reinforcements found the road completely in Arab hands. I saw the spotters' reports, always the same: "The Arabs are pouring fire into the cars; now they are throwing Molotov cocktails and grenades. British police are watching from the Police Depot (400 yards away). Our armoured car is firing back, but sparingly."

Before midday the Army was informed that a large Haganah rescue party was preparing to fight its way through. The attack died down just then. Any Haganah move would only make it flare up more viciously, said the Army; they would try themselves to arrange a cease-fire. Officers drove up, apparently equipped only for negotiation. It failed, and they retired. A British police officer then tried to intervene; he and a handful of men drove right into the line of fire. But his wireless calls for reinforcements went unanswered; he himself was soon injured and forced to withdraw. By 3 o'clock the Arabs were close enough to set fire to two buses. As the survivors stumbled away from the flames and smoke the Arabs picked them off. Finally, at 4.30, troops appeared and laid down a smoke screen.

A week ago Stubbs was saying at his Press conference: "Government is determined to keep this road open." Maybe after Deir Yassin it feels that it doesn't need to keep the road open to the Hospital and University.

When I passed the Jewish Agency building to-night a tense crowd was still gathered, desperately seeking information of relatives who left with the convoy. No one could help them. The names of only a few victims are known. Dr. Yassky, head of the Hospital, is among them.

I heard to-night of people who were due to go up, like Dr. A., but missed the convoy; of others who didn't have to, but went up. I heard of a couple, a doctor and a nurse, who were to be married this week, after four years of waiting; the doctor went up this morning to pay a last visit to his patients before his honeymoon.

While the attack was in progress a convoy of 175 food trucks reached Jerusalem, the largest we have yet had. From Etzion, reports of a heavy attack by about 3,000 Arabs; finally beaten off at nightfall. Also an attack last night on Ataroth.

Had to get back on foot from the broadcast and reached home late. Found Ruth waiting on the landing, tormented with alarm. She would have gone looking for me, but I have revealed to no one the place from which we transmit. Judy very dejected; her doctor was to have gone up with the convoy.

14 April

THE CITY IS IN mourning. At least 75 people dead in the convoy disaster, and other bodies are just heaps of ashes and bones that will never be identified.

The funeral was terrible. It took place at Sanhedria, the temporary cemetery since Mount of Olives was cut off by the Arabs in January. Haganah guards posted all around. Grave-diggers still at work when we arrived. To-day they had to work faster; the ready graves weren't enough. The bodies lay in shrouds in a shed. Everything makeshift and temporary; only death was permanent. As each body was brought out the name was called and the family came forward. Everything done hurriedly, for fear of sniping. The thousands who ventured to Sanhedria, the many more thousands who lined the streets, were sunk in horror and bitterness—bitterness above all with the British, who stood by and let this happen. But R. remarked to me, "This is the outcome of Ben-Gurion's policy." I heard an assistant of one of the victims say that he had been treating Arab peasants from Isawiye village on Mount Scopus only a fortnight ago.

M. told me that monitoring the wireless messages of police cars yesterday she heard a British constable say, "They're bringing them out now, all dead. This is the twenty-seventh, I think." There was a reply from H.Q. which she didn't catch. But the constable, forgetting himself, suddenly shouted in anger and grief: "If you'd have let us move from this spot when I asked you, we could have got them all out safe."

The loss is very heavy. Among them Yassky, Doljansky, Ben-David, three of the men most closely concerned with the new Faculty of Medicine; Professor Bonaventura, head of the University's Department of Psychology, Dr. Guenther Wolfsohn, the physicist, Dr. Benjamin Klar, the philologist, Mizursky, the cancer research man, Dr. Abraham Freimann, the authority on Jewish law.

This afternoon I looked in at Dr. M.'s, who escaped from the convoy by a miracle. Couldn't see him, but Rahel told me how it happened. He was in the immobilized ambulance with Dr. and Mrs. Yassky, six other doctors, a matron and a stretcher patient. Dr. Yassky was the first wounded. One by one, as the minutes dragged, all were hit. Through the peep-hole, Yassky twice saw Army convoys of armoured cars passing less than a hundred yards away. They shouted, but the soldiers continued on their way. Time became blurred and they resigned themselves to death. They made packages of personal belongings on which they wrote the names of their families. Then they sat awaiting the final bullet. Few were killed outright. Yassky was hit three times. He said farewell to his wife, colleagues, the stretcher patient, then asked for a morphine injection. The Arabs were steadily approaching and massing for the kill. M. decided there was nothing to lose; he would make a bid, however hopeless, for freedom rather than merely sit and wait. Although wounded, he doubled himself up and dropped out of the car. By some quirk of Fortune, he wasn't noticed rolling into the roadside ditch. Its depth saved him; he crawled forward to the Army post at the Mufti's House under a hail of shots. There he collapsed.

Government is connecting this outrage with Deir Yassin. "A very important change has been brought about in the situation in Jerusalem," Stubbs announces this afternoon, "due to the evil barbarities committed at Deir Yassin." The Arabs themselves make no such claim. Their official explanation is that information reached them of "large concentrations of Jewish bands gathering near the Hospital and University."

The Hospital is being evacuated and emergency hospitals set up in the city.

15 April

At its closing session in Tel-Aviv the World Zionist Council yesterday proclaimed "to the civilized people of the world, to the representatives of the U.N.O. and to the Jews scattered throughout the world" that the national independence of the Jewish people will come into force on 15 May. There is nothing triumphant or defiant about the proclamation. Between the lines it recognizes that independence is not a matter of resolutions or declarations, that a stern struggle against heavy odds stands between declaration and fulfilment.

"We refuse to remain a minority on the sufferance of others," the proclamation declares. " . . . While refusing entry to Jews striving desperately after a last refuge, His Majesty's Government opened our frontiers to hordes of invaders come to make a mockery of the decision of the United Nations. . . . Now the Mandatory is proposing to destroy the very foundation of our existence and leave the country in utter chaos. . . . We have resolved this day that the termination of the Mandate for Palestine shall, in fact, mark the end of all foreign domination in this country. . . . In this hour we turn to the Arab citizens of the Jewish State and to our Arab neighbours. We offer peace and friendship. We desire to build our State in common with the Arabs as equal citizens. . . . Fortified by faith, we appeal to all nations to grant us this right to our own salvation, and rest our trust in God, the Lord of Israel."

Will the nations respond? Will men who stir to the struggles of Cromwell, Jefferson, Paine, Mazzini see the kinship between this declaration and those that other ordinary men have made throughout history, the same act, rooted deep in the daily lives and aspirations of a people? Or will it be dismissed as just another political device?

To-day the Jewish Agency announced that a Planning Board

has completed the design of the Jewish Government, and a Civil Service Commission has appointed the first 50 civil servants.

News of Arab attacks all over the country—in the cities, on settlements and roads. None sustained, but dead and wounded everywhere. In Jerusalem, new snipers' nests have sprung up. Yesterday, a well-planned frontal attack on the Jewish Quarter of the Old City nearly succeeded. Haganah is retaliating, sniping, blowing up strongpoints and shooting up traffic.

A minute ago a company of Haganah boys passed my window. Some in knitted caps, some bare-headed; one wore overalls and another grey flannels; most carried rifles or sten-guns and a few had machine-guns. Nurses marched with the men. Motley in appearance, but all of them marched like soldiers. They were singing a new Hebrew marching sing, "The Song of the Barricades":

" . . . *On the barricades we will meet at the last*
And lift freedom on high from the chains of the past;
Rifle on rifle our guns will salute,
Bullet on bullet our guns will shoot. . . ."

The deep roughness of their voices and metallic beat of their tramp echo in the air for anyone to hear. Almost imperceptibly Haganah has emerged at last from its 40-year-old hide-out. I think of the elaborate forms of conspiracy that are so much part of its underground structure: its leaders, known only to the few, moving about as farmers from the settlements engaged on special duties, as members of innocuous public institutions or committees; the Government clerks, engineers, policemen who are also officers of Haganah; the labour organizers, teachers, taxi-drivers and its other contact men; the men and women of every sphere who form its rank and file. Even now at the *Mateh* you are fascinated by the suddenly revealed underground identity of people you knew as independent, sometimes vague figures, fitting like pieces into the vast jigsaw pattern. If you happen to know their personal identities, here you forget them. At H.Q. everyone is still anonymous; no one has a surname, the Biblical first names pinned up on their doors are all assumed.

The other day Z., now Operational Chief in Jerusalem, told me of his early days in Haganah, 20 years ago. He applied for membership the day he became eligible, on his sixteenth birthday. Years later he learnt that his father was also in Haganah. Your application had to be supported by two members. For several weeks Haganah checked up on you and your friends. Finally, you were called before an examining committee. Hours of waiting in a dark passage, then three men, their faces in the dark while yours was illumined, questioned you: about your ideas, home, friends, leisure pursuits.

"One question they put was: 'Can you keep a secret?' When I said, 'Yes,' they asked: 'Tell us one you've kept.' I heard nothing for two months. Then a message was delivered to me to be at a certain place and 'Ask for Eliezer.' I was sworn in alone, before a baize-covered table, on it two candles, a Bible and a pistol."

Complete secrecy was the first rule; they were to own no photographs, keep no letters. They met in cellars elaborately protected by three girdles of watchers and a warning system of electric bells. Had British police penetrated their hide-outs they would have found only groups of students with their tutors, armed with an innocent story and piles of books to substantiate it.

Long before they fired a shot, they learned to dismantle and reassemble light arms to the last screw. For two years they served as runners and watched the movements of given people. Only then came training in the use of firearms, in remote *wadis* in the wilderness of Judea a day's tramp from the city. They trained in small cells; rarely did a Haganah man know more than seven others. The hiding-places of their arms, honeycombing the country, were known only to selected officers. *Sliks* these hiding-places are called, from the Hebrew *sallek* (to dispose of). In many a building under construction most of the labourers would have been astonished to know what went on in their absence during the night: of the barrels of arms sunk into the earth beneath the floors and the dummy tiles that concealed them.

16 April

THIS EVENING DON brought me some pipefuls of tobacco; exquisite. He filched it from a friend in his platoon. Don told me about him, a young French Jew who fought with the *maquis*, came here on a visit, and decided to remain. Spoke also about the other fellows in his unit, an oddly assorted crowd, hailing from seven different countries; some of the men didn't know one end of a rifle from the other.

"It's crazy the way we're armed," he said. "We've one weapon for two or three men, and those we have are of all kinds. When we go out on a *peula* they bring us enough to go round, but some are still hot from the last *peula*. As soon as we get back, half the stuff is taken away for some other bunch."

He asked if I knew anything more of the last attack on Etzion. He tried not to show it, but I see his deep concern about Tamara. We haven't understood how much she really means to him. The others went to bed and Don and I sat up in the study talking by candle-light. He told me how he first met her in the bus going up to the University. Her profile attracted him; but when she looked at him it was her eyes that held him. Grey, and dazzling, he said, under thick, dark eyebrows. He hadn't been long in Jerusalem and just then was looking for a gay and casual affair. He knew that this wasn't it, but felt that he must talk to her. When the bus reached Mount Scopus, he attached himself to her, summoning up all the Hebrew he knew. From then on, nearly all their spare time was spent together.

"It was as though we had always been lovers, but had been long separated."

Then she was sent to Etzion on a training course of a few weeks. That was three months ago. A few days after her arrival the siege of Etzion started.

I don't know Tamara, but I can understand any girl being

drawn to Don. He is all enthusiasm, and his quick, dark eyes are full of fun. His loose limbs were hunched up now in the chair, and he spoke slowly, as though embarrassed by how the words would sound. He looked at me quickly across the dim candle-light, then spoke more easily. Everything about her, he said, was supple and firm. The experience of her face was that, under her short, curly hair, and her body, and her mind, too. That was also the way she thought.

"And the way she feels about Palestine. She wasn't born here, but came as a child with her people from Latvia. There isn't any other place for her in the world. When I tell her about the States she's interested in a detached kind of way, and because I come from there. But she hasn't any wish to go there."

He was silent for a moment, then burst out as if suddenly releasing something pent up in him.

"What's the matter with these young Palestinians? They seem decided, as a point of honour, to be interested only in Palestine. They aren't even curious about the rest of the world. If one of them goes abroad the others look at him as if he were a deserter."

I asked Don how he feels about Palestine.

"It's grand to be here, and it's great fighting for the Jews and fighting with them. And what they've done in this country, well, you know. It makes me proud to know I'm a Jew, too. But, hell, I can't live here! I'm an American. Give me the States and you can have the world. I love America's bigness and space and its scope. I belong there. I'd get paralysed if I had to live in this little country."

There was a slight cheerlessness in his voice, unusual for Don. It was nearly midnight now, and he suddenly picked himself up and left.

Sixth day to-day that we have no water. The reserve tank we set up in the kitchen is getting low. The lavatory smells, and I feel itchy. This afternoon I saw G. carrying home two kettles that he had filled at the old well near his office.

Recruitment order for *Mishmar Haam* (Civic Guard) for men and women not already in the Haganah, up to the age of 55.

17 April

A THRILLING DAY! The road is open, supplies have poured in. Five more hill villages taken during the night and others destroyed: this is the peak of the fortnight's battle for the road. All the way down to Wadi Sarar the bands have been driven off, and 350 Arabs killed. They called it Operation Nahshon, after a prince of ancient Judah.

At 8 this morning I was waiting at Romema road-block, with other newsmen and photographers. Carl G. remarked, "Haganah is beginning to learn Press relations." We expected the story to concern a convoy, but when Maccabee Mosseri's tired, broadly-smiling face peered out of the little saloon car I guessed it was no ordinary column. Behind him the first truck rounded the bend. "The tail is somewhere around Bab-el-Wad," he said. "This is the longest we've had; about 17 miles." Over 250 lorries; and not a shot fired at it. A thousand tons of food—and arms and ammunition; and more to come! Chalked up on the first lorry were the words: "If I forget thee, O Jerusalem, may my right hand forget its cunning." A bunch of wild flowers waved in the carburettor of the second; and "Cheers for Jerusalem" was painted on the third. I don't know which stirred me more, the sight of lorry after lorry, piled high, rounding the bend, or the excitement of the drivers and Haganah escort as they entered the city.

Within an hour the whole city must have known. Jaffa Road, almost empty on an ordinary Saturday morning, was thronged. Light-hearted, cheering people lined the convoy's route to Schneller's. Some still in pyjamas. They filled streets, balconies, roofs. Women with tears in their eyes. "Isn't it wonderful?" they kept repeating, as though there was nothing more to say. It was not only that food and equipment have come in, but also that freedom has been restored. Jerusalem is no longer isolated. When the column halted, children swarmed over the lorries and lionized the drivers, who loved it.

In honour of the convoy, we opened a bottle of wine for lunch and a tin of duck in wine sauce that once found its way into the larder. The B.'s joined us and we set the table alongside Judy's bed. Ruth danced with delight. English wasn't expressive enough to reflect her mood. It was *fantastisch*, she said. Everything was *fantastisch*: the boys and girls of the Haganah, the opening of the road, the convoy, the duck in wine sauce, the spring shining so cordially from the sky and earth. Judy was cheerful, too. She laughed and joked in her measured, penetrating way; and Michael made fun of Ruth's intensity. For the first time in months that prison-trapped feeling has slackened from us. And not for ages has one's heart been filled with such peace, with serenity and real laughter.

After lunch Ruth and I climbed to the flat roof of the high building across the road and looked out over the city. Spring seems real now, the red japonica and apple blossoms in the gardens, the daisies and anemones in the fields, all true; and there isn't any mockery in the fluting of the birds. Only the walled city on the hill is still a prison, grey even under the warm blue sky. And that has its own light, lit by the centuries of human longing straining eternally towards divine peace.

18 April

THE SIEGE IS *not* lifted. At the *Mateh* last night they were saying quite plainly that we haven't the forces at present to hold the road permanently. Some of the key villages remain in our hands, but the Arabs are expected back among the hills, and in greater strength than before. I hadn't the heart to tell Ruth and the B.'s.

Ruth went hopefully shopping this morning, but returned almost empty-handed. None of the convoy supplies has been distributed yet. All she got was some milk, made of milk powder, that the butcher down the road has been selling at 5 piastres (1s.) per pint.

I saw a man killed to-day in Gaza Road. Shots were coming from Katamon and Talbieh. I walked close to the houses, taking shelter when the bullets came close. Suddenly a bullet hit a Jewish constable walking on the pavement about 20 yards ahead. He fell forward like a log. If he uttered any sound, I didn't hear it. Before I reached him a man and girl ran out of a house and carried him into Dr. H.'s. Mrs. H. told me he was dead.

I walked on, hugging the houses. The street, which used to be a street like any other, now had a menacing significance all its own. A malevolent spirit seemed to have taken hold of it, lifted it out of the pattern of Rehavia, transformed it into an endless black tunnel. Shots kept cracking out. Would I reach the end of it? And why only this street, I thought. And why only snipers' bullets? We go about, telling ourselves that they will never get beyond mortaring and sniping, that Rehavia is somehow impregnable to assault. Why shouldn't they break through? Our machine-gun nests in the border buildings, our stone barricades— can those alone keep them out?

Contrast in reports: A Government hand-out at the P.I.O. to-day stated that Kaukji's forces on the Mishmar sector "have left the area." General Ismael Safwat (the Iraqi Generalissimo of the Arab forces in Palestine) puts it differently: "They have extricated themselves from the area besieged by the Jews." Haganah says the Arabs have been driven from their last stronghold on this front.

Jim H. was talking at the P.I.O. of his visit to Kaukji's H.Q. at Tubas. He calls the Arab Army of Liberation a "bunch of ragheads"; says 500 Haganah men half decently armed could beat the pants off them in a couple of days.

Had supper with Dick at the P.I.O. canteen. I don't go there oftener for fear that someone will recognize my voice from *Kol Hamegen*. But when hunger gets the better of me, I take a chance. Ahmed still serves correspondents a real egg, real milk and real cigarettes. He wouldn't give me anything to take away. Says he'd be a "ver' dead man" if he sold food over the counter to a Jew.

After supper, Dick, asking if I had a strong stomach, showed me an album of photographs of 50 dead Jews. An Arab peddler sells them outside the Y.M.C.A. Mutilated bodies of both sexes and all ages. You can buy them in folding albums or singly; one album is pinned up on the outside Y.M.C.A. wall as a display advert.

Back home (feeling embarrassingly well fed), I found Erwin A. telling Ruth of a man he met who came by yesterday's convoy. Bag in hand, he walked up to Erwin and enquired casually after "a hotel which also serves food." Erwin said: "If you find a place like that let me know, too."

19 April

Extraordinary news from Tiberias. The whole Arab population has fled. Last night Haganah blew up the Arab bands' headquarters there; this morning the Jews woke up to see a panic flight in progress. By to-night not one of the 6,000 Arabs remained. Some fled to Nazareth, others to Transjordan. I wonder what's behind it. It can't be just fear of the Jews.

Drove out this morning to Castel with Yeshurun. Stopped *en route* at Schneller's, Haganah's main Jerusalem camp. Very German it still looks, the name *Syrisches Waisenhaus* broadly carved in old Gothic, the architecture solidly German and, in its tower, the old German clock with its slow, deep chime.

Speaking of yesterday's attack by the Arab Legion on Neve Yaacov, Yeshurun said they have sworn to flatten Neve Yaacov and Ataroth. The two settlements are in his area of command; and keeping them supplied is giving him a headache. A few weeks ago he adopted this ruse: he had a 14-cwt. truck painted olive green, in British Army style, and with faked Army numbers. To man it, six fellows who could pass for Englishmen were chosen and dressed in R.A.F. uniforms. Before Ataroth, Arab road guards challenged them. They answered with a flow of English oaths that both cowed the Arabs and satisfied them that they were Englishmen. They brought through 11 tons of food, as well as arms and ammunition.

Amos was at Castel on a duty visit. Noticeably older than when I saw him a few months ago, but still a big kid; even the deep tan couldn't hide his masses of freckles. He has been in most of the fighting in the hills. Told me how his fellows march at night by forgotten paths so as not to arouse even the Arab dogs, fight till dawn, then return to Kiriath Anavim. Tired, muddy, wet with sweat, they eat and rest for a few hours, then go out again. If it isn't direct action, it's watching, reconnoitring, probing, setting up new strongpoints, or preparing for the next night's attack. So, day after day. For weeks they don't change their socks; their shirts, thick with blood and dirt, stick to their backs.

"And we've never got enough stuff. We've always got to be ready with whatever lies to hand. The fellows who don't fight never seem to be ready. The further from the actual fighting, the more disorder and slowness there is. But I suppose it isn't their fault, either," he added moodily.

I asked him about Operation Nahshon. Three battalions were in it. His fought between Jerusalem and Bab-el-Wad. They were the most experienced. One of the other battalions almost upset the whole operation; a good crowd, but with hardly any training, and knowing next to nothing about battle discipline or battle procedure.

"Once, lying in ambush for a company of Iraqis, it was all their commanders could do to restrain them from firing prematurely and revealing their ambush."

The Arabs, he told me, were already back in the hills. "Jerusalem has got to eat," he said. "We'll have to drive them out again." I thought of how jubilant we all were on Saturday thinking the siege was lifted. But, for every convoy, these boys must go out again to clear the road. How long can it be that way?

Castel is a mass of ruins. Fortifications and machine-gun nests all over. Amos swung his arm in an arc, including everything on both sides of the highway.

"From here we control the road down to Suba. The trouble is lower down, and those hills to the north."

I looked over the defiles and the hills, like nicely rounded scones. Easy to see why Castel has always been a strategic height. The Romans called it Castellum, and relics of a Crusader castle still lie about. From here you see also how harshly the gorges cut into the high Judean tableland. Recalled that episode in Joshua's days when his spies, returning from Judea, said, "Make not all the people to labour thither; let but two or three thousand men go up." There was feeling in those words, "to labour thither." Amos and the others to-day must know just what they meant.

20 April

ANOTHER GREAT CONVOY has come in—294 trucks—but this time badly mauled. Six killed, 24 injured, 36 trucks damaged or destroyed. Over half of the vehicles were safely on their way to Jerusalem when the others were attacked near Bab-el-Wad. Six hours later the last of them limped into the city. Ben-Gurion was in one of the earlier cars.

I was in Ben Yehuda Street at 11 when a shout went up, "A convoy is in." Once again everybody dashed excitedly into Jaffa Road. The lorries rumbled along, like a festive procession, with the crowd waving and cheering and the men of the escort waving back with their guns. After midday, hearing of the attack, I went down to the Romema road-block. Scout cars and armoured cars were dashing out at full speed. One by one, or in small groups, the other lorries came into Romema during the afternoon. Most of the drivers and escort were done in; black, torn, many hastily bandaged, their lorries perforated with bullet-holes. Maccabee Mosseri was among the wounded.

Yesterday, Abdul Khader's successor as Jerusalem commander, Emile Ghoury (a Christian Arab, graduate of an American University), told foreign Pressmen that his first job would be to seal "convoy alley." To-day Government announced the gradual suspension before 30 April of all postal services, internal as well as overseas. So in every way we are being cut off from the world like a plague spot. And they call it the Holy City!

Every day the town looks more of a theatre of war. New concrete strongpoints and trenches; road-blocks being converted into barricades; streets torn up for anti-tank traps. Old and young alike have been mobilized for this work. Children not yet of age for Haganah march out after school to help build defence works.

The papers that came up from Tel-Aviv with the convoy are full of death notices from every part of the country. Strange how often parents write the obituaries of their children, and the extraordinary and moving restraint with which many write them.

Encountered two attitudes to-day. The first was a refugee peddler who carries tooth-paste and other toilet articles from table to table around the cafés. While giving Michael change, he remarked that Americans and such-like were mad to come here when they didn't have to. The second was a boy in uniform who got chatting with me in a bus queue. He comes from England. "My father's proper daft," he said; "he cables me to come home. *He's* the religious one, prays for Jerusalem every day. I ain't religious, but I ain't leaving 'ere."

The Jewish Agency to-day charges the British Army with handing over large quantities of its military stores, arms and equipment to the Arab Legion. In London, Mr. Attlee tells the House of Commons that he does not think the arms Britain is supplying to the Arab States are likely to be "improperly used in Palestine."

21 April

ENDLESS SHOOTING ALL through the night. I got up early, unrested and despondent. The easy confidence I had in spite of everything has dwindled, and the outlook now seems dark. Nothing about me seems my own any more, least of all my destiny.

During the shooting from Katamon last night the whimpering of a frightened child next-door sent my thoughts again to Gail. Often, these days, I think of her, growing up in peaceful South Africa. I wish so deeply that her childhood, at least, may be carefree. Wonder if she remembers Jerusalem still, those calm and peaceful days when we ambled through its streets? She must have stopped puzzling long ago over what became of her father. I think of Doris, wondering how she is rebuilding her life there. Life was hard on her, and I, in the end, hardest of all.

I decided during the night that I must write to Gail to-day. Within a week the mails will stop; after that, who knows? By next week, anyway, I may not be here. Why should Leib Jaffe, Vita Melamed, that policeman in Gaza Street, or any of the others be killed, and not I? I am no less exposed, no less vulnerable. It goes on and on; simply a question of which ends first, the shooting or I. Every day, by the law of proportion, my chances grow slimmer. I go to my office or into town, run across open spaces, duck as the shells and shots whizz overhead, and feel all the while the helplessness of the individual, the futility of trying to avoid death or maiming here when it may be waiting for you as you turn the corner. At night I listen to the implacable accent of finality of every shot and shell and think of those for whom this night is their last.

M. asked yesterday if she could name me executor in her will. I made mine weeks ago. Everyone is writing his will. That is the only legal work lawyers are doing these days.

I find I am saying to myself, "I must do this or that next week," and adding in parenthesis, "if I am alive." Or (if it is something unpleasant), "I'll put this off. Perhaps next week I won't have to do it any more." It isn't death itself I think of: not the poignancy nor tragedy of it; simply whether I shall still exist to-morrow or next week. I don't believe I am afraid. But life has become so brittle and contingent, so little dependent on me.

22 April

I MUST STILL SHAKE myself to believe the news from Haifa, as though it were something "plucked from the moon." The whole town has been captured by Haganah. Haifa is not Castel or Biddu. It is a city. Besides its 70,000 Arab population there were Arab Legionnaires, bands of Syrians, Iraqis, Lebanese, ex-Nazi prisoners-of-war from Egypt, Yugoslav mercenaries, British deserters. How could they all crumble up like that in 30 hours? Yesterday we heard of heavy fighting; there was nothing startling in that. When the news broke this morning of the initial successes we were thrilled. But the capture of all Haifa? Exaggerated, we thought. E. met me this afternoon with the remark, "You don't have to believe it, but it's true." A great wave of exhilaration has swept the city, and I am sure the same thought has entered everyone's mind: If it can happen in Haifa like that, why not Jerusalem?

An amazing thing is the scrupulous fairness of the British in Haifa. They are incalculable. The Army moved officially out of Haifa city yesterday morning. In keeping with its evacuation plan, it occupied a small strip of the port area, and that is all that now concerns it. Yet it's still incredible that, seeing the Arabs taking a beating, they didn't intervene. Knowing their record, everybody is asking, Why?

The planning and execution by our fledgling army was, by all accounts, perfect: a three-pronged attack from Mount Carmel and a series of concerted pincer movements in the Arab sectors lower down. In the level stretches, units of our men sprang up like clock-work and battered their way into key-points like the Telephone Exchange, Railway Station, Government offices. Here and there Arab pockets are still resisting; but they were beaten, it seems, from the beginning.

About 20,000 have fled already. The sea is their only escape route, and thousands, crying out for transport, are flooding the harbour area. Their leaders are suing for truce. One of Haganah's terms is that all foreign Arab troops be handed over for deportation, and "Germans and Nazis be surrendered," a significant distinction.

Haifa wholly in Jewish hands—what a prize! Port, Iraq oil pipe-line terminal, refineries (where 40 Jews were butchered a few months ago), nerve centre of all the country's communications, road and rail junction of the Middle East, key industrial centre. I remember the old Admiral I met at Oxford last year. "I don't know and I don't care," he said, "who's going to be top dog in the rest of Palestine, Arabs or Jews. But take it from me, young man, we'll run Haifa."

Fighting all over the country. Everywhere except in Haifa the Arabs are attacking—Galilee, Sharon, Tel-Aviv, Negev—but we are holding our ground. Bad business in Galilee: 18-hour battle at Ramat Naphtali on the Lebanese border, 21 settlers killed, 15 wounded. But in the Negev, a complete rout of the Arabs, 40 of them killed. Here in Jerusalem, the endless "orchestra," as the children call it. Will ever again a night be free of that clamour?

Rations for Passover week: 2 lb. of potatoes, 2 eggs, $\frac{1}{2}$ lb. of fish, 4 lb. *matzoth*, $1\frac{1}{2}$ oz. dried fruit, $\frac{1}{2}$ lb. of meat, $\frac{1}{2}$ lb. of *matza* flour. Sheer wealth it sounds as I write it down. Ruth is for wild indulgence. We may be dead to-morrow, she says, and see what we'll have missed! To-day I'm less concerned about sudden death; it seems remoter now. Ruth says it's the vitamin pills working on me.

The special correspondents have organized two neutral Press zones in which to live. My bet is that before long one will become overwhelmingly pro-Arab and the other pro-Jewish. That's how it always seems to end. Altogether, conditions are pretty tough on foreign newspapermen. Neither Haganah nor the Arabs have proper Press relations. Government sources are hopeless. The Jewish and Arab sectors are already in effect completely partitioned and Government doesn't even know what is happening in them, other than what each side chooses to tell it. If the correspondent has Jewish contacts, he is suspect to the Arabs; if Arab contacts, suspect to the Jews. He has all the food and transportation difficulties of the resident, all the danger of the war correspondent, with none of the facilities.

23 April

THERE IS SOMETHING EERIE in the way the Arabs are running. In Haifa their leaders to-day decided against a truce, after all. They agree that Haganah's conditions are fair, but prefer to evacuate the whole population. Some unseen hand is stimulating this exodus, first in Tiberias, now Haifa. Many wanted to remain. They know the Jews, had dealings with them. They have no idea what awaits them in the Lebanon; whether there is a roof and food, what they are going to live on. But all 70,000 are leaving. The British Army is helping them with transport.

The conquest becomes the more astonishing now that we know how few casualties there were on both sides. Yesterday, while Faris-el-Khoury, Syria's delegate at U.N.O., was painting a blood-curdling picture of "Jews directing their guns towards the peaceful thousands of Arab citizens" and "corpses piled up in the streets," the High Commissioner's report to the British Government was released: another of the big surprises. It said, "The Jewish attack was the direct consequence of continuous attacks by Arabs on Jews. . . . Arabs in Haifa were thus themselves responsible for the outbreak, in spite of our repeated warnings." It adds, "There is no question of a massacre." Of the Army: "As always, the Army is completely impartial." After all Government's misrepresentation, people keep puzzling: What lies behind this report?

The great uplift that Haifa has given to Jerusalem persists. Everyone is keyed up to some big Haganah move here—to-night perhaps. *Seder* eve, start of the Festival of Freedom—what occasion more apt? The men are, in fact, under "stand-to" orders. One's first thoughts turn to the people pent up in the Old City, the siege within the siege.

More and more Arabs are leaving the city. They are feeling

very low after the Haifa news. The luxury hotels in Cairo and Beirut are already filled with the wealthier Palestinian Arabs, some of whom left as far back as December. Convoys of trucks piled high with furniture and kitchen utensils are seen leaving by the two safest routes, eastward to Jericho and Transjordan, southward to Hebron and Egypt; the children laugh, clamber about their mobile playgrounds, still insensible of the tragedy of leaving home for exile. Arabs who cannot pay the fantastic fares now demanded are crowding into the Old City.

The flight from Jerusalem is aggravating the glut of foodstuffs in the surrounding Arab villages. The first blow was loss of their Jewish market when the troubles started. What a preposterous situation—100,000 people hungry here, and mounds of food rotting a few miles away. Ruth paid nearly £2 for the 2 lb. of meat that was our joint Passover meat ration (and stood in queues for about 5 hours). At Malha, which I can see from the roof-top, they are probably selling a whole lamb for under that amount.

Because of the desperate fuel position, buses now stop running at 7.15 p.m.; taxis almost unobtainable. Most private cars have been requisitioned by Haganah. Few people have kerosene left for cooking, although I heard of some tins changing hands at £12 each. (Mrs. K.'s last half-tin was punctured a few nights ago by a shot from Katamon.) Handymen are improvising wood-burning stoves out of empty tins, bits of piping and bricks; but firewood is also becoming a problem. Street urchins hover around avenues and private gardens to lop off branches when people aren't looking. Our candles are dwindling. Fortunately, a few days ago Ruth got three small candles from a friendly beadle she once met while sketching his synagogue in Mea Shearim.

Will be at the Hyman's for *Seder*. They are having a crowd, pooling rations. The Bs. will be at Rivlin's. Judy will be carried down, first time out of bed for 7 weeks. She is as eager as a child before her birthday party.

I think of *Seder* last year. Arrived from England, reaching Mark's just as it started. Couldn't get a plane passage from Cairo in time, so I travelled by Arab taxi service across the desert. My

Arab fellow passengers were very polite. We talked about Palestine. One of them, while peeling an apple, demonstrated vividly. "In one year," he said, "all the Jews will get this . . . skrrrr," and he made a motion with the knife across his throat. Then he offered me half the apple.

24 April

It wasn't a merry *Seder* last night, but was soberly cheerful. There were 40 of us. Felt good again to see so many people gathered for a celebration. Roy and Monica also there; very few other English Gentiles can have been *Seder* guests in Palestine this year.

All the men took turns at reading from the *Haggadah*. Variety of Hebrew accents: English, American, German, Russian, Irish, and the smooth native Palestinian Hebrew. The *Haggadoth* also recalled other lands and other times; an ornate one printed in Austria half a century ago, a lavishly illustrated modern American edition, a beautiful collector's piece some hundreds of years old, the simple Palestinian *Haggadoth*, a South African edition with Afrikaans translation. The meal was a banquet: soup, two fish dishes, vegetables, dessert, wine. The fulsome exclamations were pardonable.

The Haganah Commander's *Pesach* Order of the Day suggested nothing big for to-night. "To-night is a holiday," he said; "to-morrow the struggle will go on." Intermittent shooting rang out from the Arab lines, starting up almost with the traditional words that ushered in the Festival: "They open the door as a reminder that it is a Night of Protection, and the door need not be shut, for there is no danger to-night." One did feel at that moment there was no danger. How often and in how many lands were pogroms instigated precisely on *Seder* nights! But with magnificent hopefulness, Jews always repeated, "There is no danger to-night." The longing kneaded into the *Haggadah*, the deep meaning that lies for us this year in its ancient liturgy! "Once we were slaves, now we are free men. . . . Next year in Jerusalem rebuilt . . ." My thoughts wandered, and I saw a great mass of people, maimed, wayworn, covered in dust, standing before a lake of clear water, eager to plunge in.

The battle for the road goes on. Yesterday Palmach captured
two more villages and razed the houses. But it means little if we
cannot hold them: in a few days the Arabs will be back. At Nebi
Samwil, the highest point around Jerusalem, and almost impregnable, our attack flopped badly: 25 dead among our casualties.

Visited Granovskys' this afternoon. Dr. G. still finding time
and mind for his compendious work on the agrarian régime in
Palestine. Myrian told us the strange story of Manya S.'s arrest
by Arabs a few weeks ago (before Deir Yassin). Trying to inter-
cept the Mount Scopus bus convoy, Manya lost her way and
hailed a passing taxi. Within sight of the convoy, the taxi-man
pushed her out, suitcase after her. It dawned on her then that he
was an Arab—and had stranded her in Sheikh Jarrah. In a
minute armed Arabs were swarming around, and took her to a
nearby base. The swaggering fellow in charge, bristling with
pistols and daggers, was unimpressed with the story that she was
on her way to see her sick son at Hadassah. She would be taken
to headquarters to be shot as a spy, he said.

They blindfolded and drove her away. From the sounds, she
thought she was in the Old City. When her eyes were uncovered
she found herself in a large, arched hall, the walls adorned with
banners and enormous photographs of Arab leaders, the floors
richly carpeted. At a super-size desk at the far end sat an immacu-
lately uniformed man. Manya's suitcase lay open before him. A
score of heavily armed men stood around. The officer, speaking
cultured Arabic, questioned her. Manya told him about herself,
her *kibbutz* and her purpose in trying to reach Hadassah. He
tried to make her say that the *kibbutzim* are Communist; finally
produced from her bag, as though it were the proof, her membership card in the V-League. At this stage he sent for another man,
who entered greeting him in English. The newcomer was fair,
looked like a soldier and wore an Army greatcoat thrown loosely
over his suit. Manya believes he was an Englishman, though he
appeared to understand Arabic perfectly. He took a chair at the
desk.

"Repeat what you said about the V-League," the chief

ordered her. When she finished, the Englishman rose and left.

Further questioning; then, tapping a cigarette on his thumb-nail, the man at the desk peremptorily closed the interview: "You are a spy and will be shot." Manya replied very quietly: "I shall live or die only as Allah wills it."

I could see the small grey-haired woman, her wrinkled peasant face, eyes blinking through thick lenses, standing unperturbed in that sinister room. She always had courage (and always needed it, since her Socialist days in Tsarist Russia, and later, when she helped found Kfar Gileadi in the back of the Galilean beyond). That Arab may not have believed her, but many others know how she has worked, in season and out, for Jewish-Arab friend-ship.

The chief seemed taken aback at her reply, kept silent for a few moments, then signalled his men to take her out. In the crowded guard-room the men spoke cordially to her. A European in uniform addressed her in German. Ten minutes later she was recalled. The chief stood up, turned to his men, and spoke in a loud, angry voice, as though addressing a mass meeting:

"Until now we have not harmed their women and children. But they have murdered indiscriminately. Now we shall kill them all. You hear me? All, all, all." Then turning to Manya: "I am releasing you, so that you may go back and tell your people this. We shall kill them all, all."

They released her, blindfolded, at the British police station inside Jaffa Gate.

The whole story sounded like a scene from a stage drama, hard to conceive as happening in Jerusalem even now. I don't know what struck me more: Manya's courage or the cold feeling of a Nazi-like machine behind the disorderly, primitive Arab bands.

25 April

Awakened at 1.30 a.m. by a furious din of battle. The eastern part of the city seemed convulsed. From a front-room window Ruth and I watched the flashes and flares. Once the eastern sky became pale in a sudden glare of false green dawn. It was beautiful in a fantastic, awful way, if you had a mind for it. Over the rest of the city the night was pitch dark. When we fell asleep somehow, about two hours later, the battle was still on. Slept uneasily and awoke early to the blast of explosions.

It was Palmach attacking Sheikh Jarrah. In two hours they battered their way into the heart of it. The Arabs (mostly Syrians and Iraqis), resisted stubbornly behind strong defences. Legionnaires came to their help, but later withdrew, after extricating 40 armoured carloads of Arabs from the quarter; three of their armoured cars, however, were destroyed. Only one pocket of Iraqis still held out. Palmach sappers started blowing up the Arab positions. Then the British intervened. Without warning, they began shelling the nearby Jewish bases. Only after that came their order: the Jews were to leave Sheikh Jarrah, this being the Army's projected evacuation route for 15 May. (For armed Arab bands to hold it is permissible, apparently, but not armed Jews.)

Our men didn't leave, and British shelling continued. Haganah declared it would return fire. Whereupon, the final command: withdraw forthwith or we bombard you with heavy artillery. Still Haganah held its ground. Parleys till midday, ending in deadlock. The city buzzed with rumours. On a map at the *Mateh* I saw where the Warwickshires' guns stood pointing at Sheikh Jarrah, only several hundred yards distance. No move on either side until evening. Before dark Haganah spotters reported British Cromwell tanks and 25-pounders moving up with Highland Light Infantry towards Sheikh Jarrah. At 7 o'clock the

Waiting for water rations

Refugees from the Old City

area blazed up with searchlights; a few minutes later the British guns let loose.

The city shook from the blasting. Nashashibi House, our main point, got 30 direct cannon hits in a few minutes. Haganah had only mortars and machine-guns. In 10 minutes a green flare rose from Nashashibi House, signal that the British had captured it. Haganah then left the Quarter. The British guns killed 36 men and injured over 40.

The Jews are fuming. Sheikh Jarrah is one of the strategic key-points of the city. Through it Arab bands have been pouring into Jerusalem without check. Itself, it was a poison spot long before the massacre of the Hadassah convoy. The Government did nothing to neutralize it. When the Hadassah passengers were massacred, Government just stood by. Now, finally, the Jews themselves clean it up—and Government promptly drives them out. What sickness has hold of the British?

Don (who has shaved his beard) came in last night with his French friend, a quick-eyed little fellow in the middle twenties. His name was Emile; now he calls himself Mikhael. He didn't say much at first, but then wouldn't stop, speaking in that peculiarly clear and logical French way. He was sent out by a French wine firm to the Middle East several months ago. Greatly excited by what he saw in Palestine, he decided to settle in a *kibbutz*, but got caught in Jerusalem while on a visit. He was saying that the *kibbutz* is the only place he knew which has got anything worthwhile that France hasn't. Not only real comradeship and equal distribution of wealth—you get that elsewhere, too—but that plus freedom to form and live up to your own set of values.

"If there is any future for man," he said, "it's in struggles like this for a better way of life, not by order and not by causing injustice to others, but in freedom and goodwill and without compulsion." When he paused now and then for the right word in English, his monkey-face wrinkled up and he looked suddenly quite old.

26 April

At Lake Success they want Jerusalem "set apart as an island of peace in the struggle for Palestine." So they have stopped the general Palestine debate in order to start another, on the French proposal to safeguard the Holy Places through an international régime. All the old slogans, and everybody trying to find a formula just as little more vague and less binding on themselves.

Postal services have collapsed completely. No longer any mail, inland or abroad, nor telegrams to any part of the country; cables only to England and U.S.A. No trunk calls being accepted, and hundreds of Jerusalem telephones out of order, with no attempt to repair them.

Walked over this afternoon to see the new landing field in the *wadi*, now our solitary channel of communication with the rest of the country. Because of its urgency, the Chief Rabbi sanctioned labour on the Sabbath, provided the workmen did not ride to work nor smoke while on the job. Hundreds of schoolchildren helped. It is a long strip of levelled land enclosed by a barbed wire fence. The only equipment is two wind-hoses. But it looks a little wonder. While I stood there, an Auster plane arrived, a tiny brown thing which circled once, then touched down like an outsize sparrow. It carried one passenger, some V.I.P., and a few packages of official mail.

More taxes announced by the Jewish authorities, over and above all the other taxes and dues. *Mas Lehaganatenu* ("Tax for our Defence") is the heaviest: 10 per cent. of everyone's monthly income, as well as a graded purchase-tax for every article costing 200 mils (4s.) and over. It is collected by a body called "The Executive Committee for War Needs and Rescue Fund," for which read "Haganah."

Haganah has issued a pamphlet under the title of *Upon Thy*

Walls, O Jerusalem! (from Isaiah). Lays down the principles for
assessing the military situation, emphasizing that the public must
not jump to conclusions from either single setbacks or successes.
It concludes: "Every man in Jerusalem—he and no other—must
fight this battle."

Was on barricade duty last night, 9 till midnight. Nothing
unusual, but the spot was interesting, top of Bartenora Street. On
the edge of no-man's-land, Arab territory only a few hundred
yards away. There were three of us, the third out of sight. My
companion was a big, heavy man with a gentle manner, a teacher
called Shimon. Each of us had a pistol and two hand-grenades.
The *Mateh* believes this area is one of the channels by which
information is leaking out to the Arabs. Shimon told me of a
Jewess married to a Christian Arab who used to pass this barricade every few days. He grew suspicious and reported her.
Haganah took her away for questioning. If she was released, she
hasn't been this way again. He also told me of an Englishman
who is met from time to time by a Haganah car, driven away,
and later brought back.

No suspicious characters passed while I was on duty. The cars
were all Consular or newspapermen's. The pedestrians satisfied
us about their identities. But I don't know whether our checking
system is really adequate.

Heavy shooting from Katamon, less than half a mile away,
and around Yemin Moshe. Strays struck the houses and street.
Hardly any light visible from the houses; all windows shuttered
and many sandbagged. On some of the roofs sandbagged posts
peeped out. Occasionally, a human form glided quickly along the
street. No one strolled. We warned everybody to keep close to
the walls. From a flat lower down the street there was the hum
of a party, with dance music on a gramophone. Someone told us
it was a wedding party, the couple both in Haganah. Guests kept
coming and going, many uniformed, some armed. One couple
in uniform came up to ask if we could recommend a cosy bush
hereabouts, discreet and sheltered from the shooting. At about
11 the firing grew loudest, with duels from different parts of the

city, especially around Ramat-Rahel. There were flares, and tracers drew arcs across the sky.

Shimon and I talked of the British, whom he thinks he understands, of the Arabs, whom he really understands, of Hebrew literature, which he teaches, and foreign literature, which he studies. But we spoke especially of Jerusalem. He was born in Safed, but has lived here since boyhood. Has only once been beyond the borders of Palestine; then only to Egypt. His wife wants to move to Tel-Aviv, from where she comes; she charges him with not caring what happens here to her and their two children. Shimon spoke of Jerusalem as a lover speaks of his bride. Even the four softly-falling syllables, *Yerushalayim*, when he pronounced it, held a world of feeling.

I cannot love Jerusalem the way he does. Its traditions are part of me, but as a city it is too remote and melancholy, too weighted down with the hatreds, fanaticisms, bloodshed of thousands of years. I feel that I live here within a kind of halo, woven of splendour and majesty, fed by a deep inner fire, but with scant promise of earthly warmth or serenity.

27 April

Bɪɢ ʜᴀᴘᴘᴇɴɪɴɢꜱ ᴀᴛ Jaffa and Acre. Etzel are breaking through the Jaffa outskirts, and Haganah is boring into Acre.

Jerusalem remains worst off. The Arabs have now built a road-block 100 to 200 yards deep near Bab-el-Wad. Government reports say hundreds of men working many days will be required to remove it. A Jewish plane dropped explosives, but made little mark on it. That seems to put an end to food convoys for the present. To show they are still preserving law and order, British police to-day raided a small Haganah post near Princess Mary Avenue; arrested two men and carried off the arms.

The mild suggestion of festive season at the beginning of *Pesach* week has disappeared. The second lot of Passover rations has been distributed, and who knows when the next will be. I hear that the city now has iron ration supplies for a maximum of one month. The exhilaration which the convoys brought with them has gone. The wisest prophet in this city of prophets can't tell what will happen to-morrow. All lines cut with the outside world (except the little plane), endless shooting, a Government vanishing in a trail of chaos, Abdullah declaring war on Zionism and fierce threats from the other Arab countries, tension everywhere—in the street, in your home, in the air; and U.N.O. dithering. Rina Nikova is putting on a ballet show to-morrow in Rehavia. Good for her!

Abdullah's star is in the ascendant. All Arab roads now lead to Amman. Even the Mufti has gone to see his arch-enemy. Despite the help from the Arab countries, the Palestine Arabs are failing utterly. Their only hope lies in full-scale intervention. Abdullah is the first to offer it; and it's easiest for him. He is nearest, and his Legion is already in Palestine under the guise of a British force. Even if they leave on 15 May, all they have to do is cross over the Allenby Bridge at Jericho and cross back

again. The other day Dick was complaining to Ahmed at the
P.I.O. canteen about the half-sweetened tea. "Sorry; sugar
finished," Ahmed grinned. "But wait few weeks, King Abdullah
be here. Then you have sweet Turkish coffee, plenty sugar."

Abdullah's lustrous black eyes must be shining more brightly
than ever. Lawrence describes him somewhere as a man "with
his eyes fixed unblinkingly on the better chance." One way or
another, the big chance is coming to him at last, I suppose. At
the least he should get part of the Arab partitioned area. He may
try to reach agreement with the Jews. Long ago he recognized
that the Jews are in Palestine to stay, and he has always been the
Arab leader least hostile to them. Had the British not stopped
him, he would have gone through with that land sale to the Jews
in 1934.

He struck me as a very subtle, cautious politician when I in-
terviewed him at Shuneh five or six years ago. A plump, ex-
uberant little man who spoke fast and emphasized his points by
waving a chubby forefinger at me. Is said to be a man of parts,
a scholar, something of a poet, a great horseman and a keen
chess-player; also a keen military tactician, especially on a chess
board. He had a chess set made with tanks and planes in place of
regular chess-men, and double their normal number. In our
talk he got on to the subject of music, one of his passions, it
seems. The most perfect of all arts, he said, "pure, sensuous joy."
(I remember the phrase coming haltingly from the lips of the
interpreter.) A remark of mine on the agreeableness of his
winter quarters at Shuneh got a lofty reply that it had nothing
to do with comfort: the spirit requires direct communion with
Nature; only thus can the body and soul achieve perfect harmony.

Etzel is henceforth to operate as a unit under the overall
direction of the supreme Haganah command, on which it will be
represented. That is the outcome of the World Zionist Council's
intervention. If it works it will be a big thing. *If* it works . . .

This evening Leo C. brought me a handful of tobacco which
I mixed with dried figleaf; also brought Judy three eggs which
he got from an American in Talbieh who, in turn, got them

from an Arab in the same quarter in exchange for cooking oil; must have been some time ago.

Sylvia came in after 11 from her *tafkid* (duty) of intercepting the wireless messages from British police patrol cars. A number of English-speaking girls are on this duty. Doesn't take them long to learn the code. Jews, for instance, are "Jigs," Arabs, "Ables" (and the police are pretty uncomplimentary about both, but especially about Jews). The Americans found it harder at first to follow the English slang. This monitoring has long been a useful source of information for Haganah.

The police apparently began to suspect the interceptions only recently and changed their code. There are few British police left now, anyway, and Sylvia says discipline among them has almost collapsed. M., who also monitors, told me last week how Police H.Q. signalled madly for a radio car that disappeared while on duty. When it turned up the policeman coolly told the angry officer that they had gone to the canteen to buy some cakes.

U.N.O. Security Council has appointed a Palestine Truce Commission consisting of the local U.S.A., French and Belgium Consuls-General. No one very sanguine. But they, at least, are men on the spot.

28 April

THE PAPERS ARE FULL of the Arab flight from Jaffa. Vehicles on the move day and night, packed like fish-cans; and, by sea, anything that keeps afloat. Fares are fantastic. Most cars are making for Egypt or Lebanon by circuitous routes. The local Arab National Committee yesterday threatened severe action against runaways from Jerusalem. But they can't stop them, especially as most of the Arab leaders themselves have fled. It has become panic now, all over the country, even from places not directly in the fighting line.

Dick, just back from Allenby Bridge, was telling to-day of the shuttle service of cars and lorries crammed with Arab families fleeing into Transjordan. About 600 people are crossing there daily. Prices in Transjordan have shot up sky high. Many families, unable to afford hotel or other accommodation, camp in the hills like Bedouin.

Arab leaders have no doubt painted terrible pictures of what will become of the Arabs if they fall into Jewish hands; and Deir Yassin has done its part only too well in support of this propaganda. But not all can believe it. That can't be the whole story. The Hebrew Press says the British are interested in stimulating this panic and creating a vast Arab refugee problem. Easy enough to blame the British; nothing seems beyond them once they get "crazed with the spell of Arabia." But deliberately, as a political weapon, to stimulate this tragedy involving the lives of hundreds of thousands of people whom they claim as friends! That even the most crazed of them must jib at. It remains a puzzle. In Haifa, Aba-Hushi has got in touch with the authorities in Lebanon to try to persuade some of the refugees to return.

The Jaffa attack looks like the real thing. Haganah is now in it in full strength. The British Army has warned the Jews it will intervene if the attack continues. Pity it didn't warn the Jaffa

Arabs during the five months of their attacks on Tel-Aviv.

The Arab Legion has been firing again at the Jewish sectors in Jerusalem. The whole position of the Legion is incongruous. Government says all Transjordan troops here are under British control and "their conduct is not in question."

Emile Ghoury has been trying to explain on the Ramallah radio the discrepancies (they can't be hidden any longer) between Arab reports of military triumph and their defeats. This is one line: "You know how the peasant sells his crop in the ear because he can't wait for the money until after the harvest. So with us. We need money for arms. So we must sell our harvest of victories now to our brethren abroad and Allah will help us reap it in time." The gallant deeds of the heroes of *The Thousand and One Nights* were not meant to be taken literally, he said, but to warm the hearts and rouse the spirits of the warriors. . . .

Westerners forget sometimes that truth is not the primary moral rule of the Eastern mind. Allah alone knows where the truth lies. So it is up to men to make the presentation, at least, pleasant and vivid.

Hear that Yigal B. was wounded by a sniper's shot this morning, travelling in No. 3 bus, reading a paper. A mortar shell from Katamon struck the house opposite us this evening; no casualties. *Mishmar Haam* orders that all World War II shelters in Jerusalem (mostly improvised basements) must be made fit for use again.

Got hold of a copy of the April number of Ramat-Rahel journal; poorly multigraphed and shows signs of the stress under which it was produced. The settlement has been having a rough time these past three months, and the attacks are growing. The first page has this: "We are right in the battle area, and the war in our section grows fiercer daily. A workers' settlement finds it hard to reconcile itself to a situation in which we must curtail our productive work and give more and more attention to war." A settler writes to express the fear that the children are growing up thinking and speaking only "of force, of armies and armaments" and might come to think too lightly of the labour of the fields and the village. Another settler who signs himself *Tarbutnik* (slang for "one concerned with culture") pleads for the maintenance of cultural activities in spite of the demands of defence. I find a bit exasperating this worship of culture in every kind of circumstance; like the people who feel dirty if forced to miss a day's bath.

29 April

ARAB AND JEWISH representatives at Lake Success agreed upon a temporary cease-fire for the Old City. Something from U.N.O. at last. That should mean more supplies for the Jewish Quarter. The last food convoy allowed in was a fortnight ago. And the search the British made then to ensure no arms or ammunition getting through! They pierced sacks with bayonets and used mine detectors even on the bread. I think some stuff found its way in, nevertheless.

Like another planet, the Old City is to us now. I was there last in February, with a food convoy. Remember the impudent stare of the Arab guards at the Gate; the deathly quiet in the Jews' Street, only the echo of Army patrols tramping on the cobbles. Wondered where all the people had gone to, till I found them crowded in the courtyards behind the buildings. That brought home to one again how much the Old City has been moulded by its stormy past. The high, embattled ramparts; then the stone houses, massed and huddled around narrow lanes, the entrances to them squat, narrow, and usually double-gated; finally, the broad squares (supplied with wells) girdled by piles of houses. All evolved for protection. And the lanes themselves, none running straight for more than a score of yards, but twisting and angled in order to hide you from a pursuer.

Haganah has accepted a truce in Jaffa, after Government's warning that full-scale military and air action will be taken against Tel-Aviv and other Jewish centres if they don't. But the Arab flight from Jaffa continues.

Only 30 British officials are left, including the High Commissioner and Chief Secretary. Others are winding up the affairs of the Palestine Government in Cyprus, having taken mountains of files with them.

Going into Si.'s to-day to buy some typing paper, I found Si., a large, sleek man of much property, bitter with despair. He had just taken a big order from two British officers. "What's going to happen to us when they go?" he said. "We'll be lost. There'll be no holding the Arabs back."

"Do you see them holding the Arabs back now?" I asked.

"No; but their very presence is a lot."

A few days ago I met another defeatist, a German Jew who had been through Dachau. He gave a shrug of hopelessness: "That is our fate, wherever we live, even here."

Found a letter to *Kol Hamegen* (sent through the Jewish Agency) at the "news-room" to-night, written by an anonymous British officer. Says he is a regular listener, and offers suggestions for improving our service. He adds: "I know your cause is right. So do many other Englishmen. Be assured that not all of us approve the policy of our Government. I have learned a good deal since I arrived here. . . . Some of us also remember that the Jews were faithful allies of the British people in the war, while the Arabs were traitors."

We are looking for another continuity announcer. Esther C. is finally getting transferred to the Old City, will get in with a food convoy. I know she has been trying to smuggle herself in for weeks. Says she feels that is where she can do most good. Perhaps she is right. That calm faith of hers and sense of duty may be needed more in the Old City in the hard days ahead than any-where else. Shall be sorry to lose her here.

Spent part of the evening with the B's. Found Judy looking wistfully at the adverts in old American magazines: at all the luscious foods and comforts we haven't got. Ruth calls it "escapist literature." Michael is out for long hours these days and Judy, all alone, must be very miserable lying there doing nothing. Michael comes home full of cheerful talk, even when he feels low, and odd bits of information. He told us to-night of a recent issue of the Army's *Fortnightly Intelligence Newsletter* that came into his hands. It reports that an American plane belonging to Haganah flew from Prague to a secret landing-ground near Beer Tuvia early this month with seven tons of arms and ammunition.

We talked of Haganah's public parade in Jerusalem the other day, the first in its history. A heart-warming sight; uniformed units, flags flying, band playing, the Commander taking the salute; every man of them still under shadow of imprisonment if caught by the British, yet watched by thousands, and no one giving a damn any longer about secrecy.

P.'s son was killed yesterday at Mekor Hayyim. Third Jerusalem family I know bereaved in a week. Ann, whom we are trying out as continuity announcer to replace Esther, told me about it this evening. She looked very worried; Jonathan, hardly 16, is already in full training. Most parents of adolescents are full of anxiety.

Unusual stir around Rehavia streets to-night. At first only single movements, motor-cycles, cars travelling swiftly; then the coming and going of lorries. An hour ago two columns of men marched by in the street below. In the headlight of an oncoming car, I saw them in their olive-green, all armed, some carrying packs, a few girls, also in battle-dress, the "walkie-talkie" swaying in the air, closed lorries in the rear.

Midnight. Waited up till now for something to break. But all's quiet.

30 April

IT WAS KATAMON they were bound for last night. The fighting is still on and goes well. Tremendous elation everywhere. What one awaited so long has started; the battle for the city. One hardly dare believe it; but there it is.

All the forepart of the quarter has been cleared, right up to St. Simeon Monastery. The Arab strongpoints on the boundary, the stone buildings of flats turned into little fortresses, have been blown up. The Arabs are on the run. It is 10.30 p.m. now and the echo of the firing comes from deep inside the quarter. No longer from the edge! For five long months, day in, day out, we heard the shots cracking down on us from the hilly border ground between Katamon and Rehavia, less than half a mile from our house. One went about one's business, shopped, visited friends in the intervening streets, always with half an ear cocked for those snipers' bullets. And now we are free of it!

The Palmach went into action at 1.30 this morning; the same boys who have been fighting in the hills without a break for the past month. The mortars laid a screen ahead of them. The explosions as sappers blew up the end houses of Katamon rocked Rehavia. Not much sleep for anybody in these parts last night. It took only a couple of hours for the spearheads to break through to St. Simeon gardens from two flanks. There must have been Germans there as well as Iraqis, for standing orders were later found in both German and Arabic. The Iraqi commander, Ibrahim Abu Dayyeh, made an early getaway, but his men fought hard. St. Simeon was not only their chief Katamon base, but it is the main strategic height in all the 10-square mile stretch of southern Jerusalem.

Before dawn the Iraqis strongly counter-attacked from Beit Safafa. They approached to within 30 yards of St. Simeon. But Palmach, expecting it, made a surprise assault on their flank.

The Arabs turned and ran. Most of the day their mortars roared at St. Simeon's and armoured cars bombarded it with light cannon. But they got nowhere. At sunset Palmach resumed its advance.

Late this afternoon I was at the forward command post. The commander is a slim, earnest young man, Yosef T., a settler of Ain Harod. One of his staff officers explained what had happened. It sounded so simple. As his finger travelled over the map, I could see the rough road to the Monastery winding across the floor of the valley. A little stream waters it in winter and the green hills encircling it are dotted with trees. The slopes must be gay with flowers at this time of the year. "It's going according to plan," he said in English, smiling. A tall, unhurried, quiet-spoken fellow, with drooping, red moustaches, and a polo shirt beneath his battledress; had been with the Jewish Brigade in the War.

St. Simeon firmly held, Abu Dayyeh fled, the Arab forces falling back—it seems only a matter of time before all Katamon is in our hands. To-night Y. told me that several days ago the Arabs were planning a gigantic assault on the city, the main thrust to come from Katamon. They hoped to repeat here our conquest of Haifa, only to do so with overwhelming forces. As soon as we learned of it, Palmach units were recalled from the hills and sent into action against Katamon; but the assault failed. Last night's was thus the second attempt; and, said Y., it wasn't too soon. A few days more and Rehavia might have been in the position of Katamon to-day!

Shabbath to-morrow, and people will be strolling along Gaza Road with their children—and no bullets. In a few days we may even walk through the gardens of St. Simeon. Two years since I walked out there last; Ruth was with me. The chapel bell was ringing—bells were always ringing in those days—and the cool, dark buildings, sunk in the trees, seemed the very home of serenity. One knew that the great walls were built as a shield for times of trouble. But then the thought of violence in this place could only be the vision of a stricken brain. The sun was sinking and its glow was lighting up Siloam and the Mount of Olives in the east. From Beit Safafa we heard the shrill call of a shepherd's pipe. Through a chapel window we saw a priest march slowly down the aisle swinging a censer towards the candle blaze. The blue cloud of incense drifted out in clouds, hung about the trembling candle-light, and rolled between the ikons. We sat in the grass on the slope above Beit Safafa. There was so much sky and air and openness among the hills, and so much peace. Then Ruth's voice, suddenly sad, broke the silence: "One thing Jerusalem has done for me. It has made me afraid. Afraid of people, of Arabs, of going out into empty places in the dark." The wind rose and the evening turned cold. We got up and walked back into town. . . .

The Consular Truce Commission has made its first move: a cable to U.N.O. reporting impending battles all over the country "on a larger and more important scale than Haifa," and anarchy prevailing outside the Jewish areas. Meanwhile, the Trusteeship Council is looking for a kind of U.N.O. "super-mayor" for Jerusalem "to ensure its peace" and run all its municipal services (which are crumbling from day to day).

To-day the Arab High Command announced it would kill the Jews of Jerusalem from thirst by cutting the water supply, which has been restored after a 6-day break, unless Jewish attacks on the Jaffa surroundings cease. Haganah is holding its fire in Jaffa, in accordance with the local cease-fire, but is attacking surrounding villages.

1 May

Two hours ago, at 20 past 1, we had our first direct shell hit. It struck the house like the blow of a colossal fist, crashing into the B.'s bedroom. I was in the study, typing. Ruth was working on her maps. A few minutes earlier Michael came in to ask what we thought of his opening another tin. "After all, we are winning in Katamon," he said. I remarked that he had already opened a tin on that score this morning. "Anyway, Judy has to have more food," he added. "She can't go on like this." All the time, from a distance somewhere inside Katamon, came the echo of firing. Then came the crash. No whistle, no shriek, just a monstrous shock. The house gave a shudder. A tinkling sound of shattered glass. A little plaster fell from the ceiling. As I ran to the B.'s room I saw wisps of smoke rolling under the door. The room was faded out in a pall of white smoke. Judy lay stiffly curled up, the coverlet pulled tightly over her head. Michael tore it down. She was lying motionless, eyes shut, face deathly white. Twice he cried out her name. She didn't reply, but as his hands gripped her, her eyes slowly opened. She was dazed, but not hurt.

Lumps of concrete, plaster and jagged bits of shell casing covered everything in the room. The floor was a carpet of debris and glass. The pall subsided, and I saw it wasn't smoke, but plaster dust. A clean-cut hole, about 18 inches long, was torn in the ceiling. Through it we could see another hole in the roof. Complete confusion about the room, but the damage was slight; it seemed strange. Then beneath an over-turned chair Ruth found the charge, unexploded. On the fragments of casing we read the marking: "3″ mortar, 10 lb."

Anxious neighbours crowded the passage. D. said he saw the shell come looping over on to our roof from Katamon. Judy is bearing up splendidly. She asked us not to make a fuss and wouldn't hear of a doctor; all she wanted was hot soup and rest.

Night

Judy slept all afternoon. This evening she said she felt fine and insisted on our keeping to our plans. So this evening Ruth and I joined Dick's party at Salvia Hotel. It is the only place where there is still dancing one evening a week. I forget when we danced last—it seems years ago.

Salvia has a border atmosphere. It is precariously poised on the edge of no-man's-land; Katamon and Talbieh here, Rehavia and Kiriath Shmuel there. You find the kind of people you expect: special correspondents, the odd Rumanians, Greeks, a couple of non-official Englishmen, a few attractive young women. The waiters are Sudanese. The proprietress wears evening dress and jewels. Dinner is served late, and the menu—if you are a resident—has items of real food. The bar is always full.

The little room and terrace were crowded. Music by a one-man band, a sad-faced Hungarian accordionist who is a wizard with his instrument. Besides Dick and his plump Jewish girl friend and us two, our party included a shy German-born Haganah lad and a sultry Oriental girl. Dick was full of tall tales. The German lad, after a few drinks, turned out to be a mine of humour. It was a warm, still night. Katamon, less than half a mile away, lay in perfect quiet. At the bar, Eliot Fielding was analysing the Katamon situation. Everybody was drinking too much.

We got home half an hour ago, soon after midnight. As we walked in, the B.'s door stared wide open at us. The room was in darkness. We looked in, alarmed. Judy's bed was empty. A hastily scribbled note from Michael said he had taken her to hospital. We got him on the phone. He told us that Judy started bleeding heavily soon after we left, and before midnight had a miscarriage.

2 May

WITH HAGANAH ALL SET to complete the capture of Katamon (only the rump of the Arabs remain and their main arsenal is blown up) Government ordered a local 48-hour cease-fire: "to facilitate negotiations for a permanent truce in the whole of Jerusalem." British troops will take action if "either side" violates it.

Now that Katamon is almost all in our hands, it seems inevitable. How could it not have happened? That is, either we in Katamon, or they in Rehavia. Yet with no more resistance, no more fighting than that? I wonder what has happened to the Arabs I know who lived in Katamon. Some of the houses are the pleasantest in the city; spacious, comfortable, many built in excellent taste, with pretty gardens. Most Katamon Arabs were dead set against the fighting, at any rate around their quarter. Some even had the temerity to say so to the Arab military leaders. But I doubt if they repeated it, especially the Christians. They never quite forgot the old cry of the Moslem fanatics; "After Saturday comes Sunday," after the turn of the Jews comes that of the Christians.

To-night, Haganah radio in Galilee was full of the fighting on the border. Syrian and Lebanese soldiers, dressed as irregulars, attacked five settlements with artillery and tanks. Haganah has rushed up reinforcements. We have suffered losses, but are holding the attacks. Fighting also on the edge of the Sharon and in the Negev.

L. has been telling about the refugees he met on the road to Amman. He calls it "a road of Arab despair." "Criminal" is one of the more polite epithets they apply to their leaders.

There is quiet in the Old City to-night. Some of the old men in the Jewish Quarter probably see the direct hand of God in the advent of cease-fire precisely at the end of Passover week.

Strange tales are leaking out of the Old City. There is an ancient legend that when the Temple was destroyed by Titus the priests threw the keys of Jerusalem to the heavens, crying out, "God, henceforth be Thou the guardian of the keys," whereupon a hand stretched down from heaven and took the keys. Now the talk among the old men is that God has given the keys back to the Jews.

Less buoyancy in the New City, in spite of Katamon. Shooting even more rampant in the other parts. For the second evening running, Arabs shelled the western suburbs with 25-pounders. That's new. The rumble of it reaches us here, like distant thunder, then the echo of the crashes. Most unpleasant.

Food position also uglier. Ration to-day: olives, about 8 per person, and 1½ oz. of jam. Supper to-night: asparagus soup and half a dried herring (imported from Turkey; used to be food of the poorest of the poor, sometimes also given as animal feed). Ruth's latest "shopping" expedition yielded 2 packets of bran flakes and 2 tins of asparagus soup. If life were not so full, I would try to plumb the bottom of the Great Asparagus Soup Mystery. How do tins of it still show up when everything else has vanished? . . . Besides the earlier cut in electricity two nights a week, it is cut daily now from 2–6 p.m.

Judy is picking up. Tough luck, having a miscarriage, after what she went through. Yet I dare say, in these conditions, she and Michael see it as relief. Friends have been looking in to examine our shell-hole and congratulate us on our escape.

First signs of a Jewish Administration: postal services in Jewish-controlled areas, including Jerusalem, announced for the interim period between now and 15 May; the plan is to get the mail to and from Jerusalem by the little Auster planes. There will be Jewish postage stamps. The first Jewish-operated train, flying the blue-white flag, arrived at Hadera from Haifa (25 miles) with an all-Jewish crew; great excitement reported.

This afternoon we cleared out our basement as a shelter; sandbagged the window.

The garden is aglow with geraniums and pink hollyhocks.

3 May

GENERAL MOBILIZATION order issued yesterday for all men under 40. It has caused some despondence. The outlook must be grave. Full-time service for women is still voluntary. Pay (men and women), £2 a month.

To Katamon this morning, with other Pressmen. A bare 300–400 yards from the limit of Rehavia. Curious that they never forced this narrow passage. Katamon is battered, but less than I expected. Many of its border buildings are piles of rubble. Here and there a house that served as a post is a complete wreck, its walls and roof crazily suspended at impossible angles. The air still smells of pounded mortar and crushed stone. The streets are animated with Haganah men, driving, marching.

We passed Z.'s house, that once stunned me with its fabulous ornaments and colossal furniture, life-size portraits, agonized gold clocks, crystal chandeliers, bright blue ceiling dotted with a host of silver electric bulbs representing stars and a large one for the moon. Through the gaping emptiness of a shell-hole I could see the ceiling and its constellations staring out in incongruous splendour. Another house I knew, H.'s, was an unrecognizable heap; but in the trim little garden the flowers bloomed undisturbed.

St. Simeon is intact, only its walls heavily pock-marked. Haganah men now stand behind the Iraqis' emplacements. Over the chapel entrance a Hebrew notice: "Holy Place—No Entrance," and before it, under the Greek cross, a Haganah man on guard.

Someone asked our conducting officer about the looting, of which there is much talk: not of little souvenirs, but of things like carpets, even refrigerators. He said it was under control.

Casualty figures published in to-day's *Post* for the past five months: 5,014 dead (1,256 Jews, 3,569 Arabs and 152 British) and 6,632 wounded. No way of knowing the real Arab losses, as many are never reported. Not much by atomic standards, but a dreadful toll for this little land; and far worse when spread out, day after day, over five months. The greatest single disaster is more easily forgotten than those dreadful daily casualty lists.

This afternoon, sheltering in a doorway from a sudden spate of sniping, I found my old hatmaker from Ben Yehuda Street, shrivelled and grey; only recently recovered from his wounds in the explosion. He was pressing hats on an improvised trestle under the passage stairway. His stock, about a score of hats and caps, were displayed in a portable cabinet on the pavement. Nothing is left of his old shop. Slowly, life of sorts has come back to part of Ben Yehuda Street. Some shopkeepers have established themselves in holes in the walls: rubble excavated, a simple doorpost built across the opening, shelves and a counter fitted in— and there is a new shop. On some of the empty plots where buildings once stood, large wooden vans do service as business premises.

The horror and cold fury of that day of the explosion! It was a rainy February morning. Before dawn, British policemen and Army deserters planted the lorry-load of high explosives in the middle of this street in the heart of the city. From top to bottom Ben Yehuda was wrecked, 60 people killed, hundreds injured, damage spread in all the streets around. That night we improvised our first underground broadcast. We transmitted from a fashionable private drawing-room, the walls lined with old oil paintings. Nothing about the room or ourselves seemed conspiratorial, least of all the dignified German lady who was our hostess. At first I felt that every word I uttered filled all space like a bell. Then I began to wonder whether anyone was listening. I saw the impression it had made when I got home. Ruth and Michael were deeply moved, said it came as a voice of authority, angry but firm and measured, giving direction and restoring assurance. But Ruth was shocked by the ease with which they recognized my voice. All day she expected me to be arrested.

Judy is coming home to-morrow. The hospital needs every bed.

4 May

Arabs continue to flee. About 50,000 have left Jaffa. (In Haifa 4,000 have remained or returned.) The roads of Galilee are crowded with them, fleeing from Safed and Acre. Surely this will make it easier for the Jews, in the long run, as well as in the short?

Heavy fighting around the Etzion Bloc, where the Legion suddenly attacked with artillery and heavy machine-guns. The defenders claim they disabled 20 Arab vehicles in reply. To-night's report is that the Legion and irregulars are trying to storm the settlements. In Jerusalem, firing all over. In Galilee, more Lebanese troops have crossed the frontier.

Rumours continue: that the large British armoured column just arrived in Jerusalem is the forerunner of a new British army of occupation; that Haganah is getting 40 planes from South Africa; that plans have been unearthed of an impending outrage by British deserters far exceeding that of Ben Yehuda Street; that beef being sold on the black market is donkey meat; that Etzel is preparing for an all-out attack on British troops before they leave; that Brigadier Glubb, British commander of the Arab Legion, has been closeted with the British G.O.C. in Jerusalem. The facts we can at least attest to are that a regiment of British tanks, headed by 34 Cromwells, yesterday moved suddenly into Jerusalem from the Suez Canal Zone; and that Robert Finnigan, giving an interview on the B.B.C. as one of the British officials evacuated from Palestine, told us this evening that while driving to the aerodrome yesterday he saw Glubb Pasha a mile outside Jerusalem with a heavily armoured escort, reconnoitring the road.

On my way to office this morning I bumped into Bertram C. in the Security Zone. He once told me why he prefers Arabs to Jews: their gracious movements and gestures, the flowing lines of their clothes, give him a sense of repose. The Jews make him

nervous; he finds them furtive and ungainly. To-day he said that
the new troops have come only to cover the British evacuation.
He laughed when I suggested that Bevin might want the British
to remain at least in Jerusalem. "I don't know about Bevin, but
ask any Tommy," he said, "and he'll tell you the sooner he gets
out of this bloody place the happier he'll be." Then he added:
"But it's *you* who will be sorry that we left. You think you can
keep your toehold on Asia? You'll find soon enough how precarious it is."

Michael brought Judy home this afternoon. In her welcome,
Ruth used up our last ingredients for a cake. We found Judy
examining the shell-hole in the ceiling with an almost proprietary
air. She was cheerful and full of plans. I told them about my chat
with Captain C., and we talked about the British soldiers. There
are tough elements among them, and Fascists, but on the whole
we agreed that if they hadn't been used to enforce Government's
policy the Jews would have got on pretty well with them. There
probably would not have been a terrorist problem then; certainly
the terrorists would have had precious little public sympathy
and would never have remained more than a tiny group. Judy
thought that had American soldiers been shot at by terrorists
they would have behaved worse.

All along one has had the feeling that the Army was the un-
willing instrument of Bevin's hostile, blundering policy. We
recalled instances of how soldiers have behaved: on the one hand
the H.L.I. party in Jerusalem that arrested four Haganah boys
and deposited them in an Arab quarter, where their bodies were
found next day; on the other, the party of soldiers who rescued
two Jewish drivers from an Arab mob in Haifa at risk of their own
lives; the Irish Guardsmen who came to search a Haganah post,
had a drink with the boys, presented them with a bottle of
whisky and left. Occasional such stories even about British police.
A few days ago a British police sergeant ran up to a camouflaged
Haganah post in Princess Mary Avenue and shouted to the
fellows through the door, "Hide your stuff! A search-party is on
the way." Ten minutes later a police search-party duly appeared.

But how many will remember isolated acts of individual goodwill amid the welter of bitter memories of official injustice and ill-will?

Prices are going up. Newspaper, bus fare, cup of coffee, laundry, even the miserable rations that you can still buy, all suddenly cost more.

A quiet run on the banks, which, people fear, may have to close their doors before the 15th. Institutions have given their staffs a month's salary in advance and are holding reserves of three months' salary in their safes. The Red Cross is organizing three "Geneva Areas," to provide refuge for 15,000 women and children.

Midnight. Am writing this by lamplight. Ruth has gone to bed. She must resent this diary. It takes so much of the little time we have together. Shooting has started up on the city's outskirts. I try to pinpoint the shots. The only sounds I can place are the cannon shots rolling in from the north-west. Here in Rehavia it is so quiet that I can hear the slight rustling of the pine trees outside, the tick-tock of the grandfather clock in the flat below. But beyond these peaceful sounds, those others beat incessantly on my mind like a hammer. Which is the more real? Neither, I would say at this moment; both feel like the strands of a nightmare, enmeshing night.

5 May

LAST NIGHT THE first session of the Jewish People's Council, the forerunner of the Council of the Jewish people, was opened in Tel-Aviv. The Jerusalem members among the 37 weren't present because of the blockade (the little plane service isn't working well). The glorious privilege of those men, to be the godfathers of the State re-born, after 2,000 years! Ten more days to go before the British leave. . . .

Ben-Gurion said, in his opening, "We shall exercise the powers of a State whether we are authorized to do so or not." He also said later that 150,000 Palestine Arabs have fled or are in flight. "That shows who the people are who are really bound to the land." I wonder? The Arab runs because he thinks he has the whole of Arabia to run to; the Arab countries always speaking up for him, promising to fight for him, to liberate him. The Jew has nowhere to run to, even if he so wishes.

Bitter fighting at Etzion; lasted 36 hours. Some Jewish positions fell, but were re-captured. Eleven Jews killed, 27 injured; Arab casualties very heavy, but number unknown.

Less shooting in Jerusalem to-day. But behind the half-lull one feels something hellish brewing. The cosy talk at Lake Success about the Truce Commission may be intended to comfort us, but fails. Beginnings of a *hamseen* adds weight to the foreboding. For the great mass of the people there is no wish to turn back; and, they know, no possibility. There never has been a parting of the ways for us. It may be more tortuous or less, but there is only one road. And because nearly all feel that way, it somehow divides the burden and foreboding among us.

Death notices of 24 Haganah men posted up in the streets.

More rumours; that Haganah is preparing to seize the vastly important Generale Building (still held by the British) in the centre of the city; that the Arabs are ringing the eastern and western outskirts, as well as the northern, with heavy guns.

On waking this morning, I saw Ruth staring into space. She said she woke up thinking of England:

"I dreamed I was paging through a favourite book of stories and suddenly opened it at a particular place, and there was England . . . Birchington and its white cliffs and stormy sea, so different from our Mediterranean; the children standing around the piano singing 'Robin Adair.' Hastings and its peacefulness, the courteous people, seldom in a hurry or harassed. . . . London on a winter's morning; riding on a bus top through Oxford Street, Piccadilly, across the Thames, all misty and grey, Westminster and Parliament, the factories showing in dim outlines; the red little ball of a winter sun low on the horizon; beautiful Westminster. . . . The slums of the south side, picturesque in spite of the dilapidation and soot. Oxford, serene and remote, its beauty so different in rain and in sunshine, its honey-grey buildings, the Isis and fantastic college barges. Blenheim Park, the old trees wrapped in fog and dripping with rain. The old inn at Woodstock with its black beams and brass and copper on the walls. . . ."

From the day she came there as a student, Ruth loved England and hasn't yet spanned the gulf between the England she knew and the England for which Bevin speaks in Palestine. She kept on, slowly, as though talking to herself:

"My little room overlooking Norland Square, drowned in blue twilight when I came home. . . . School in the morning, and the friendly fellows and girls, never probing or bothering too much with you. The whole day before you, the only demand that you draw and paint as well as you can. Coffee at Charley's with your friends, talking about art and painting, joking, gossiping. Everything so easy and quiet and unconcerned. The people, like their country, cool, dim, indifferent, and so restful. They sometimes left you lonely and unsatisfied. But now I think back to it longingly, as one thinks of a cool bath on a hot summer's day. . . ."

She turned to me:

"Do you think there will be friendship again between us and England?"

"I suppose it depends on how they treat us when they have gone."

They never seemed to understand, or just weren't interested in the deep tradition of good feeling that existed among Jews for England. For Jews everywhere, Britain was a standard bearer of human worth and dignity. I remember the Yiddish folk song Mother used to sing to me as a child about the dawn of a new day of freedom with England as one of its lights. Even the bitterness of the Afrikaaners she knew in South Africa could not dim that tradition in her.

6 May

*H*AMSEEN FROM EARLY this morning. The heat blowing in from the dry, parched desert pierces every nook. No refuge anywhere from its incessant presence. Breathing is hard; your body limp. Everything looks grey. At midday the grey congeals into a hot whiteness. Even the stones seem flattened in the vibrating air. You remember on *hamseen* days that Jerusalem lies within the great circle of the desert; the bleak, brooding, immense nothingness just over the border. Lest you forget, comes the *hamseen*. And to drive it home, come the men of the desert, Transjordanians, Syrians, Iraqis, product of those sterile wastes.

Peculiar crackle to a shot in this heat, as though it labours to tear through the haze. And a bit more sinister. Shots were fewer to-day. In the south, Arabs fired at Katamon; so much for the extended truce there! Cannon fire again from Nebi Samwil. Stern Group blew up part of an Army convoy on the road near Givat Shaul, and the Army retaliated by shelling Givat Shaul for two hours.

Stubbs had his last Press conference at the P.I.O. to-day, a pathetic affair, and Stubbs most pathetic of all. He admitted that Government refuses to allow a food convoy in to the Old City until two rifles and three pistols stolen by "unidentified Jews" from an Old City police station are returned. He admitted that Arabs are shelling Jerusalem from Nebi Samwil, but "the people concerned in the shelling over the last period have been warned. Aggression will be stopped by strong military action." No one even smiled.

Don met me at Tuv-Taam Café. We had coffee, half-cold (probably from a thermos flask). He spoke of the feeling in his unit. They are full of fight and confidence about 15 May. But they are all worried about the shortage of arms. The old story: our few effective weapons always on the move, rushed from one emergency to another.

"As far as I can see, there's not much to fight with except our guts and bodies. When I think of all the stuff my unit just squandered in the Pacific . . .!"

He told me about his visit to Tamara's people. Her father was polite, but has no interest in anyone who is not religious. Her mother was friendlier, and her kid brother was swell. "And he showed more interest in the States than almost anyone else I've met here."

Walking back, Don told me his family cabled last week urging him to come home. "But I'm in this with both feet," he said.

He talked of his family, schooling and Princeton days. His father is a fairly successful paper merchant, nothing distinguished in his life or interests. Pulp and market conditions absorb him more than events. Apart from *New York Times*, a weekly journal of current opinion, a trade journal and Book of the Month selections, which he gets but doesn't read, he reads nothing. "Plays a moderate game of golf, goes to Temple twice a year, and is particularly sensitive," Don smiled, "to Jewish faults."

Don's mother is a lively woman, interested in music, art, women's clubs, bridge, and organizing. Don says she is always planning; when there is nothing else to plan, she plans summer holidays for her friends. Don was almost solemn this evening, but I was struck again by the cheerful lightness with which he can talk of most things—even subjects that, for him, are not laughing matters.

Persistent stories of continued looting in Katamon. Jewish Agency has appointed a Custodian of Enemy Property. Haganah's Hebrew broadcast carried another warning to-night of severe action against looters.

Shooting stiffened to-night. Coming out of the "news-room," we found ourselves in the midst of a hiss of bullets. We edged low along the outer wall, then took cover behind the new defence wall before Yeshurun Synagogue. (Similar walls erected to cover the entrances to public buildings all over town.) We got on the air four minutes late.

Don was the only bright person I met to-day. Everyone else irritable, depressed, washed out by the *hamseen*.

7 May

YESTERDAY, ABU EL HUDA, the Transjordan Premier, told his Parliament in Amman that Arab resistance in Palestine has collapsed. But you don't feel it in Jerusalem. Here almost every Arab wall, roof-top, mosque, cemetery seems to have become a snipers' post, and most of them spat fire all day. Mortaring heavy, too, especially at Rehavia towards dusk. That is when the little plane usually glides in.

Jews and Arabs announced their truce terms for Jerusalem. Jewish terms: (1) opening of the Jerusalem–Tel-Aviv road and access to the Old City "from Tel-Aviv to the Wailing Wall," as Eytan put it at the Press conference; (2) withdrawal of all foreign armed Arabs. The Arab terms are: (a) Jerusalem–Tel-Aviv road to be kept closed, and they will supply the Jews with food and water; and (b) both sides to return to the areas they held before the troubles. Each side wants the same things, only the opposite.

Saw Colonel L. at the Y.M.C.A. this afternoon to learn what the Truce Commission is doing. It wasn't pleasant crossing the short stretch from the P.I.O., which lies wide open to Arab snipers on the Old City walls. I ran fast across it, ducking. L. is now U.N.O. representative with the Consular Truce Commission; a live wire and very shrewd. During World War II he was head of the Norwegian Intelligence in England. He says the Truce Commission is meeting all kinds of people who might help; secular and religious heads of the communities, Consuls, Government people. He thinks truce prospects are promising. But he believes, privately, that only force of arms will settle the issue in the long run, with the Jews having a good chance of coming out the winners. He thinks they should try to come to terms with the British. If they were convinced that the Jewish State would tie up with them, the British would swing round full cycle behind the Jews, says L.

Not all Britons are leaving Palestine unsung by Jews. The Press to-day refers appreciatively to a few men like Sir William FitzGerald, the Attorney-General, and Richard Graves, Chairman of the Jerusalem Municipal Council. The *Post* calls FitzGerald's report on Jerusalem "a genuine labour of love, even if it was labour lost." Graves was also a champion of Jerusalem; if all the municipal services have now collapsed the fault is not his.

Eric Mills is another Englishman who loved Palestine and might have done much for it were he allowed. They probably suspected him of partiality to Jews; perhaps also thought him too clever. Came in 1920 and was happy then; inspired because he saw in Palestine opportunities unequalled in history for display of the essential dignity and generosity of humankind. Allenby had entered the Holy City on foot, and that was the symbol of a new way of conquest. Now Mills leaves as Commissioner of Withdrawal, an instrument, if not the organizer, of chaos.

Saada, our Yemenite washerwoman, came at last to-day. Everyone is having only minimum laundry done to save fuel and soap. Saada said the shooting in their district is very bad. People are afraid to leave their houses by day. She told Ruth that two of her sons are in the Haganah, and one—she hesitated—in Etzel. She sighed as she told of the bitter way they quarrel when at home together.

"But they are alive and well, *Baruch Hashem*" ("Praised be the Lord").

The eldest, Yihye, nearly lost his life in January, "but the Lord looked after him." I remember Yihye, a skeleton of a boy with leathery, coffee-coloured skin drawn tightly over his hollow cheeks, and his large white teeth showing in an enormous, almost perpetual smile. Saada related how a Haganah escort of which he was a member was ambushed while returning from Etzion, and ten men killed. Yihye jumped from the lorry to rescue a wounded man who had fallen. A new storm of bullets lashed down at that moment on the lorry; the driver was ordered to start up again or all would be killed. So Yihye found himself in Arab territory with a dying man on his hands. The Arabs, concentrating their fire on the speeding lorry, failed to notice him crawling into a ditch and dragging the wounded man with him. The Arabs left, and the wounded man died. Yihye moved cautiously across country, hoping to find a hiding-place for the day and to advance by night. But, coming upon the body of one of the attacking party, he had an idea. He exchanged clothing with the dead man, shouldered his own rifle, and marched confidently forward. At the turn of the road was an Arab check-post. Yihye speaks Arabic like a native Arab. "I've come from my village to fight the Jews," he said. "My rifle has been lying in idleness for too long and cries out to kill the dogs."

The guards directed him to a house where a band was preparing for an attack. Yihye joined the band, a mixed group of local villagers and cut-throats from Transjordan and Syria. He invented answers about his village; when difficulties loomed, he side-tracked questions by entertaining them with Arabic love songs. He had a good voice and a wide repertoire learned from the wireless and gramophones of Old City coffee-houses. By early morning when the band left, Yihye was a great favourite. He marched with them towards Ramat Rahel. As soon as the attack started, he escaped.

Saada said she knew he would return. From her bosom she drew out a much-fingered little booklet. "This *kamea* (talisman) did it," she said. Its title was: *Laws and Prayers concerning Means of Preventing Influences by Evil Spirits as Unfolded for the Benefit and Consolation of the Elect in the Holy City and the Holy Land. From Ramban and Other Authorities*. It was assembled by the *Haham*[1] Saadya Gedalya and was printed in Jerusalem "In the year 5701, viz. 1873 Years after the Destruction."[2]

Saada said it was intended against evil spirits, but it was also good against snipers. Only it is not enough then to say the verses in the given order. Certain signs must be made. Behind the closed door, she demonstrated them to Ruth. When you leave the house you cover your right eye with the right forefinger and

---

[1] *Haham*—Rabbi (lit., wise man).   [2] Destruction of the Temple.

place the left middle finger to the left of your nose. The index finger of the left hand rests beside the left eye. Something like that; then you whisper, just under your breath, the verses indicated. It is useful, but not essential to carry the booklet with you always. Saada said her sons don't believe in it, but she repeats all the verses and makes all the signs for them, too. That's why Yihye was saved.

Later

Wonderful news; cease-fire for Jerusalem as from to-morrow. P.B.S., which just announced it, said it was arranged through the High Commissioner. Nothing about the period or terms. But the word itself is a dazzling promise. Even the *hamseen* seems easier.

8 May

I T REALLY IS CEASE-FIRE, and the tormented city is catching
its breath. We know it is not the same as a truce, and there is
little hopefulness that it will last long. But here and now the
tremendous fact is—it's quiet. Not a shot all day. Makes one feel
almost uneasy, like a toothache that persists even after removal
of an aching tooth.

Negotiations were conducted secretly, almost surreptitiously,
between Government and Arab League representatives. Even the
Truce Commission knew nothing about them; as though Government wants to show the world that it can achieve what U.N.O.'s
Truce Commission can't. No conditions fixed. The siege remains.
The Arabs merely agreed to stop shooting, and the Jews, though
not consulted, will conform. Haganah Order of the Day, however, regards it only as "a temporary instrument for a short
period of time," and the Jewish Agency says it is not prepared to
accept cease-fire as a manœuvre to enable the Arabs to consoli-
date their forces.

This morning I heard a woman across the road send her young
children out to play. They were not to go far out of call; if there
were shots, they must hurry in at once. That's the general feeling.
The Arabs took it more freely. The coffee-houses in Mamilla
Road opened to-day for the first time since January, and the
main streets in the Arab sectors are crowded as on a holiday.
But Abdullah remains defiant. "I have not accepted the cease-
fire. I will invade Palestine after 15 May," he told newspapermen.

Ruth and I honoured the occasion by walking to Romema.
(*Hamseen* is breaking.) Other people had the same idea. One
young couple ahead of us, their arms around each other, were
singing; the man was in khaki and had a rifle slung over his
shoulder. We noticed, as though it were a new discovery, how
the grey slopes have become deep green and the pale green of the

olive contrasts with the dark emerald of the cypress. The *wadis* shone whitely like highways. Behind us lay the town, the compact substance of the Eternal City. Beyond, on the eastern horizon, rose the many-coloured range of the Moab Mountains, a wall marking the boundary of another world. Like the cliff that surrounded the Lost Continent in Conan Doyle's story of Professor Challenger, guarding its desert mysteries from curious eyes, so the Moab Mountains guard Abdullah's desert mysteries from our eyes. Returning, we saw the little plane circle four times and land. "Primus" is what people affectionately call it, because, like the cooking-stove, it is a slight thing and makes a lot of noise. We watched some small boxes off-loaded and taken away by uniformed men; hoped it was arms or ammunition.

Completed our celebration this evening by taking Myriam G. and Erwin to a cinema. An ancient film, but it was stimulating merely to be out in a crowd.

The Old City got a food convoy to-day, after waiting 8 days. Government's honour was satisfied when the Jewish Agency turned over two rifles to the British Army in place of those stolen.

Haganah has reopened the battle of the road; fighting again in the hills around Saris to drive the bands from the same villages as before. Learnt this evening that when the city was cut off in March, Jerusalem Haganah could spare only 400 men for the battle of the road. But for Operation Nahshon in April, Haganah H.Q. in Tel-Aviv threw half its mobile fighting strength into the battle; in one night 1,500 Palmach men arrived in Jerusalem in a secret convoy.

To-day is Palmach's seventh birthday. We broadcast a Palmach programme last night (with a piece on Orde Wingate, that strange, lovable Englishman who laid the foundations of Palmach). In the history of these days the name of Palmach will stand for some of its greatest, bravest, most precious memories. They are the stuff of to-morrow's legends, but their name is a legend already. Not a partisan force; nor uses partisan methods. It is a military brotherhood observing strict military discipline and employing orthodox methods in action, but with amazing mobility and fanatical fighting power. Their secret weapon is their spirit. In peacetime they spent two weeks of every month in gruelling and diversified training, and the other two weeks in agricultural work in the settlements. Badges of rank, decorations, military pomp don't exist; uniforms are unimportant. Complete intimacy between commanders and men. They regard one another by elemental standards, with a searching eye and a stringently sincere judgment; judge a man, above all, by his loyalty, courage, and his cameraderie. The great bulk are Palestinian-born. I know their faults, the faults of Palestine's youth. Too many are self-centred, intolerant and uncompromising. Their brightness is often that of the glittering surface that throws back the light to which it refuses access. But when I think of them now, how they are measuring up to this crisis in the life of our people, I feel very humble before them.

9 May

Last night Ruth kept waking up, feeling something uncanny. The quiet still doesn't seem quite real, and the streets to-day were only slightly more animated. I heard Reuvy and his young friends in the garden gravely discussing the problem of supply of spent bullets if the shooting really stops. The air was not completely quiet, however. Over the few miles of hill and valley from Ain Karem the echo of shooting floated in to remind us that the cease-fire is only for Jerusalem.

Fighting is unabated in the hills along the road. Also news of fighting from other parts, especially Galilee. Abdullah announced again that he will invade Palestine on 15 May; becoming a daily habit with him. General mobilization in Transjordan. The other Arab states are also loudly talking of invasion. If it is only bluster, they risk pretty serious repercussions at home when their bluff is called. Or do they really think their threats will bring the Jews to their knees?

The great event to-day was inauguration of the Jewish postal service. Everyone elated by the prospect of resumed contact with the outside world, and, nearly as much, by the birth of the first Jewish mail service in history. A great fillip to morale. In place of talk of fighting, food and what will happen on 15 May, talk is of the new postal service. Long queues at the post offices in Jewish quarters buying the provisional stamps, a Jewish National Fund stamp showing a map of partitioned Palestine, overprinted with the word *Doar* (Post). I heard an old man loudly pronounce the *Sheheheyanu*[1] blessing before sticking one on an envelope. Letters posted this morning were delivered in the city during the day. To places outside Jerusalem, letters will be forwarded by the little plane.

[1] "Blessed art Thou, O Lord our God, King of the Universe, who has kept us in life, and has preserved us, and enabled us to reach this season."

More reports of Jewish services steadily evolving in the Jewish areas of Palestine. Latest are Law Courts, Import and Export Licensing Department, Income Tax Office, Food Control; a temporary Jewish airport is already in use near Haifa and arrivals there pass through Jewish passport and Customs control. A new Administration is arising on the ruins of the old, and the surprising feature is how everyone accepts it all without surprise. When the Mandate ends next week, the Jewish State will be an established fact.

Of course, we are not really starting the Administration *ab initio*. Whether the British wish it or not, the framework of the machine they built up remains: the Jewish staffs they trained in every department, the systems they introduced, even much of the equipment they brought. An Indian once said to me that when the British quitted India one bond would remain that neither Indians nor British could easily break: the railways. And in the Jewish State for a long time to come many services will bear a British pattern.

Went through Katamon this afternoon with Amihud G., who is civilian officer in charge. The looting is driving him frantic, in spite of restraints. The Haganah Commander has failed to curb it. Somehow, one never expected this: men who in ordinary life would not dream of touching another's property don't hesitate to lay hands here on whatever takes their fancy.

Passing one house, we saw two men slink out carrying hastily-wrapped bundles. Amihud challenged them. One replied indignantly: "I've been in that *emda* over there for three months facing death every night and you quibble over my taking these souvenirs from them!"

The loss from looting is enormous—in demoralization even more than in goods.

Looked into F.'s house, remembering the spectacular house-warming party a few years ago. A beautiful house, with a medley of ornaments in a mixture of exquisite and excruciating taste. First F. commissioned an interior decorator, a refugee from Vienna, then added his own selections. I was aghast at the sight of it all now: ornaments shattered, pictures slashed, clothes and finery scattered about, carpets of glass across the floors, shreds of silk littered like flower petals on a dust-heap. That's how our home would have looked, worse probably, had the Arabs got there first—again I think how easily it might have been—but it was a shock to see Jews behaving that way.

Some houses bore large Hebrew notices: "Danger. This House is Mined." Amihud thought Jews who know the Arab owners put the signs up to deter looters.

Third day without water; the pipeline from Ras-el-Ain has been punctured by Arabs in four places. Jerusalem Municipality promises it will soon be repaired.

The People's Council in Tel-Aviv has launched a £5,000,000 countrywide national loan: "the first national act on the threshold of our independence," Ben-Gurion calls it.

10 May

SAFED HAS FALLEN to the Haganah. Another wonder, and another of those Arab mysteries. No one is dumbfounded now, as when Haifa fell; but it remains extraordinary. Here were 12,000 Arab civilians and about 3,000 irregulars, including seasoned Iraqi and Syrian soldiers; heavy guns supported them from Syria and Lebanon. Against them stood 1,500 Jewish residents, mostly middle-aged and elderly, and a few hundred Haganah men, with mortars as their heaviest equipment. The Arabs held all the dominant positions, the police fortress commanding the city, the citadel in the heart of the city, the hills around; all the roads leading into it were in their hands. The Jews were caught in a narrow trough. A month ago the British offered to evacuate the Jews; said all would be killed when the Government left. But the old orthodox Jews of Safed declined. "It is all in God's hands," they said. Now, attacked by several hundred additional Haganah men from the outside, the city falls after only 15 hours of fighting! Can't make it out.

The skirmishes around Safed in the past 10 days, though we didn't know it then, were part of Haganah's campaign for the city. The main drive was launched by a Palmach column that penetrated the city over mountain paths. At first they were beaten back, but after that reverse they smashed their way forward, driving the Arabs first from the fortified positions, then from street to street. In one quarter the battle raged from house to house and from room to room. Then suddenly Arab resistance collapsed. They fled pell-mell into the valleys, most of their equipment abandoned. The last of the Arab civilians fled as soon as the battle started.

They key of all Eastern Galilee in Jewish hands. What it will mean for those 30 isolated settlements and for the old sacred city

of the Kabbalists itself! Whoever hoped that Safed's centuries-
long battle for surival would be won in a night? Once it was the
glory of Jewish learning. Every Arab outburst left it another
stage nearer extinction. We had come to look upon it as a relic
belonging to an age gone by; a beautiful relic.

I can see it now as it looked when I stood on the opposite
mountainside last year, its white-walled houses spilling over the
slopes and into the valley; the distant dark line of the Mediterranean beneath a sky of old gold; the snowy top of Mount
Hermon in the rear. A sense of space and freedom enveloped one,
of height and openness, of being above the mundane world and
away from it. If there ever was a natural birthplace for the mystic
teachings of the Kabbala, this was it, with nothing but the
heavens between man and the greatness of God. I stood there as
dusk grew into night. Above was a black sky; the stars—nearer
to earth than I have seen them anywhere—winked over Galilee,
and the valleys lay in utter darkness except for the glow of a
solitary fire deep in a distant mountainside. . . . Somewhere
among these hills, Tanchik now lies buried. He has his share in
the victory of Safed.

Jerusalem truce talks continue, but very confused. Both
Consular Truce Commission and Government are working inde-
pendently to the same end. Whatever others might wish, the
High Commissioner, I believe, would be happy could he leave
the Holy City at peace. The Red Cross Delegation has put forward a lofty scheme to make the city a "hospital or place of
refuge" under the Red Cross flag. U.N.O. is still talking of a
United Nations Emergency Mayor of Jerusalem and a "neutral
authority" for all Palestine.

Fighting growing fiercer along the Jerusalem road, but
Haganah still blacking out all information. Obviously they are
making a determined effort to open the road before 15 May.
P.I.O. reports heavy Haganah losses.

Kaukja's Liberation Army will be disbanded on 15 May; then
the regular Arab armies will strike. All the Arab broadcasting
stations carry this news. Any hope that this is only idle talk is

dwindling. Reports also coming in from all Arab capitals of feverish war preparations. Nobody has faith in U.N.O.'s ability to stop them. The grimmest part of the struggle is only starting, and the Jews stand alone. There are differing estimates of the worth of the Arab armies, but everyone agrees that their equipment is formidable. Dr. G. button-holed me this afternoon to pour out an inchoate jumble of hope and apprehension, defiance and defeatism; then his flickering confidence collapsed completely. The country will become a heap of ashes, was his final opinion, and that will be the end of us.

No water in the taps yet, and our reserve running low. In some quarters a black market has sprung up in branches and twigs for cooking; the papers are telling people how to make fireless cookers. Rations distributed to-day, miserable portions, mostly 3 oz. each of dried fish, dried beans, lentils, macaroni, and 1½ oz. of margarine.

Worried about Ruth; noticed again to-day how much weight she is losing. She is nervy and irritable. Everyone is thinner; some look gaunt. Mrs. B. warned us she may have to stop serving lunches, as her supplies are running out. Her meals leave me nearly as hungry at the finish as at the start; a mackerel remains a mackerel, however camouflaged with a little dough and sauce. But how are we going to manage without it?

Heard to-day of Shemaya's death. An ascetic who avoided the pleasures of life, fasted by day and ate at night, and constantly exhorted his friends to return to God and His Law. The last time I saw him was on *Pesach*, on the way to synagogue, his flaming red hair showing beneath his Palmach beret, his red beard trained to a point in honour of the Festival, and his prayer-shawl carried under his armpit. Must have been killed in the battle for the road.

Judy took her first walk to-day. She was thrilled, especially by the air-strip. "Isn't it exciting?" she said. "Why, La Guardia Airport just doesn't compare!"

11 May

THE QUIET WAS shattered to-day by Arab snipers. Everyone restless and uneasy, like prisoners awaiting sentence. We might be living in a tiny, padded world, our thoughts and images going round in circles. Yesterday Ben-Gurion said in Tel-Aviv: "I believe that the Jewish State will arise in a few days, after an interval of over 1,900 years." It will seem incredible when it happens. But now it is almost assumed, and the question that beats against our minds is: How will it come about? What will happen on the 15th?

I notice how people are startled at realizing, quite suddenly, that their conception of the future has been altered. Until recently their thoughts of May and June were illumined by a brilliant if undefined picture of freedom from foreign domination, of independence. But now they find themselves caught up in all the implications; unforeseen anxieties begin to loom large. I doubt if anybody thinks of his personal life or plans after the 15th. I catch myself looking at the spring blossoms and wondering how life will be when spring turns to summer.

The battle for the road goes well. News black-out on Operation Maccabi (after Maccabi M., who died of his wounds) lifted to-night. All down to Bab-el-Wad the road is in our hands. In four days Palmach captured seven dominating heights between Jerusalem and Beit Mahsir, and capped it to-day by taking Beit Mahsir itself (one of the main Arab bases for sealing the road). For nine hours they battled ,through fog and strange, wild, mountainous country to reach the village from the rear. At dawn the Arabs suddenly found them entrenched in the hills above. It's a large village—normally 6,000 population, now swollen by 1,000 Iraqis and others—and all day they tried desperately to dislodge our boys. But Palmach held fast, and at sunset launched their own assault. By 4 o'clock this morning the Arabs had fled. Next phase for the battle of the road will be at Latrun, the last and strongest Arab stronghold.

Some people have started asking uneasily whether the British will really leave on 15th. The preparations seem conclusive. In Zone C I saw them nailing down huge crates, burning papers, all the commotion preceding departure. Other people fear that some soldiers may have a last-minute crack at the Jews. Army also seems nervous; has strengthened its precautions and taken to blowing bugles every half-hour.

Everyone is concerned about the Arab Legion. The British have undertaken to send them back to Transjordan. If they remain, or return at once, will their British officers also fight?

Jerusalem is bound to be Abdullah's first objective. To be master of the Holy City, that's a prize for a desert king! Speaking about it, R. drew my attention to-day to the passage in Ezekiel about the old King of Babylon who had the same idea: "He stood at the parting of the ways to use a divination; he shook the arrows to and fro, he consulted with images, he looked in the liver. In his right hand was the divination for Jerusalem, to appoint captains, to open the mouth in the slaughter, to lift up the voice with shouting, to set battering rams against the gates, to cast up mounts, to build forts." And Ezekiel adds: "And it shall be unto them as a vain divination." I wonder if Abdullah ever reads the Old Testament?

N., French Consul-General, who visited the Old City a few days ago, says it is choked with Arab refugees; and armed men everywhere. He was indignant to see groups of Arab soldiers wearing blue reefers and round sailor hats with pommels of the French Navy. N. is anxious about the Christians and their property in Jerusalem when the British leave. For the first time in 100 years they are left without protection. Latterly Britain, before that France and Russia, were considered their protectors. Most Christians have fled to the Old City and Bethlehem. Some have remained in the Jewish sectors.

What will happen now to the torn little Russian community and its £20,000,000 worth of Church properties? The Russian

Palestine Society administered them, under control of the Government. Now most of the Russians (some first-class Fascists and anti-Semites among them) have fled to the Arabs in the Old City; Father Lazarus has also gone, the weird English convert who is one of their leaders. Only the splinter group of monks and nuns who support the re-established Church in Moscow remain, and side openly with the Jews. The aged lay nuns in the Russian Compound (who still won't believe that the Tsar is no more) have also remained.

Had an exciting windfall to-day. The M.R.'s left for England, taken by air by the British. (A few other British Jews were also "rescued" that way.) Before leaving, they sold their stocks of tinned food. We got part of it. They felt very grieved for us who are staying on; which didn't discourage them, however, from charging us three to four times normal prices. What does money mean to us now, anyway?

B.'s and we decided, for economy, to share supplies and cook together. Their superior maid has vanished, like our Ada.

12 May

Events moving swiftly all over the Middle East. Only here, a kind of hush of preparedness has descended. The Truce Commission has published an Appeal to the People of Jerusalem. The High Commissioner announced his proposed truce terms. Lake Success still searching for a Mayor for the Holy City. All, all unreal. Arab firing at Katamon last night and at the western suburbs this morning struck the only note of reality. Moving from a kind of nameless war into the full thing.

In Egypt a "state of siege." In Syria the army goaded on by talks of *Jihad* (Holy War). In Lebanon (where Christians fear the Moslems far more than they fear the Jews) the Minister of Interior says they will first occupy the Arab areas of Palestine. In faraway Saudi Arabia the Monarch of the Desert has spoken: "My troops will also be there." From Iraq, regular troops moving steadily into Transjordan. In Transjordan, Abdullah's daily declaration: "We are coming to enforce peace against the Jewish terror bands." Three more days to go until the 15th. . . .

The Etzion Bloc is in a life-and-death struggle. Savage fighting since 4 this morning. The Legion's heavy tanks, field guns and mortars battered it from all sides; then infantry, wave after wave. Once they got to within a few hundred yards of Kfar Etzion. Each time they were driven back. A lull since dusk, but still fiercer fighting expected to-morrow. How can they possibly hold out? Completely cut off from reinforcements, while the Legion has only to call for all it wants. When the Jewish Agency demanded that the Army order back the Legion, which is directly under the British G.O.C., the reply was: "Give us the numbers of their vehicles."

Water rationing started to-day. We have had none for six days. Yesterday, just as the damage to the pipeline was repaired, the British guards suddenly left the spring-head at Ras-el-Ain and

Iraqi soldiers walked in. So we're cut off at the source! Fortunately, the contingency was foreseen, and the Jewish authorities quietly sealed up all Jewish private and public cisterns in Jerusalem a few months ago. How long this reserve will last is another matter. The daily ration, two bucketfuls per person, is distributed from lorries. The queues to-day were disorderly, everybody anxious lest there wouldn't be enough to go round. Nor was there. Judy and Michael were jostled out of their places; when finally their turn came, the supply was exhausted. They were promised an extra ration to-morrow. A doctor's wife came to fetch hers in her husband's car. Another woman carted her buckets in a pram. I passed two queues in town, one waiting to take part in the £5,000,000 national loan; the other, on the opposite pavement, waiting for water.

Drove down the road with Y. this morning as far as Bab-el-Wad. Only a half-hour's drive, but a real tonic. Immediate danger has been driven back from all this part. One can move—a mile, 3 miles, 10 (if you have Haganah business). You realize what a weight bears down on you in the city; how your breath is pent up. The air out there is less hot. I remembered my last night drive from Kolonia and the muffled menace among the hills. Now the road is full of Haganah traffic. The summit of Nebi Samwil and the hilltops towards Ramillah are still danger spots. But it felt less potent as we sped along the hot, dusty road, past Kolonia, Castel, Suba, Beit Surik, all ruined and deserted.

At Abu Ghosh we saw Arabs—live Arabs!—friendly, smiling, driving hard bargains with Haganah men for fruit, vegetables, English cigarettes, sugar, that they were selling by the roadside. At the sight of all that food I wanted to stop at once. Y. said we'd stop on the way back. Of all the Arab villages in the Judean hills, Abu Ghosh, the notorious bandit village of a generation ago, and Beit Nakuba have resolutely kept out the Arab bands and remained friendly with their Jewish neighbours.

Mishmar Haam (Civil Guard) road-gangs from Jerusalem—portly business men, professional men, clerks—were sweating and

panting at clearing Arab road-blocks and erecting new fortifications. Haganah encampments have sprung up among the hills.
The police fortress opposite the towering Virgin statue beyond
Abu Ghosh is now a Palmach camp. In the roadside ditches are
the skeletons of a score of burnt-out lorries. Nobody has disturbed
them, only spiders have woven their webs over the rusted bodies.
We came to deep, half-cleared road-blocks. Y. said: "That's the
famous road-block, 200 yards long and 2 yards high, that would
take weeks to destroy"; so said the British report. In fact, there
were half a dozen loose barriers barely a yard high and together
perhaps 40 yards deep.

We heard the echo of heavy guns. Other echoes grunted in
reply. "Yes, we have some guns now, too," said Y. A patrol told
us there was heavy fighting west of Bab-el-Wad. We reached
Bab-el-Wad, sprawled between the paws of the mountains, with
the Shephela lowland rolling westward towards the sea. You
felt the breath of a frontier.

We could see the tips of the groves at Latrun where the Arabs
are piling up men and equipment to keep the further road closed.
Among the Bab-el-Wad hills Haganah is making its preparations
to force the road open. Birds were flying frenziedly backwards and
forwards between the two lines, frightened by the shelling. In the
no-man's-land I could see the carcase of a camel that had been
shot or had trodden on a land-mine and lay rotting in the
blazing sun. Among the trees on the slopes around us a great
stir was going on. Movements, vague and widespread, like the
muttering in a forest when a storm is rising. Y. recalled that once
before Jews ambushed an enemy among the wooded gorges of
Bab-el-Wad and killed thousands of its soldiers. That was in
A.D. 66; the enemy were the Romans.

Stopped at Abu Ghosh to buy a pile of real, fresh vegetables
and other foodstuffs from Arabs. (Everything else was sold out.)
When I got home, Ruth, recovering her speech, said it was the
most wonderful sight she has seen for months. Judy blinked and
asked if it was real.

Erwin came over this evening, pessimistic and hungry. He is

working on personnel selection for the Haganah. He had a letter to-day that was posted in Haifa 10 days ago; wonder how it arrived. Clara writes him of a neighbour whose children are in Jerusalem. The woman said to her: "I used to weep because my children in Jerusalem were hungry. Now I pray to God they may be left alive to continue feeling hungry."

13 May

ONE DAY TO GO.

Kfar Etzion has fallen. In these circumstances it was doomed. But one hoped that somehow . . . One's heart is heavy. Yet one does not mourn. There was so much courage. Of its 164 men and women, at least 62 are dead, 42 seriously wounded. All four settlements of the Bloc had a combined defending force of 500, of whom 100 were women. The Legion attacked with 2 battalions of infantry, 2,000 irregulars, 20 tanks and 20 gun-carriers and armoured cars. Sixty thousand Arabs inhabit the district and groups of them kept coming over all day and night to join in the fighting.

A few details of the desperate battle have come through to the *Mateh*. Monastery Hill, Kfar Etzion's advance post, was held by 26 men for six hours against hundreds of Legionnaires, three 25-pounder guns, 6 Sherman tanks, 6 gun-carriers, seven 3-inch mortars; it fell when only one officer and 2 men were left. The column of 18 tanks that attacked Kfar Etzion village was repulsed 16 times; when the Legion overran the settlement the settlers fell back fighting towards the second settlement of the Bloc, Massuoth.

I saw some of their wireless messages: The last one was: "Hand-to-hand fighting. Tanks penetrated our rear into the farm-yard. . . . Overrunning the dining-room and children's house. . . . Swarming in from all sides. . . ." Late last night a wireless message from Massuoth: "We broke through the Arab lines and rescued Kfar Etzion's survivors. Kfar Etzion buildings all burning." This afternoon the remaining three settlements are locked in a savage battle, each cut off from its neighbours. They are finished; they must have known it yesterday. The Red Cross was asked to arrange evacuations of the wounded men and the girls from the settlements, but so far without result.

Jaffa has fallen, the largest all-Arab town in the country, over

70,000 population. This morning the four notables of the Jaffa Emergency Committee came to Tel-Aviv to sign the truce terms with the Haganah. They said the Iraqi and Syrian soldiers and all but 2,000 of the civilians have fled.

At Latrun, Bedouin units under their tribal sheikhs have come from Transjordan to support the Legion and irregulars in the growing fighting.

The Jerusalem truce is crumbling, as one expected. Sporadic firing throughout the night and day. Now Haganah is replying. To-night is ominously quiet.

No electricity; few people therefore heard our broadcast to-night. Hava didn't turn up. I hope nothing has happened. Maybe the Etzion news is preying on her; since her brother was killed there, she can't take anything about Etzion.

As I walked home the city was black and deadly still. It seemed shrunk into the shadows. You felt it taut, crouching, like an animal. Or perhaps it was time that crouched. The whole world seemed gripped in darkness, toneless, blotting out everything, invading even your mind. Some thin slits of candlelight or lamp-light peered grudgingly from between shutters. Once a Haganah's car's headlight cut like flashing knives through the blackness. Then darkness and silence again. I said to myself, it was the silence preceding birth. . . . I quickened my pace, longed for a noise, a shot, anything. I thought of the Etzion settlements fighting hopelessly, of Tamara (was she alive?) and Don. I wondered what it was like to-night in Tel-Aviv and Galilee and the Negev. And in Cairo and Damascus. Then as I passed Ratisbon Monastery the chapel bell tolled out, calm, measured. How my heart went out to that bell!

At home I found Ruth tidying the closed porch by the light of a candle. For months she talked of turning it into a studio. To-night she chose to do it. The grand, delightful irrelevance of it! A spark of the happy-go-lucky creature of whims she used to be.

We joined the B.'s, sat talking by candlelight about the 15th, our chances against the Arab armies, how the British will leave, what kind of State ours will be. I left them still talking to write up these notes. The candle in my study is flickering and its light casts strange forms on the books and carpets. Not a sound outside. The world is a far-away planet in a bottomless well. Are people thinking of us, of what will happen here in 24 hours?

In one day's time a nation will be re-born, a new State will arise. As I write it down, the fact has a meaning I have still to fathom. (How does a nation get re-born? Is it a new essence?) Because Jews lacked the attributes of statehood, the world could make pariahs of them. Now they will have statehood, and be judged by what they make of it. Will it be a corner of the West, Western thought and values projected into the East? Will it become corroded by the slick superficiality of the Levant? Will it express the old Hebrew social idealism? Maybe the new ways of life on the land are already a presage of what it may yield. And what of the militant Dissidents, full of admiration for totalitarian energy, for its "monolithic" concentration upon the supreme goal of achieving power; the large backward sections of the Oriental community; the fanatical clericalists; the D.P.'s who survived Hitler's Europe only because they developed survivor's wits?

Whatever we evolve, it will, at least, be our own. Being ourselves instead of explaining ourselves, what a relief! If we also contribute something worthwhile, build that bridge our leaders speak of between the old prophetism and a new internationalism, that other bridge between West and East, so much the better. . . . I, meanwhile, here am I, a particle in this miraculous process, living it, watching it, the spanning of 2,000 years before my eyes!

14 May

IT IS DAWN of Friday. To-day the British leave Palestine. One can still barely comprehend it. It was ominously still during the night, and I slept fitfully. Straining my ears, I heard the grinding creak of tanks from the Zone, and, in the distance, a dull, indistinct, receding noise, like the rumour of a river. The British Army stealing through the night, as though in complicity with the darkness.

The sun is low over the Mountains of Moab. Its first rays are lighting up the slopes of Scopus and Mount of Olives. It is going to be a hot day, perhaps *hamseen* again. From the window a few minutes ago I watched a young boy furtively break branches in the avenue, then run with them to the stove made of stones and tin-piping in the backyard of his house. Ruth is still asleep. I am writing these lines now because I don't know if I shall be able to write anything more to-day. For the moment time hangs suspended. Any minute it may break into violent motion. At 8 I am going on to the high roof opposite; perhaps from there I can see the High Commissioner leave. At midnight he will sail from Haifa on a British cruiser, to a salute of 17 guns. Last night he broadcast his farewell to the peoples of Palestine; it was a sad farewell. He pleaded for the isolation of the Holy City, at least, from the conflict.

Later

Through glasses I have just watched the High Commissioner's Residence on its grey hilltop. Its massive white austerity was lit up by the sunlight. From its tower waved a Union Jack. A few minutes past 8 I saw the sleek, black Rolls Royce drive out of the gates. The little procession of cars is on its way now to Kallandia airport with three Spitfires zooming before them. In half an hour Sir Alan and the last of the 6,208 British civilian personnel will board planes for Haifa. At that moment the Union Jack will be hauled from the Residence and a Red Cross flag hoisted.

So ends the adventure that started bravely 30 years ago. They came humbly then, Allenby on foot, but proudly, too. Thanksgiving and prayers from millions of Jewish hearts accompanied them. They shuffle out now in darkness and chaos, almost unnoticed. The more tragic because it need never have been a tragedy, had Britain only remained true to her trust and to her own traditions and wisdom. Those who know the real England, who have thrilled to the turbulent story of English liberty from the days of its rough and obstinate growth, for them, too, her record here and the manner of her going is a sad thing.

Afternoon

3 o'clock. Am snatching an hour for a bite and to write these notes. Events moving too fast to keep pace with them. Know only there is fighting all over the city, and going amazingly well for us. Jews and Arabs both poised to spring the minute the British left, but we got in first, advancing everywhere, the Arabs nowhere. Tremendous excitement, and rumours tumbling over one another.

Within 10 minutes of the British evacuation, "Bevingrad" Zone completely under Haganah control: Generale Building, G.P.O., Anglo-Palestine Bank, Police H.Q., Central Prison, Russian Compound—all of them, and without a single gunshot. Just like that; everyone thinking the main clash would come here, Haganah streaming in at one end, Arabs at the other!

Arranged with Dick yesterday that I cover "Bevingrad" and Zone C, he the southern districts. At 9 I was at "Bevingrad" perimeter. Neighbouring shops were closed. Young men and girls standing about in the side streets. Main Haganah troops hidden in surrounding buildings. (For weeks Haganah has been keeping close secret watch on the moves of the British.) Small Union Jacks fluttered from upper windows; also a freshly-washed white shirt that looked like a flag. Two British armoured cars parked near the Gate. A party of Jewish constables came up Jaffa Road;

some parleying with an Army officer; 6 of them, unarmed, allowed in. Surprising. I caught quick glimpses of Arab spotters on roof-tops at the other end.

Asked a British policeman when they were leaving. "Don't know any more than you. Some time to-day I expect," he said laconically. Twenty minutes later, at 10, the British troops and police moved out, and Haganah rushed in; as though a single spring directed both. A blue-white flag from the window where the Union Jack had been. Men and women running into Jaffa Road to see the sight, cheering, laughing, some even embracing each other. Whoever thought it would be so simple. From Mamillah Road and the Old City walls came bursts of shooting, and the crowd scattered.

The last of the Army was pulling out of Zone C when I arrived. Tanks, armoured cars, lorry-loads of soldiers, staff cars, all flooding down King George Avenue. Pavements and windows dotted with people (careful to keep out of sight of snipers from Old City Walls) standing in silence, watching the dramatic spectacle, the final migration of the British. Joy, irony, bitterness, animosity, incredulity on the faces of the watchers. Some betrayed no emotion, just watched intently. "Is it possible? Are they going?" M. called out to me.

Few, I think, felt anything against the individual Tommy. Most would have wished to be friendly. It was the collectivity they loathed. A couple of soldiers waved goodbye; a couple of Jews waved back. Then the last car disappeared. The street suddenly became deserted. It has happened. The British are gone. . . .

Into the Zone a host of children started madly to drag sandbags; it seemed the kids were taking it over. Suddenly, already within, Haganah men appeared. They were there all the time! J. told me the Zone O.C. agreed that joint British-Haganah patrols guard the Zone last night as a measure for deterring a last-minute Dissident raid. (Wonder whether the rumour of the raid was true or planted?) As their spells of duty ended, British soldiers and Haganah men ate, chatted, slept together. (Wonder

what they talked about?) Has it ever happened before, since the
war? And this morning, when the British left, the Haganah men
remained in possession. Arabs, massed on the eastern flank,
opened heavy fire the minute the soldiers left. They were all set
to swarm in. Haganah, already inside, replied.

No word from Dick. I handed my story to the Haganah censor.
All despatches being sent by plane to Tel-Aviv (thence by normal
wireless). Rushed to the *Mateh* for latest developments. Atmosphere in Y.'s rooms electric; Y. himself calm and undistracted.
Haganah advancing strongly east and north, squashing Arab
resistance. Part of Sheikh Jarrah is in our hands. Etzel occupied
the Police Training Depot on Scopus. Stern Group is pushing
into Barclay's Bank, the border line in the city's centre; Iraqis
are entrenched in the great Notre Dame Monastery 100 yards off,
and Arab irregulars hold the Tancred Lane flank, 20 yards away.
All-out attacks expected on our "Bevingrad" positions this afternoon. Arabs pouring out of Old City through Jaffa and Damascus
Gates. In the Old City, Jews have seized evacuated Army positions and Arabs heavily attacking them. On the western outskirts,
the Arab bombardment is ferocious. Explosions everywhere, and
pillars of smoke mounting lazily in the *hamseen* air. Running
through the incessant noise of detonations is the constant rattle
of machine-guns.

Flags all over. Israel flags on public buildings; foreign flags, as
signs of neutrality, on church buildings, hospitals, schools, consulates, private dwellings, giving the city the appearance of a
gigantic international fair. I notice the Vatican flag among them;
and the Mexican flag over the Consul's house in the heart of
Shaare Hessed, one of the most ultra-orthodox Jewish quarters of
the New City.

Rumours upon rumours: Arabs have sued for terms; Jews of
the Old City have surrendered; British troops ordered back to
Jerusalem; the whole Arab Legion speeding up from Jericho and
Ramallah. None seems true.

Whatever happens later, the morning's successes remain
astounding. Less than 6 hours since the British left, and the key

areas of the New City are in Haganah hands. In our imagination, Jerusalem has been fought for in many ways, but never as smoothly as this.

The rest of the Etzion Bloc has fallen. They wirelessed the *Mateh* after midnight for orders: Would they be evacuated? (By whom? The British? They couldn't have known that the British were already on the way out.) Or were they to carry on a last-ditch fight? They were ordered to surrender; didn't appear to expect that. While they negotiated with the enemy, the rabble from the Arab villages poured in by the thousands. How many were left to surrender? What has happened to Tamara, Eldad P., Joseph L., Amos F., G.'s boy, "Mosh"? For how many families the triumph of this day is darkened by personal anguish! Etzion settlement carried out their task. For five months they held up thousands of Arabs who would otherwise have been at our throats in Jerusalem. Now they are wiped off the map. The southern road into Jerusalem lies open to the enemy. Within the city, we are more firmly entrenched; outside it, the knife is cutting all the strings.

The Jewish State will be proclaimed to-day, to-morrow being *Shabbath*. Place and hour are secret. What will it be called? The National Council of 37 will become the Provisional Council of Government. Twelfth-hour U.S. Government pressure on Jewish leaders against proclamation of the State is reported. At Lake Success, U.S. now recommends a U.N. High Commissioner for all of Palestine.

Michael has just come in, brimming with the latest rumours. I can hear Judy's voice, overjoyed. Ruth is out, working on maps. Haven't seen her since early morning, but found a note from her, saying: "Please, please, don't get yourself killed to-day of all days."

To the *Mateh* again. Perhaps I can get out with one of the columns. No proper Haganah arrangements yet for reporters to cover the fighting. And what a story!

Night

Exhausted, physically and mentally. So is everyone else. But I must put down what happened.

The tension of weeks burst to-day. A tremendous weight has been lifted from us. The war may only be starting. But we are our own masters in our land. Can't fully grasp it yet. . . .

At 4 o'clock in the Museum Hall in Tel-Aviv, Ben-Gurion proclaimed the establishment of the independent State of Israel. Few people were present; in Jerusalem even fewer heard the broadcast, the electricity being completely cut. I listened on the *Mateh's* battery set as Ben-Gurion read the Proclamation. ". . . Accordingly we, the members of the National Council, representing the Jewish people in Palestine, and the Zionist movement of the world . . . by virtue of the natural and historic right of the Jewish people and of the resolution of the General Assembly of the United Nations, hereby proclaims the establishment of the Jewish State in Palestine, to be called Israel. . . . With trust in Almighty God, we set our hand to this Declaration . . . on this Sabbath eve, the fifth of Iyar, 5708. . . ."

Hatikvah rolled out, a hymn of thanksgiving. Rabbi Fishman, his voice choked with tears, pronounced *Sheheheyanu*. A deep *Amen* from the throats of the assembly like a congregation at worship. A minute's silence; among us, too. You could feel the taut self-restraint in each one gathered around the wireless. Then Ben-Gurion read the first Ordinance: "All the laws enacted under the Palestine White Paper, 1939, of the British Government, and all laws deriving from it, are hereby declared null and void."

So the lamp snuffed out nearly 2,000 years ago was relighted to-day. A miracle as great as any that ever happened in this land. The whole world must sense its drama, though many hate it.

In the *Kol Hamegen* commentary this evening I said *Shalom* to the British; recalled the selfless good many have done in these 30 years; expressed the hope that Jews and Britons will still come to recognize each other as friends. I was saying that the celebration of Jewish independence must be left to peaceful days when a

shrill whistle sounded, like a driver's lash descending, a shattering explosion, sudden darkness, and our five-story building
shuddered and rocked. No one was at home in the flat it penetrated. Z. thought it was a 25-pounder.

Home at 10.30. Found a group of neighbours round our
battery wireless eager to pick up something new. All worn-out,
but too keyed up to go to bed. Exaltation, anxiety, weariness,
everything mixed up.

"Whoever really believed we'd live to see it. . . ." "A personal
triumph for Ben-Gurion. . . ." "It's Bevin we really have to
thank for it. . . ." "We've got to hold out for a couple of months
against the Arab states, until we get arms; then we'll thrash
them. . . ." "The Arabs must be holding their attack. . . ." Bitter
reminiscences of the British. . . .

The faces of the group caught the pale glow of the candlelight.
How tired they looked, with the ingrown tiredness of years;
years of struggle for nationhood; years of bearing punishment
inflicted on the whole community for the doings of the terrorists.

12.15 a.m. Am completely done in.

15 May

No morning news bulletin; the wireless "dead." Lack of current at the broadcasting station, or something worse?

First day of Israel. A radiant day. Short lull this morning after a night of incessant fire. I slept through most of it, the din a kind of nightmare backdrop to a confusion of dreams. Woke up feeling a great restlessness throughout my whole body. In the street below a thin, cracked voice ended an over-the-fence chat with R.: "Your old men shall dream dreams, your young men shall see visions." How many thousands of times the Prophets will be quoted to-day! A natural impulse; who does not feel that the days are prophetic? Reuvy and his friends are arguing in the garden whether we shall have a king or president; Leizy says it will be a president, because a king's crown costs too much.

What are people thinking, feeling? Are they saying to themselves that now everything is going to be different, like starting all over again? The romantic, I suppose, believe that all will be more beautiful. And the pessimistic that we're in for a new kind of Arab-made hell. How do I feel? Strange excitement fills me; all at the same time I am uplifted, moved, and anxious. My thoughts rove between a new life, and war, first one in the foreground, then the other.

What will that new life, independence, freedom, mean for me as a person? I don't know—except that it will be my own. For the moment, I feel poised between the pressure of a past wherein one was seldom allowed to forget the Problem of the Jew, and an unknown future that also may be grim, but largely of my own making. That was always the difference between the Jew here and in the Diaspora. There he is a compound of theory and dream. Here he became an instrument of action. But henceforth action on another plane. . . .

The State: we start with fragments—of a people, possessions, national services; even the land that Jews hold is in fragments, disconnected stretches. Only the central idea is whole, but that is everything. . . . A tangle of ideas. I have a lot of thinking to catch up with, when the time for thinking comes.

Midday

Our whole southern line is linked up, and in a single night and morning. Magnificent! That's the main section that made Jewish Jerusalem a "strategic monstrosity." Three Haganah columns this morning captured the southern Arab links—German Colony, Railway Station, Allenby Barracks.

Despite the raging battles in the south, people are wandering, heartened, around the Zone. Concrete pillboxes, dragon's teeth, sandbagged posts, miles of barbed wire—and no British soldiers! Instead, Haganah men. Relics of the Army's occupation strew the once-fashionable quarter: guide-posts, traffic signs, oil-casks, piles of half-burnt rubbish and papers, patches of deep-soaked oil on pavements, gardens overgrown. Rumours of two British deserters who stayed behind. House-owners, evicted by the British when they seized the area for a Security Zone two years ago, already enquiring when they can move back.

K., on duty there, told me they are calling their newborn daughter Etziona, in memory of the settlements.

Went round to Dick, who was caught in the cross-fire yesterday near Yemin Moshe; he lay in the gutter, bullets whizzing over him, from 11 until after dark, when a Haganah armoured car rescued him.

The cleavage between correspondents accredited to Jews and Arabs is now complete. Only Williams (B.B.C.) is trying to retain a kind of independence in St. George's Close in the neutral zone under the Anglican Bishop. He is using an amateur transmitting set. About all he will see there is the Cathedral and the Bishop.

All of us are furious about our despatches. Haganah is *not* getting them through to Tel-Aviv, or only with great delay. *Mateh* promises wireless facilities in a few days. What we've

missed already, and what we shall miss before it gets going! And
there's no one to howl to. Haganah G.H.Q. are in Tel-Aviv, and
at the *Mateh* here everyone is too preoccupied to listen.

Heavy shooting echoes from the east and north as I write, and
a great confused din from the Old City.

Night

By arrangement with Y., Dick and I were taken to the Italian
Hospital this afternoon; crawled across some patches on our
bellies. The officer in charge, a morose fellow who looked like
a labourer, but controlled the situation like a professional soldier,
viewed us as a nuisance. He gave us a guide and told us to keep
low and silent. Through peep-holes and between sandbags, we
saw the battle area. St. Paul's Road and the Street of the Prophets
where we were, is a kind of cross-roads for mortar shells and
bullets, and the building itself shook with the rattle of machine-
guns. Hardly a minute of quiet. We seemed to be in the centre of
a circle of fire, one semicircle Jewish, the other Arab. A couple
of score of yards to our right a battle was going on across St.
Paul's Road, between Haganah in the Russian Compound and
Iraqis in Notre Dame across the way. To the left, our men were
driving their way from building to building.

Three hundred yards further down, the Sheikh Jarrah battle
was in its final phase. Arab armoured cars and trucks were pulling out towards the Old City. One armoured car lay sprawled
on its side. From a gutted building the Arab flag was still
flying. Then the last Arabs retreated, pursued by fire. Sheikh
Jarrah, the death-trap, is ours at last, and the road to Scopus
lies open.

Every point of the compass was in it. Confused shooting down
the Street of the Prophets and Godfrey de Bouillon Street.
Another battle along Suleiman's Way. More shooting around
Jaffa Gate, and the echo of still more near the Station. On its
lonely hilltop the High Commissioner's house looked down on
the city. Through our glasses, we saw the Red Cross flag hanging
lifeless on its tower. Yesterday the building was the heart of the

Government; to-day, a lone and silent witness of the bloody battle for Jerusalem.

Just behind us lay Mea Shearim; not a soul in its warren of streets. We looked straight down into a house that seemed to be a first-aid post. Two stretcher-bearers and a body disappeared within it. Then a man came alone, limping heavily. Through a dirty glass pane above a sandbagged window we saw into the corner of a synagogue; vaguely our glasses showed a man swaying in prayer. In a shade-dappled corner of a courtyard in the Hungarian Houses, a woman was dragging in two children dressed in their *Shabbath* clothes. From the forward houses of Mea Shearim we saw the sudden flashes of shots: some of our snipers' posts. Flowers sparkled ironically on the slopes of Scopus, anemones and cyclamen in close patches amid the lush green of new grass.

A girl in khaki trousers ran into our room with a message. The machine-gun stopped its crackling. The man in charge wiped the sweat from his terra-cotta face. He turned to us beaming:

"I've settled a few accounts to-day."

He had been on duty for 36 hours with only two breaks of three hours each. Told us that some of the units fighting hereabouts were Etzel men, among them fellows straight from the *Yeshivoth*. He said it was funny to see them run forward, their *peyot* (side-curls) swinging under their steel helmets; but they had guts. With him was a small pale fellow with silver-rimmed glasses, who spoke with a lisp. Dick to me in an aside: "Ever seen a less likely-looking soldier?" His arm was bandaged, and the corners of his mouth were marked with the half-dry froth of saliva mixed with dirt.

Nearby, a loudspeaker burst out in Arabic. Haganah broadcasting to civilian Arabs, urging them to leave the district before 5.15 a.m.: "Take pity on your wives and children and get out of this blood bath," it said. "Surrender to us with your arms. No harm will come to you. Or get out by the Jericho road, that is still open to you. If you stay, you invite disaster."

The Commander was glad to see us go: he even smiled. "Come

Workers on the "Burma Road"

Young woman guarding the "Burma Road"

back when we've captured the rest of Jerusalem and I'll tell you all about it," he said.

Got home in time to hear the wonderful news broadcast from Tel-Aviv: United States has recognized Israel. But also that Egyptian Spitfires bombed Tel-Aviv three times last night and again this morning, and Egyptian forces have crossed the Palestine frontier. They came up over Sinai, the same desert through which the Israelites once fled from Egypt to the Land of Promise. That's how it is: half your emotions rejoicing, the other half distressed. After all its vacillations, who would have expected the U.S.A. to be first to welcome the birth of Israel? And the Egyptians, who grow angry when you call them Arabs and affirm their descent from the Pharaohs, the first to fight for the Arabs?

The first call of the Israel Provisional Government to its citizens was issued to-day. ". . . We are called on to defend our State. . . . Everything must be given for victory and for peace. . . . All of us—to arms!"

In his Order of the Day, the Jerusalem Haganah Commander declared a state of emergency, adding: " . . . Henceforth we are no longer unknown soldiers of an underground army who must hide their arms. We have become soldiers of the free State of Israel which has won its place among the nations. . . ."

Sounds so simple: Haganah into Army of Israel. Who can stop to think of it now, but what a tale! The 40-year, illegal building up of an underground self-defence; years of exhausting struggle against the Ottoman Turks; the cold, frustrating struggle against the British; the secret assembling through the years of light equipment, armoured cars, a few heavy guns, some light planes, getting it wherever they could, paying fantastic prices, stealing it where they couldn't buy it, smuggling it into the country by every ruse. (Remember stumbling once upon a consignment of meat imported from Syria that had machine-gun parts in the carcases: learning on another occasion, that lorry-loads of bee-hives, all menacingly a-buzz, held ammunition); manufacturing bits of equipment in under-cover workshops; training its men (from a score of countries) in cellars, caves, farm settlements;

half their energies given to maintaining secrecy. Now, overnight, it is an Army of a sovereign State. It needs time to train in the tactics of full-scale war, to arm, to knot together its disparate elements, to shake off the conspiratorial habits. And straight away it is challenged by regular armies, squadrons of planes, tanks, cannon. How much the iron of their wills must make up in the balance!

Ataroth has been evacuated. Only little Neve Yaacov lies now between Jerusalem and the Legion at Ramallah.

The road battle continues; two more Arab villages captured in Latrun district, 50 of our men killed.

In the midst of it all, this morning, a boatload of 500 Jewish refugees from the D.P. camps land in Tel-Aviv. Yesterday they would have been called "illegal immigrants" and deported. To-day flags wave in their honour.

16 May

ANOTHER DAY OF bitter fighting, and Jerusalem is all hypertension. Main battle now is in the Old City. Hell let loose there since Saturday. About 40,000 Arabs, against 1,500 Jews, most of them old men, women and children. Some Jewish positions have been overwhelmed. A message came through to-night: "Morale high, but cannot hold on without reinforcements." The Arabs still command the immediate approaches to the Old City, and, the main thing, the Walls. Those ramparts once kept the might of Rome at bay for three years. Some say we should evacuate the Old City: lives are more important than antiquities; that it's bad tactics, with our limited strength, to cling to it for prestige reasons. But most people don't feel that way.

The fury unloosed against that tiny space echoes in my ears. During the day we saw pillars of smoke rising sky-high. Even the children are full of that battle; in the garden they were playing at relief of the Old City.

"Leizy, *ata meguyas* ('Leizy, you're conscripted'). All exemptions withdrawn. We've got to save the Old City."

The Consular Truce Commission and the Red Cross are striving to renew the Old City truce; but the Arabs are not interested. And the world outside, so large and self-absorbed, what does it care! All the proclaimed distress at the threat to the Holy City; the piety and adoration (Sunday to-day, and in how many millions of churches millions are singing "Thy light shall shine, O Jerusalem," maybe thinking of the Holy Sepulchre, Via Dolorosa, Brook Kidron, the Golden Gate)—all together haven't stopped a single bullet in the Old City. And the climax of U.N.O.'s deliberations: a Quaker Mayor for Jerusalem—and he still in Philadelphia.

Haganah drive through the southern quarters continues. Everyone more confident with this incredibly swift capture of so many Arab-held sectors. A group of Haganah men marched jauntily down the street a few minutes ago. You can see they are on the upper end of things now. They carried a captured Iraqi flag, black, green and white; it fluttered and quivered as though it were alive.

But the big questions in people's minds are: Will the Legion attack? Will the Egyptians come up from the south? Will the planes bombing Tel-Aviv and other places come over Jerusalem as well? Some still try hard to believe that the Legion will keep out. British-trained, British-equipped, largely British-officered, Transjordan bound by the closest treaty with Britain, almost a British Protectorate, in fact—how could Britain let the Legion attack the Holy City? Self-delusion!

The heavy guns blasting the western suburbs must be the Legion's. This sound of shell barrages is new and frightening. At sunset yesterday they let loose 100 shells in 15 minutes; to-day, again. You hear the sound like the lonely roll of an approaching thunderstorm, a kind of portent that makes you grow cold, and a few seconds later, the rapid crashes.

The radio has just announced: the Syrian and Lebanese armies have struck across the northern border. Well, here it is! Any minute we'll hear of the Iraqis and Transjordanians attacking from the east. How shall we hold them all at once—stretch our ill-armed, outnumbered force to stem the flood across all the frontiers? What a tunnel of bloodshed lies ahead!

Night

First blood to us! Nirim settlement in the Negev has beaten back two Egyptian assaults. In the north the Lebanese retreated with 200 dead. If we had their arms, the lashing they would get!

Again found a crowd in my study twisting the wireless knob from station to station trying to squeeze out something more. Martin Buber among them, looking very sad. From Cairo, Nixon of the B.B.C. reports a feeling of "restrained joyfulness" among the Egyptians over the decision to invade Palestine. "This is like the Crusades all over again," says Nixon. "Only this time

the Arabs have gone out to save the Holy Land." And Azzam
Pasha, Secretary-General of the Arab League, told the Egyptian
Press: "This war will be a war of extermination and a momentous
massacre which will be spoken of like the Mongol massacres and
the Crusades."

The city's stocks of flour and fuel, C. tells me, are nearing rock
bottom. For lack of fuel, no buses have been running for five
days now, and water-lorries are soon to be replaced by donkey-
carts. Water rationing is working badly; insufficient yesterday,
none to-day, and the *hamseen* still burning us up. Electric current
cut completely; only the papers get it for a few hours to print
two pages each. *Mishmar Haam* has issued identity discs for
children up to the age of 8.

A Haganah man brought me a message from Don: Can I find
out anything about Tamara? I wish I could. I imagine his feelings, the feelings of hundreds of families who still have no information about Etzion: Who is dead, who alive? The men
prisoners have been taken to Transjordan. Eighty-six women are
being held in Bethlehem; Red Cross is trying to take them over.

17 May

THE OLD CITY IS in the fourth day of its agony. The crackling and roaring echo through the town. All we can do is hope that Haganah breaks through in time. A feeling of awful helplessness presses down on one. If only one could contribute to the outcome. Fires throughout the Quarter. The Arabs are pumping mortar-shells into it from close range, but Haganah's fire from the New City is obstructed by the Holy Places. If some Holy Places *were* hit, the nations might act instead of talk. But I'm not sure; there is no oil and not much strategic value in churches these days.

Arabs still withholding their reply about renewing the truce for the Old City. Saw Azcarate, back from Lake Success as U.N. representative with the Truce Commission. An embittered man, but deeply concerned to help save Jerusalem. Says the Truce Commission is powerless, and almost in despair. He and N., the Commission's Chairman, asked the British last week for tranport to interview the Arab leaders in Amman and Damascus. Got the reply that all British planes were engaged in evacuating the British.

Thought to-day of Esther C., wondering how she is faring in that Gehennum. Her wish is fulfilled; to help defend the Old City. Last week I had a scribbled note from her (a British soldier must have smuggled it out) saying how happy she was to be there.

Transjordan and Iraq troops have crossed the Jordan. Now at least we know. They're all in it, and it can't be worse. (Remember the remark of the club commissionaire to Churchill during England's black days: "Anyhow, sir, we're in the final, and it's going to be played on the home ground.")

Transjordan started off gaily, as though it were a *fantaseeya* (a celebration, with shooting in the air), Abdullah firing the first shot across the border. . . . Arab artillery and bombers attacking in the Jordan Valley. But in the north, Palmach raided 10 miles into Lebanon, blowing up installations, equipment, bridges. In the Negev, Nirum still halting one Egyptian column. Cairo announces that another column is nearly halfway to Tel-Aviv. Here everyone is waiting nervously for Egyptian guns to reach Jerusalem. Since the fall of Etzion, nothing stands in their way.

Met Edward J. returning from operating, terribly distressed. The shells are falling where they cause most damage, in the poorer, congested sectors. Ghastly injuries, and the emergency hospitals working under fearful conditions; fuel, water, electricity, food, all short. Shelling to-day the heaviest we have had.

Dr. B. has stopped serving lunches, but agrees to let us have a plate of soup each, daily, on condition that we provide some of the water. This week's rations distributed to-day: 3 oz. dried beans, 1½ oz. margarine and two onions.

Went out last night on defence works, midnight to dawn, at Talpioth, the direction from which we expect the Egyptians. Most of the party were elderly Kurds—husky, bearded porters, bootblacks, building labourers—a half-blind Greek shopkeeper, officials, a University professor, three *Yeshiva* students, teachers, and some middle-aged Germans who called each other "*Herr Doktor*." Divided into three groups, erecting barricades, digging trenches and filling sandbags. I was in a stone-carrying party. Ahead, under cover of a hillock, Haganah men were laying mines.

There was shooting all over the town. Ramat Rahel was under heavy attack, and several times we had to fling ourselves down when shots came our way. Heavy guns flashed out in the west and north. From the city, the conglomerate sounds of mortars and machine-guns; but in the Old City there seemed to be a lull.

After two hours' work, a brief rest, tea and a sandwich. We spoke about the Old City, the shelling and invading armies. The calm and determination of these people were splendid. The Greek told us his shop had been wrecked by a 25-pounder on the first day. Someone diffidently repeated a rumour that Latrun was in our hands and a secret convoy had come through. A Kurd uttered an excited "*Baruch Hashem*" ("Praised be the Lord"). "Now we'll have food and water and I'll get work." The others were sceptical. One of the *Yeshiva* boys, a bit of a chatterer, was full of fighting talk. A Kurd asked him why, then, wasn't he fighting.

"I'm being trained," the boy answered, as though he had waited all night to tell us. "This is extra."

"My two big sons and daughter are fighting," said the Kurd. "I also wanted to fight. I was a great fighter in Kurdistan. I used to fight robbers and raiders. Now all I am good for is fortifications."

Another Kurd asked for a second sandwich, but there weren't any. He said he was hungry. I believed him; so was I. The Greek said, "Food won't save us. It's guns we need. Big guns! Plenty of guns. And more men." The Kurd nodded and said, "That's right. But still I'm hungry."

Got back home at 6 a.m.

18 May

THE LEGION HAS COME. The thing Britain couldn't let happen is happening. They are advancing from the east and north. Their artillery pounded the Old City all morning, and since early afternoon their mechanized infantry has been moving in through St. Stephen's Gate and up Via Dolorosa. Another column is bombarding the western suburbs. They came up during the night.

A Haganah unit was preparing to break through towards Herod's Gate and the Walls when the news was flashed of the Legion's advance in its rear. The *Mateh* believes this is the column that smashed Etzion. Everyone is expecting the full force of their guns to-night. B.B.C. reports that Glubb Pasha gave the Legion a final inspection this morning. They must be at about the same place as Titus' cohorts when he "gazed upon Jerusalem the day before its destruction and wept for the sake of the beautiful city." I doubt if Glubb Pasha is weeping.

The Legion is only one mechanized division in strength, but reputed to be good soldiers. Their equipment is first-rate; it has cost Britain millions. They know the country intimately. Being men of the desert, they respect nothing but a mosque and tombstone. If they should get into the city . . . a frightful outlook.

The whole Jewish Quarter of the Old City seemed to be burning this afternoon; long tongues of flame rose through the smoke. Our men yielded more ground, but fought for every room of every house. Reports to *Mateh* that some of the older people can't stand any more and want to surrender to the Legion. Haganah is trying desperately to relieve the Quarter. To-day they got right up to the Walls. During the night Palmach seized Deir Abu Tor and immediately pushed across the Vale of Hinnom and captured Mount Zion. Furious resistance, but they beat it down. Without a pause, they went for Zion Gate with bazoukas,

their heaviest weapons, but failed. Another unit stormed Arab
strongpoints around Jaffa Gate, but couldn't breach the Gate
itself. Last night's objective was a concerted attempt to smash
through three gates; none of it was achieved.

Fighting all day around Musrara, the only New City quarter
still held by the Arabs. Some progress, but stiff opposition.
Jewish evacuees are flocking into the farther parts of the city from
the areas under shelling. Most are being accommodated in the
captured Arab quarters. An old couple, dragging a few suitcases,
have come with two grandchildren to the R.'s. How is Mrs. R.
going to feed them?

Acre has fallen to us, after a 22-hour battle. Haganah, with
Dissident units, are attacking Ramleh and Lydda; we have old
scores to settle with these places. Gloomy news of ceaseless
artillery attacks and air-raids on the Jordan Valley and Galilee
settlements; much damage, but no loss of ground yet. More
Egyptian air-raids on Tel-Aviv.

Y. tells me of a document Haganah captured, which sets out a
combined plan of campaign by Glubb Pasha for all the Arab
armies. An Egyptian force is to join up with the Legion in
Jerusalem. Syrians and Lebanese to keep the Jewish forces on
the move in Galilee. Transjordan and Iraq forces to drive
through the Jordan Valley to Nazareth and Haifa. The British
Government would at once recognize Abdullah's sovereignty
over Haifa as a Transjordan harbour. Date set, 21 May. Tel-Aviv
is to be captured by the Egyptians; no date fixed for that.

In the midst of the war, the State of Israel takes shape.
Weizmann has been elected Provisional President. That great
leader who has guided his difficult people with such controlled
intensity of purpose in an inimical world, how must he feel in
these days!

U.S.S.R. and four more countries have recognized us. Israel
has applied for admission to U.N. Diplomatic delegations are to be
sent overseas. Eliyahu Epstein will represent Israel in Washing-
ton. Strange to think of these friends I knew a few months ago
as officials of the Jewish Agency serving now as Ambassadors and

Ministers. They, too, will grow with the new stature of Israel.

I long to see more of the State emerging from its chrysalis. It grows daily, but only the barest facts of it reach us. "The Government in the plain has forgotten Jerusalem," shriek the Dissidents' posters. We do feel utterly alone, closed in by a ring of steel, fighting for life, without a spark of inspired leadership in the city. Even our indomitable *Palestine Post* is struggling for existence; no current at all last night for its presses. This morning it appeared in four small, illegible multigraphed sheets. I couldn't decipher half of it, but it was good just to know that it is holding on, our sole remaining link with the world outside.

J. R. tells me a strange tale that might have come out of a political thriller: how a plan by the Mandatory Government to enact new, far-reaching measures on the eve of its departure was defeated. I don't know how far they would have been binding on the Israel Government, but they certainly held the seeds of complications. Among the measures was a grant of new facilities to the international (but British-controlled) Iraq Petroleum Company. Another gave the British Government ultimate authority over the £20,000,000 worth of Russian Church properties in Palestine. A third empowered the Mandatory to promulgate summarily any further measures it wished in the remaining days of its régime. The *Gazette Extraordinary* containing these enactments was printed under armed guard by a Jewish printer. (The Government and Arab presses weren't functioning.) Completed on 11 May, the sheets were taken, still under guard, to a binder. In the early hours of 12 May a party of 30 armed Jews forced their way into the binder's shop and removed every copy. J. R. assures me they have been destroyed. The *Gazette* never appeared, and the Ordinances it contained remain unpromulgated.

19 May

I T I S N E A R L Y M I D D A Y, and I got up only a short while ago. The city is full of the shriek of shells. Ruth says it has been like that all morning, but I slept through it; even now it worries me little. I am still exhilarated by the happenings of last night, an unforgettable night. I watched Palmach break the siege of the Old City.

After the Haganah Press conference last night a party of us were officially taken to eyewitness a battle. Driven to Yemin Moshe, where a 25-year-old Palmach man they called Uzi was in charge. They were not out to capture the Old City, he said, but to break the siege of the Jewish Quarter. The *Portzim*[1] were on Mount Zion, awaiting the signal to attack. With them were reinforcements and supplies for the Quarter.

I saw the Commander's Order of the Day, just two lines. It read:

"*Portzim!* You stand before the walls of Jerusalem. For 1877 years no Jew has climbed them. To-night you will mount them."

All the centuries that have brooded over these battle-beaten walls since that time, the bitter ages that have dragged over the Jews, their undying hopes for the future, all seemed gathered up in those few words.

A white night, and the Old City looked congealed and impenetrable in the moonlight. It looked infinitely lonely, too. Perhaps the magic light helped also to give it an air of gallantry to-night, but a petrified gallantry. The air above it seemed heavy with menace. Beyond the battlemented ramparts rose the cupolas, minarets and spires. On Mount Zion the cypress and olive trees stood up like black stains in the white light. Zion Gate was hidden in a pool of shadow. Nearby, the wall turned sharply, then, from where I stood, seemed to plunge into a void and

---

[1] *Portzim* – "The Stormers" (a unit of Palmach).

disappear towards the Valley of Jehosophat. I don't think I
was ever so moved by the sight of the Old City as on this night.

Operational H.Q. at Yemin Moshe consisted of the two rooms
of a former dwelling-house. By candlelight the youthful staff
officers studied the maps on the table. I wondered if any of the
maps were Ruth's work. A "walkie-talkie" stood in the corner.

A message was sent over.

"Everything O.K. Awaiting orders."

"I repeat. Awaiting orders. Over to you!"

Uzi gave an order. Then he sent us, with an accompanying
officer, crawling along a trench to a forward parapet to await
developments. For nearly two hours the city had been resounding
to the shooting. Within the walls a pattern of constantly moving
flashes from the shots. An Arab shell struck the tower of the
Dormition Abbey on Mount Zion and broke into a hundred
fragmentary specks of light; but the tower took it. Arab fire
switched nervously, but mostly concentrated around Jaffa Gate.

Dick, standing beside me, said:

"They must expect an attack around Jaffa Gate. That's where
the Romans breached the wall."

Which reminded me that a few weeks ago I found H., an
Operational Officer at the *Mateh*, engrossed in Flavius's *History
of the Jewish Wars* while lunching off a sandwich. A long glance
back to eleven centuries ago, but, except for the upper layers, it
is still much the same wall.

Our accompanying officer, eyes on his watch, suddenly
whispered:

"Now you'll hear the Davidka in action." He was trying, not
very successfully, to keep his tone matter-of-fact. One heard talk
of Haganah's hush-hush weapon, a heavy mortar firing something like a rocket-bomb, but it has never yet been in action in
Jerusalem. It must have come by the plane. Who the David is
who invented it, I haven't discovered. Possibly a farmer in some
remote settlement; so many of the bright boys of the Haganah
are farmers.

We waited expectantly. At 2 o'clock we heard a gathering of

sound over our heads like the race of an incoming wave, a fearful
shriek, then a shattering crash; a great flash lit up the sky beyond
the wall; a plume of smoke spread up and sideways. More and
more came over; a pause, and still more.

Dick turned to me:

"Now, if the Romans had something like *that* it wouldn't
have taken them three years. . . ."

Above the dying echo of Davidka's crash, an anguished cry of
"Allah, Allah" floated across to us. I pictured the folk at home
tossing sleeplessly, their hearts beating fast for the outcome of
this battle they heard, but knew nothing about.

My thoughts turned back to the Old City across the ravine.
How would it emerge from all this? . . . Not a city as much as a
symbol of the passionate beliefs, prayers, hopes of mankind
through the centuries. Benedictions that have been poured over
it, and the blasphemies! The emperors who have desired it—
with little Abdullah of Transjordan the latest of the line! Beyond
the ramparts that ancient rulers built to hold it, its fingers
flicked out far beyond this land. . . .

But for the people of Old Jerusalem who live there it is still a
city. Their roots and homes, their children's schools, their liveli-
hoods are there, the treasures of their faiths. Every man living
in Old Jerusalem feels himself the guardian of his faith, whatever it may be. Nowhere in the world is any man more jealous
of that privilege than he. . . . The tightly-bound little Jewish
Quarter, walled within the wider walls. Mixture of splendour and
debris, huddle of synagogues and houses of sacred learning,
squeezed beside and on top of each other; blue-washed dwellings
with Rembrandt interiors, flush with narrow sordid lanes.

Whenever disturbance breaks out in Jerusalem, it starts in the
Old City. When there is tension, the first place one avoids is the
Old City. And of all restrictions of movement the one you resent
most is that on the Old City. For some Jews it means denial of
access to the Wailing Wall. For me, denial of access to the relics
of ancient ways; forgotten years that still live on here as though
nothing had happened since; old streets where every stone seems

hardened with age and every crevice seems to hide a secret; where men live with their God behind furtive, mildewed walls in strange corners not of this world. Grace, beauty, colour, sordidness, magnificence, amid endless confusion of centuries.

Some of the people I knew there; old R., who lived like a pauper all week and like a king on Sabbath. Moishe, the pimply, weedy young *Yeshiva* student who dreamed dangerous dreams. Rabbi M. and his beautiful wife and very Continental daughter. Brother F., who never quite forgot that he had been born a Jew, and would steal to the Wailing Wall when not too carefully observed. The beadle of Nissinbek Synagogue with his laugh "like a thousand beeves at pasture" and his magnificent purple caftan. Father T., soul of charm and courtesy, guarding his precious old manuscript that nobody had the heart to tell him was a fake. Our little Persian maid who lived two lives poles apart, one in our New City western home, the other in her own home which was pure Orient.

The flash of a shell lit up the Armenian Quarter, close to Zion Gate. I hoped no harm was coming to it; another walled city within the walls; fortified like a fortress of the Middle Ages, with cisterns to hold water for four years and store-rooms to match. Friendly folk, these Armenians: suffering has made them sharp and wary, but kindly still. . . . My last Easter visit to their archaic Cathedral, with faience and mother-of-pearl, rare treasures brought out on that festival from their Treasury, ancient missals covered with gold, mitres with emeralds and pearls, gold tiaras dazzling with precious stones, exquisite brocades; their Patriarch with the bearing of an Oriental prophet, the unsmiling priests with peaked black hoods like little pyramids. . . .

Firing from both sides rose and fell. At 3.15, a lull. Strangely, only one Arab heavy machine-gun kept up its ratatat near Zion Gate. The Jewish guns were silent. Were the Arabs deceived into thinking we had called it a night? Their machine-gun paused in its spluttering; then swept the road between the Abbey and the Gate. A kind of duel, machine-gun *versus* silence.

The officer turned to us:

"The sappers must be close now. Should be crawling along the foot of the wall. Only 30 metres from the Dormition garden to Zion Gate. Watch out for the explosion!"

Suddenly, from the Abbey, Jewish machine-guns burst out.

At 3.22 it exploded. A fantastic flash and roar, the earth beneath us quaked, a great blanket of smoke engulfed the wall and billowed heavenward. I moved my fingers from my ears and listened to the dying rumble. A full five minutes before the smoke and dust cleared. The wall was still there. We waited, chafing, until a message was brought to our officer. Then he led us around the ravine and up Mount Zion. We followed in single file, twisting and threading among the mines and boulders. A new motif of sound from the Old City now, machine-guns and grenades.

At Bishop Gobat School a Palmach officer told us:

"They're there. Took less than 20 minutes to get through."

His face was drawn, but his eyes were triumphant. We crouched, and, keeping close to the wall, ran to the gate, our limit. Bullets from David's Citadel whistled over our heads. Within the city fighting had dwindled. The heavy gate, overlaid with iron, stood wide open, dangling on its great hinges. Part of the masonry of the wall had sagged. The stone barricade behind the gate was flattened.

We crouched in the shadows. The moon was waning and a faint breath of day lit the sky. Then we saw the first *Portzim* return, singly or in twos and threes, not unduly worried about the snipers. Some waved easily and others smiled as they passed us. With them came a few Haganah men from the Quarter. One, his head bandaged, paused for a moment and looked down over the New City. "I never believed I would see this again," he said slowly. Back at Bishop Gobat School, I talked to the boys about the big moment of the link-up. There was nothing demonstrative, they said. One of the Old City men at a forward post was ready with a grenade, one of his last, in case they were Arabs. They met and shook hands.

"It's good you've come. We have been waiting for you. . . ."

A girl had come out, too, with the *Portzim*. She was limping.
Under a steel helmet she had long, straggling blonde hair, rib-
boned at the nape of the neck. She arrived in the Quarter as a
teacher in April, she said. Not much teaching possible, so she
took a greater share in the Haganah. Some of the pupils, boys
of 10 and 11, were also using firearms. Yesterday everything
seemed lost. The Iraqis and irregulars seemed determined to
finish them off before the Arab Legion got started. For 36 hours
they battered the Quarter and set fire to houses abutting on
Jewish positions. Some of the old inhabitants of the Quarter lost
heart, first wanted to surrender, then asked for Red Cross protection. They were transferred to the Misgav Ladach Hospital,
over which the Red Cross flag was hoisted. When the attack
passed its climax the Jews counter-attacked. They recovered
some of the lost ground. But their ammunition was almost
exhausted. To-night's supply came in the nick of time.

I don't think the *Portzim* numbered more than 120. They had
been in continuous action, in the New City and the Old, for 28
hours, and showed the signs of it. A few chatted in a casual and
workshop manner, but I think they were very proud.

One said: "You should have seen Yeruham! The old *shwitser*
[busybody—*slang*] had a hole in his belly you could stick your
hand through. But he wouldn't let them take him away. Kept
on saying he had to polish off that Iraqi."

A 17- or 18-year old red-head was telling his companion:
"When the old greybeard embraced me I thought he'd never
let go. Then something started crawling down my neck and I
thought, Aha, I've caught something already. But when I put
my hand there, I found the old man had been crying."

I find it hard to think of these lean, tough Palmachniks as the
kids I used to see strolling to and from school a year or two ago,
the friends and contemporaries of Tanchik. There is something
so complete about them. Palmach is not a name any more. It has
become a kind of character or state, a state of nervelessness,
reliability, audacity, skill. I wonder if these boys ever think of
death. What do the Arabs say about them?

Behind the Old City the eastern sky was light when we turned towards home. A heavy silence hovered over the New City. I walked softly into the bedroom, but Ruth was awake, dreadfully worried about me. "I thought the whole city had crashed," she said. When I told her the siege of the Old City was broken she said nothing, but I think she wanted to cry.

Evening

A ghastly day. The shelling has started in terrible earnest, crashing into every part of the city, in salvoes and singly. The victory at Zion Gate warmed the hearts of the city this morning, but this fiendish onslaught has already driven it from people's minds. I have no idea of the number of casualties, but it must be large. Heard of three killed in one family; of a woman killed but her children unscathed while running for shelter. In King George Avenue I saw a stretcher being carried towards an ambulance, a coarse grey blanket covering the body. Returning from the Jewish Agency's Press conference at midday I twice took shelter in sandbagged doorways. Other people were there too, all tense and many frightened, but no panic. When the shelling moved away they slipped out in ones and twos, keeping close to house-walls for protection.

I don't think there is a person not fully awakened now to the enormous danger to the whole city. All vague, thoughtless confidence has been blown to bits.

At Latrun, the struggle goes on. The lines change a bit here and there, usually in our favour, but not much. The main thing, the road, remains closed.

20 May

As TERRIFYING TO-DAY as yesterday. The distant boom, the fiendish whistle and crash, the echo of one shell hanging in the air with another already on its way, scattering death, injury, destruction.

The whole city is the target; this sector, then that, then back to the first. Houses mutilated, streets strewn with shattered glass, torn telegraph wires, broken stones. What are they doing to Jerusalem!

In Rehavia we got it first last night. I didn't hear it in the beginning. When I awoke Ruth was sitting up stiffly. "Listen to that," she said in a small voice. Her whole body was shivering. The B.'s were whispering in the next room. In the adjoining house a child was screaming in terror. The shells kept on coming over, their long, slow, terrible whine growing louder and deeper-toned as they approached. The very air seemed sick with it. Then crash, a colossal fist pulverizing an unresisting body. Every time that scream whistled overhead, nearer, louder, lower, something inside you rose up to meet it, while the rest of your body grew rigid. Ruth hadn't been in town during the day. The full hideousness of it was new to her. I lit a candle and saw that she was all drawn up inside, waiting for the blow with an awful, helpless anticipation. Somewhere in the city machine-guns were rattling away; it was music against this appalling thing.

We all ran down to the shelter and found the neighbours already there. We spoke little. For an hour we listened to the shells landing all around. Once there was a grinding explosion in the street outside. Our building shook and bits of shrapnel struck the walls. We knew that our improvised shelter, half above the street surface, was little protection against a direct hit. At 3 a.m. it was quiet again, and we returned to our beds.

How welcome was the dawn! It was a bright, cheery morning.

In the immediate neighbourhood a crater in the street, telegraph wires pulled down, the corner of a house shot away. Later we learned there had been 30 direct hits in Rehavia. But this Jerusalem stone of ours can take it; there were few casualties.

Michael said:

"If that's the best they can do, we don't have much to worry about."

He meant that for Judy. At 9 a.m., as I was on my way to the office, it started up again, swinging in one after the other, in a series of monstrous bounds. Each one made straight for me. I felt that any second the earth would disappear suddenly under my feet. Then the whistle overhead, and the crash a block or two away.

It isn't only the shelling; it is the consciousness of our awful vulnerability that is devastating. No defences, few shelters. You just walk along, exposed to shells from before and behind and above you. Each shell seems to have its own diabolical volition. When it misses you, it is only by virtue of some whim or mistake.

The usual people at the office. Most away on duty, and of those present some had been on duty earlier, or would be on duty later in the day. What made them come to the office? Feeling a need to keep busy? Duty? It needs enormous effort to work. And what is the work worth? Calls for a strong dose of something—more than courage, mysticism perhaps—to go on working, planning for the future when its practical value is probably nil.

Abdullah is boasting that it will be a 10-day war; that the Egyptians are about to make juncture with the Legion in Jerusalem. Difficult to know what the situation really is. How long can any city stand up to continuous bombardment with no means of warding it off and no heavy armour for counter-attack? And the Legion's tanks are massing. . . .

To-day we suffered some bitter losses of ground, but also made important gains. We have lost Sheikh Jarrah and the Police Training Depot, both held by Etzel. The Legion bombarded them mercilessly. Scores of casualties within an hour. Now Scopus is isolated again and another Arab path opened to the Old City.

Then the Legion turned its guns on Mount Scopus: on Hadassah Hospital and the University. Red Cross and the Truce Commission intervened, but to no effect. It is quiet there this evening. The Hospital has ceased to function. Some of the most valuable medical equipment in the Middle East has been destroyed. Perhaps the Arabs, from King Feisal II of Iraq down to the local *fellaheen* (peasants), who have blessed Hadassah for its services to them, will feel the better now for its destruction.

Among our gains, however, is Notre Dame, one of the three main objectives in the Haganah plan to defend the city. An absolute fortress, built by the French in Turkish days to house— and protect—their pilgrims, and dominating some of the main cross-roads of the city. Abdullah's Legion and the Egyptians are going to find it hard to join hands as long as Jews bestride their path at Notre Dame.

About 200 Iraqis held it; 30 Haganah men took it from them at 2 this morning. Deafening fire was going on all around. Under cover of this tumult and a diversionary assault, the attacking party broke through neighbouring walls with explosives and then through a rear wall of Notre Dame itself. While some set up a fearful din suggesting hordes of attackers, the others pounced upon the Arabs in their forward positions. So they swept from corridor to corridor. (For pattern of the battle, see Gideon *versus* Midianites, about 1200 B.C.E.) The Arabs fled through any and every opening, mostly windows. Eighteen Arabs were killed, 30 taken prisoner, and more found hiding in cellars this morning. Jewish losses, 2 killed. The attackers were a tough crowd, most of them Orientals. Their commander was a 22-year-old University student.

In spite of our reinforcements that went into the Old City with the *Portzim* on Wednesday (only about 60 could be spared, I'm told now, and a very mixed bunch) the balance of forces within the Old City is worse for us than ever. This afternoon spotters saw wave after wave of Legionnaires advancing through Sheikh Jarrah into the Old City. Another vain Haganah attempt last night to pierce the walls, this time through a little half-forgotten gateway near Jaffa Gate.

The Truce Commission cabled a report to-day to the United Nations: "A bitter battle is being waged inside the Old City. . . . The Arabs are continuing their violent attacks on the Jews, whom reinforcements from the almost entirely Jewish-controlled new city are endeavouring to reach. We heard that as many as 300 combatants and 200 non-combatants are besieged in one synagogue. The situation of the Jews in the rest of the city, who are deprived of water, electricity and provisions, is extremely difficult and precarious."

This afternoon we heard the drone of planes. Everyone was certain they were Arab. From where have we planes, except the little "primuses"? A cold feeling crawled up my back. I know there isn't a single anti-aircraft gun in the city. I tried to shake the noise of the planes out of my head, but it persisted, grew louder. Then I saw them, steadily looming larger. Most people scattered to the shelters. I watched the planes come lower. Suddenly they dipped sharply, soared again, and flew away. They were four Spitfires; and they were ours.

21 May

Now the Egyptians are also upon us. Their artillery is pounding Ramat Rahel from Bethlehem. The Legion has brought up more guns. Even worse to-day than yesterday. The streets vibrated endlessly with explosions. Tactics are the same; to bombard every corner of the city, but to keep us guessing where the next shell will fall. Only the Jewish Agency block seems to be a consistent target; yet it has come through so far with no more than a few holes in the walls. Ambulances are tearing through the streets all the time. The *Magen David Adom* (Red Shield of David) is working feverishly to organize more mobile first-aid units.

But the great news is: We have met the Legion's tanks and repulsed them. . . . Word flashed round the city this morning that the Legion was launching its heaviest armour against Beth Israel. The same thought must have shaken everyone: this is the most critical day of all; our first taste of tanks—and what have we to hold them with? . . . If they get through Beth Israel, they're in Mea Shearim; after Mea Shearim, the centre of the city. . . . The Legion opened up with a terrific artillery barrage; 30 dead and I don't know how many injured in under two hours. Then the armoured cars and tanks advanced. Battles were in progress in other parts as well, but I couldn't forget Beth Israel for a minute. Late this afternoon the news flashed through: the tanks have turned tail; three of them knocked out, two more disabled. I think many of us realized then that we were holding our breath.

To-night I heard about it from Y. A newly-appointed officer known as Zohar was commanding our northern line. His entire force consisted of 3 companies, one of officer cadets, one of *Palam* (youth attack groups) with a week's training, and one of *Gadna* (under-17 auxiliary youth corps), besides a detachment of garrison troops normally considered unfit for front-line service. Their heaviest equipment was 2 Beza machine-guns which arrived in the city by air a week ago (only one man was found in Jerusalem who knew how to handle them; he taught a few others). Zohar, who was an armoured car officer in the British Army in the War, observed the entire operation of the Legion's advance into Sheikh Jarrah yesterday. He noticed that they followed the British manual of operations to the last detail. He also observed that by their formation they seemed anxious to avoid risking their infantry. He decided to scrap the old defence plan, and instead to ambush the enemy's armour with his one armoured car, 2 Bezas and one Browning machine-gun, and a volunteer squad armed with Molotov cocktails. He ordered that anyone who fled the line of battle was to be shot.

The Legion launched the attack with four batteries of heavy guns, smaller artillery units, two infantry regiments, and large units of tanks and armoured cars. After the artillery barrage they advanced in massed strength, tanks in the lead, acting exactly as Zohar expected. Well before Beth Israel, his tiny force was waiting for them. Electric mines and Molotov cocktails started the Legion's confusion; heavy machine-guns brought right under the tanks noses (where, by all the manuals, they should never have been), increased it. Machine-gun fire began piercing their chinks. Ahead of them stood the forward positions of Beth Israel, of unknown strength. The Legion decided they had had enough. . . .

Hideous pandemonium all through last night. Shells that come screaming over in the night have a terrifying quality of their own.

O. told me this afternoon of a unit he saw at Yemin Moshe last night preparing for another attempt to breach the city wall. All religious, some with *peyot* under large American steel helmets; many bearded. They held a short prayer service before leaving. Some hours later they were back, their mission unachieved.

For a time last night Rehavia was an island of quiet in the uproar. I stood by the window and looked out on the solid grey stone buildings bathed in moonlight and at the scattered pines. A broad space of stillness seemed thrown like a protective arm around the quarter. The pines stood perfectly still and aloof, and the light of the moon seemed to heighten their chill, ascetic look, like cowled, motionless figures. Then suddenly the whistle of the first shell. More followed. We went down to the shelter.

The landlord's family lay in bunks that they have fixed up for themselves around the walls. They practically live here now, which accounts for their unexpected munificence in installing a small oil lamp. The rest of us sat on the stools we brought down. Ruth has tried to brighten the place by hanging up large coloured travel posters. "Come to Switzerland for Rest and Pleasure," "Tulip Time in Holland" kept staring down at us from the wall.

"Like invitations to holiday on the moon," said Michael.

All of us were tired and sleepy, but no one seemed frightened. The old couple from Beth Israel sat huddled together, silent and sad. I asked them about Beth Israel; a quarter of catacombs, they said, everyone left there lives in the shelters, the women keeping them clean, the men reading Psalms.

Michael brought his gramophone and records to the shelter; he thought hill-billy songs would liven the atmosphere, but they weren't a success. K. gave us a disquisition on the Hebrew word for 'shell," *pagaz*, derived from the Book of Jeremiah. Once we thought our building had been hit. But the crash was in the street.

After an hour Rehavia was quiet again. The street looked as indifferent as before. The pines still stood inscrutable; concerned not with time, but with eternity. When we awoke at 7 this morning the roll of the shells had died down, although the shooting still blazed away in the distance. From Ramat Rahel two great pillars of smoke rose to the sky: the Egyptians smashing at our back door.

Hamseen still on, and people's bodies are beginning to smell. The other night we thought back to when we had our last real baths: Ruth and I, in Tel-Aviv, about two months ago; the Bs. still earlier. When there was water, in winter, there was no kerosene to warm it. When spring weather came round, there was no water either. For laundry, we lack soap as well as water now; I wear my darkest shirts. *Mishmar Haam* had distributed a leaflet illustrating the most economical use of our water ration. Posters in the streets bear a large picture of two drops and the word "SAVE." The precept isn't necessary.

For the first time we hear officially of the Israel Air Force. Yesterday its aircraft bombed Samakh in the Jordan Valley. Wonder whether they are real bombers or makeshifts. Meanwhile, Arab bombers are raiding us almost at will all over the country. Yesterday the Egyptians bombed Tel-Aviv four times.

Looked in at the Es'. to collect from Roy a commentary for *Kol Hamegen*. It's the last he will write for us. In a few days *Kol Hamegen* in English will come to an end. It has served its purpose. For those who have battery sets there is now the official *Kol Yerushalayim*, with programmes in English, besides Hebrew and other languages.

Roy's "Column One" in the *Post* has made his *nom-de-plume* (David Courtney), almost a legend. Nothing else written in Jerusalem these days carries so much weight with the man in the street. Most don't know that he is not a Jew. Sometimes the column is stickily sentimental, but usually it's first-rate writing. I think he is kept here to share our hardships and whatever lies in store for us, not only by friendship but by a feeling that, somehow, he is also thereby faithful to the real spirit of England.

Shots were flying over from Malha, so we avoided the balcony. Through the window we saw the box-like plane come from the west, glide low through the crackling of fire, and circle four times over the landing strip. Each time it dropped a parachute supporting a bulky package.

Roy is dejected about the situation of Jerusalem (which he calls "the holy no-man's-land of the nations") but tries to hide it. He told us of the old Russian priests at Mar Salabe Monastery in the *wadi* who sell buckets of water from their cistern. The price at first was two or three cigarettes per bucket; now that no one has cigarettes, they accept money. He told us also of a Polish Gentile painter whom the priests harbour in their monastery. Haganah allows him to be there, but not to leave the premises. Several Polish *émigrés* who have remained in Jerusalem are suspected of spying for the Arabs or British, and are watched. There are rumours of a Jew and a Pole caught spying a few weeks ago, tried by Haganah, and shot.

22 *May*

EACH DAY IS LIKE a week. The shelling still beats down
implacably. Same persistency and uncertainty where it will strike
next. But now they also seem to have the range of some important
Haganah targets. One workshop where they have been repairing
captured Arab armoured cars is under constant fire. Clearly there
is something to the spy talk.

Shelling starts at 8 or 9 a.m., goes on until dark, stops until
midnight or the early morning hours, then continues intermittently until dawn. The fighting, however, has no fixed hours;
machine-gun fire, punctuated by the rattle of other weapons and
explosions of mortars, beats sporadically on your eardrums all
day and night. But the shells are the monstrous thing. From
rising to bedtime we talk of little else. How get your mind off it
when it encroaches on you wherever you are, whatever you try
to do? Life has lost all shape. Long ago its rules, customs, attributes, the things one used to take for granted—food, water,
light, traffic, human relations—just melted away. One paused
sometimes to wonder how such a thing was possible. And now,
overtopping all that, the terror of the shells.

Another victory to-day over the Legion's armour, but this
time, Y. says, it was a very close thing. They sent in their infantry
first, behind an enormous smoke screen; we drove them back
only by a tremendous effort. Had they persisted another half-
hour . . .

The neighbours downstairs have been urging us to sleep in
their flat. For the present we have declined. However, we are
sharing the Bs.' bedroom (though it's the one that got the mortar
shell from Katamon); that's the safest room in the flat. We placed
two wardrobes between their beds and ours. Silly; who cares now
about privacy, anyway.

Everyone has chosen the least-exposed room for sleeping in,

the ones with the fewest outside walls. Some people sleep in their passages. *Mishmar Haam* has ordered that all glassware and pictures be removed to avoid glass splinters. Ruth is compromising by taking the pictures down at night only; says she feels there is less chance of a direct hit by day. At night she also rolls up the carpets, and transfers to the passage cupboard all the other articles we value. We have detached our windows altogether. As soon as the distant roll of shelling draws near, we close our shutters; as does everyone else. Banging shutters is a sound of the times.

A mortar has been set up on a roof not far from us. Every night the gunner fires a lone shot or two as if to say: "Just to prove to you I'm here"; occasionally, he fires one or two shells also by day. People say, with bitter irony, that the gunner makes the shells himself and it takes him all day to make two. We hear them tearing the air to pieces, wait eagerly to hear the echo of the distant crash six or seven seconds later.

Don came in this evening. His left arm in a sling; wounded in the hand, but he says it is nothing. They wanted to send him to the rear, but he insisted on remaining with his unit, saying he could still be of use. Was sent to-day to base hospital for examination. His unit is at Beth Israel. He has changed; gone older, his face harder, less boyish-looking, and he is thinner. The sparkle that used to light his eyes, like points of light on little waves when they catch the sun, has dimmed. But the biggest change, perhaps, is in the way he speaks of the country. He speaks of "us" and "we" and "ours"; no sign of being on the defensive as before. He doesn't know whether Tamara is alive or dead. Speaks hesitantly of her and his eyes are full of anxiety. He only knows, as we all do, that the women from Etzion who survived are still in the Legion's hands in Bethlehem.

He told us quietly about his French friend, Mikhael. He was killed during the attack of the Legion's tanks on Thursday. Don was near him. A shell exploded in their *emda* and tore half Mikhael's back away. He tried to lift himself, leaning on his Sten gun. His face was all twisted up. All he said was *"Merde!"*

then "*Tuez! Tuez!*" and fell back dead. Don sat staring at the table for a few seconds. Then he got up suddenly, as he did that night he first told me about Tamara, and said *Shalom*. It strikes me now that this was the first time I heard him use the Hebrew word.

At Lake Success they are still debating how to arrange a cease-fire. Britain does not want the threat of sanctions invoked. "We should not attempt to reach any far-reaching conclusions," says Sir Alexander Cadogan, "except on the basis of detailed information from competent and impartial observers such as we do not possess." (The Consular Truce Commission will appreciate that.) And while the armies of six states have crossed our land frontiers and an arms embargo invests us on our sea coast, Cadogan rises to ask the Jews whether they are letting in men of military age and, if so, where they come from. He is trying to imply Russia. He wouldn't know about the D.P. camps.

Yesterday Count Folke Bernadotte accepted the role of U.N. Mediator. He says he believes there is "only a 1 per cent. chance" that his mission can succeed, but he adds that, although slim, the chance is worth taking because it offers the one hope of extinguishing a spark that may set the world on fire. Not much known here about Bernadotte except that his life has been spent in humanitarian work, that he is religious, and that he is a nephew of the Swedish King and the son of a father who renounced a throne.

We have a new member of the household, Karamba, Ruth's boxer bitch. She used to be with E., whose flat has now been shelled out. A new mouth to feed, and a large one, when we ourselves are hungry all the time. Ruth loves the animal and says she will find a way to feed it. Mrs. R. has promised to bring kitchen scraps, such as they are, from the Etzel Hospital. To-day we got some half-mouldy bread for Karamba from a nurse. And water? Everyone tells us we are mad. I think they are right.

23 May

MET RUTH AT 11.30 behind the security wall in King George Avenue—large printed signs identify it now as King David Street—to try our luck at the restaurant Erwin told us about. The morning hammering, in full swing, seemed directed mainly at the centre of the city. We decided, nevertheless, to chance it. Through the peep-holes in the 10-feet high wall we could see the little park on the other side, where children used to play. Eastward, the angular profile of the Old City rose above the walls, uplifted and withdrawn on its hill. We could hear the endless firing there. What hell they must be going through! "There . . . the great number of the damned . . . are heaped together in their awful prison." Through the peep-holes we saw the bursts of smoke, little curls, quite impersonal and somehow unrelated to the noise of the shells. Through the opening it looks more than ever like a gigantic prison fortress, yet also like a remote and unreal backdrop on a stage.

Posters with Bible quotations are pasted up on the walls and hoardings. The lettering is modelled on ancient Hebrew characters. One passage from Isaiah: "For I will defend this city to save it. . . ." Another from Zechariah: "And in that day will I make Jerusalem a burdensome stone for all people; all that burden themselves with it shall be cut in pieces." Biblical days never seem so remote to those who live in Jerusalem, and now the prophetic reassurances of other days touch not only the pious. On the day that Abdullah announced in Amman that his troops were attacking Jerusalem, two new posters appeared: "I will cause an alarm of war to be heard in Rabbah of the Ammonites; and it shall be a desolate heap" (Jeremiah); and "I will make Rabbah a stable for camels, and the Ammonites a couching-place for flocks; and ye shall know that I am the Lord" (Ezekiel).

The few people about the street walked fast, as we did. Only

near Bezalel Street a small crowd had queued-up with their pails
and tins beside the water-cart. Everyone was anxious to get it
done with us quickly as possible, and the overseer was shouting
to them not to shove.

"It's all right for you," he said. "In a few minutes you can
get back into your houses, but I'm exposed all the time."

Windows and doors all along the street are barricaded with
concrete blocks or sandbags. Most shop windows are boarded up;
all the stores in this street are closed. On the roads, only military
traffic. No civilian transport of any kind (except doctors' cars)
for the past fortnight. Piles of rubble and chipped stone everywhere. Gutters full of rubbish and shattered glass. Turning into
Ben Yehuda Street, we see a long, irregular brown band of dried
blood running into the gutter.

Still can't get accustomed to the sight of Ben Yehuda Street.
The damage of the shelling is jumbled up now with the wreckage
of the February explosion. Some of the buildings partly rebuilt
are now damaged again. From top to bottom it stands maimed
and mutilated, some walls obliterated, others gashed and ripped,
with gaping sockets that once were windows. Holes torn in roofs
and iron work grotesquely twisted. Telephone wires curl crazily
across the shell-pocked road.

We passed Hannah's old flat. The room in which I used to
play with Yael and Yehudit is now a yawning emptiness, open
to the sky. Lower down, the Atlantic Hotel has disappeared completely; that happened in February. Lucullus, where one used to
go for a meal after midnight, has two walls left and half a ceiling.
In the side street leading to the Orion Cinema stands a hoarding
with old posters, pasted on top of each other. One, partly hanging down, advertises as "Showing shortly," Tyrone Power in
Nightmare Alley. Around it are some of the old underground
broadsheets, Haganah's *Hahomah*, *Maas*, the Sternists' *Heruth*,
and an Etzel announcement that they have shot Eva Dukas, a
Czech Jewess, as a spy. Newest is a Haganah calling-up notice
to men aged 18–45.

Across the road a half-demolished façade and a torn

signboard reading MICHEL RA is all that remains of old Michel
Rabinowitz's bookstore. A world of its own it used to be, utterly
remote from the rest of the bustling street. You wondered if he
ever sold his dusty books or kept the store open mainly as a
meeting-place for the learned.

Futter's Delicatessen, the complete façade blasted out of its
new premises, a wine-shop, and a pharmacy were still open.
Futter's had no non-rationed commodities except a glutinous
mixture they called Chocolate Spread, one jar per person. At the
pharmacy we bought sleeping pills and disinfectant for the water;
and at the wine-shop a bottle of dry wine and cognac. Wine is
all that may still be had freely. There was pleasure just in spending money. So long since we have been able to use it, except the
few piastres for rations, that it has become almost meaningless.

The restaurant menu was incredible. Meat! Portions only just
visible, but meat all right. The waitress said it came from some
of the cows evacuated with the settlers of Neve Yaacov; no feed
in Jerusalem, so the animals were slaughtered. Word had got
around that Ophir was serving a real meal and it was packed.
We waited over half an hour for seats. By the time our turn came
round—12.30—there were queues of three or four people round
each table. Besides meat, we had some watery soup, dehydrated
potatoes, half a slice of bread and two tinned plums; charge,
750 mils (15s.).

Conversation revolved around food, shelling, Old City, and
the battle for the road. A woman at our table, who had a loud
voice, a big face and flaring ears, told us of twins born last night
in their shelter during the shelling. The father is away in the
forces and the mother was before her time. None of the phones
in their district were working. A young boy volunteered to go
for the doctor; but the woman couldn't wait. The neighbours
put up a sheet as a partition, and the other women did what they
could for her. When the doctor finally came, the twins were
already there.

All the while we ate, the shelling was going on somewhere
behind Jaffa Road (now re-named Herzl Street), within a radius

First food convoy reaches the city

Jerusalem liberated

of about half a mile from the restaurant. Nobody took much notice until one shell crashed up the road and shook our building. A few people paused in their eating, but most didn't stop. A bent little man with a long beard and swinging side-locks hopped in for cover through the half-open door. The scared look on his face gave way to mild disgust when he guessed that the restaurant was not *kasher*. The proprietor pulled down the heavy corrugated iron shutters and we ate in semi-darkness. A few minutes later two shells crashed just outside. More people paused in their eating and some looked frightened. I wondered vaguely whether it is more comfortable to be hit on an empty or a slightly filled stomach. Then the shelling moved off a bit, perhaps a few hundred yards. After that there was a lull and I thought perhaps the Arabs had knocked off for lunch. But Ruth reminded me that they haven't put their clocks forward as we have, and by their time it was hardly 11.

The woman at our table asked if we had noticed that before a particular area was shelled a single rifle shot rang out. She said that was a signal given by some spy.

"There are spies all over the city. Some are Germans and Yugoslavs posing as Jews; others real Jews."

She had known Eva Dukas, who came of a good family in Czechoslovakia, and fled with her husband and infant when Hitler entered. For years they struggled in Turkey to earn a livelihood and a few years ago found their way, at last, to Palestine. She could not get a job at once with Jews because she knew no Hebrew, but she knew English and was employed by the British. She made friends with some of them, and after a time had an English lover. He got her to work for the C.I.D. as an informer against the terrorists. Our table neighbour said she was sure there were other Jewish women from Europe, especially those who hadn't made any Jewish friends, who had become involved as spies through English or Arab friends.

The lull continued and we made a dash for home. We noticed that Tuv-Taam Café was open and, hoping it was a sign that they had something to eat, we looked in. They hadn't, so we had a cup of watery coffee. Weren't out a minute when the shelling started again. We dodged in and out of doorways and ran across street inter-sections. The few other people about also ran and dodged for cover. Behind the security wall in King George Avenue we had a narrow escape. Ruth was saying, "I miss the little park on the other side," when the pavement about ten yards ahead of us sprang violently into life with a loud wham. There was a pungent whiff to the air. We fell flat on our faces. When we raised ourselves we saw a young man in khaki sitting dazedly on the ground a few yards ahead, bleeding from the shoulder. We helped him into a first-aid post. Ruth said:

"If it came out of a gloomy sky, it might seem less unnatural. But I'll never get used to its shrieking down on us like that out of a soft, silky sky."

24 May

A DAY OF MIXED emotions and tensions.

Yesterday the Security Council called for a cease-fire, under threat of direct action. From morning, people have been talking of nothing else. . . . A door opening on a golden dream. To-day the Israel Government ordered fighting to stop at 8 to-night. No reply yet, however, from the Arabs. Haganah Intelligence reports say Glubb is opposed to it, and Legion reinforcements were this morning driving on Jerusalem and Latrun.

The Legion seems to be all out to score a signal victory by Wednesday, which is the second anniversary of Abdullah's coronation as King of Transjordan. The Arab Radio at Ramallah predicts he will be crowned King of Jerusalem on that day. The battering of the Old City has grown even more savage. For two hours to-day the Legion hurled a 15-gun barrage into the tiny area we still hold there, the size of a single block; in it 1,700 people crushed together, the dead with the living. Desperate calls are coming in for ammunition and medical supplies; five smoke-rockets were sent up as distress signals during the night.

Ramat Rahel fell yesterday evening. I watched it burning, livid flames against the darkening sky; barns, cattle, poultry, workshops, homes—how much labour and sweat went into that inhospitable hillock! Artillery from Bethlehem plastered it round the clock for three days. Tanks and armoured cars drove in at sunset. For four hours the defenders fought amid the flames and smoke; late at night they got away. But after a few hours they returned with reinforcements and drove the Egyptians out. Many of the enemy dead were carried off, but 31 bodies were left.

I learned about its recapture as soon as I got up this morning. A man on a donkey was riding up the street, his face black with grime. His body and head kept jerking forward from weariness. One arm was bandaged. He wore a khaki sweater and his long legs, in torn khaki trousers, dragged along the ground. The donkey's hooves went clacking on the road like tired castanets. A passing woman called *Shalom* to him.

"Where do you come from?" she asked.

"Ramat Rahel," I heard him reply. "It's ours again."

The news spread through the street. Shutters opened and heads craned out. Children, shouting the news, ran after the donkey.

On the wireless to-night we heard a message from the parents of Ramat Rahel to their children, who were evacuated to Givat Brenner. It said simply, "We are well. *Hizku v'imtzu*" ("Be strong and of good courage"). Only the skeletons of the settlement buildings remain. The defenders (who include an Etzel unit) are in dug-outs. There will be more bloody fighting here. If we lose it, the southern suburbs of the city are sunk.

Yesterday the Legion almost captured Notre Dame. For two hours they unleashed against it an average of 7 or 8 shells a minute. The eastern wall was holed like a sieve. At the *Mateh* to-day I saw Oded, who was right in it. "Like a continuous earthquake," he said, "sandbags, stone-work and timber raining down all the time. In the midst of it, ten Legion tanks and armoured cars come storming up Suleiman's Way, a long string of infantry lorries behind them. All we had was mortars and machine-guns. At the last minute we got two piats (anti-tank guns). We'd been howling for them all week. But just as the first tank reached the building one of the piats conked in. . . . We were cornered all right. We gave them all we had, but it looked hopeless. Then suddenly the tanks turned and went home. *Pashut* (simply). We rubbed our eyes. Our commander thinks they suspected a trap because we fired first with two piats and then, just as they reached us, with only one. To me it was a plain miracle."

He said that some of their fellows had next to no training. Four, not long out from Buchenwald, learned all they knew of automatic weapons only after they came to Notre Dame. Two of them were brought out dead the first day they were posted. They were so intent on the rules of firing that they forgot the rules of defence.

All the correspondents feel utterly defeated by the cable

position. Sent a bitter joint protest to-day to Ben-Gurion saying
that for ten days "one of the greatest stories of history" has
reached the world entirely distorted and one-sided because
Jewish channels fail to send out our news despatches from
Jerusalem in time. The censors work fast and try to be helpful. The
postal officials also keep up the pretence that every minute counts.
Then our cable forms pile up somewhere waiting for a plane, which
may come some time to-day or to-morrow or the day after.
Flaming, pulsing stories, but they turn them into dead letters on
sheets of clean white paper. Indescribable feeling of frustration.

At 10 o'clock last night the electricity suddenly came on. Light,
the most ordinary light of incandescent lamps, but what cheer
it brought us! Echoes of the excitement came also from the
neighbouring flats. We hardly knew what to do first. Put water
on to boil; Judy tried to cook some soup; Michael plugged in
their absurd little wash-machine; Ruth ironed. And all up and
down the street wireless sets blared out to heaven. The current
was miserably weak, and lasted only an hour, but a crammed,
blessed hour. No one knows when it will come on again.

No bread to-day. Drew on our iron ration of *matzot*. Still getting
bean-soup from Dr. B.; we add a little water and leave part of
it for supper. For Karamba, who springs up with pathetic eager-
ness when anyone enters the kitchen, Mrs. R. brings scrapings
from the Etzel Hospital kitchen.

Yesterday Ruth saw a pedlar sitting in the shelter of a doorway, some oddments of foodstuffs in a suitcase beside him;
bought two small tins of sardines, 50 piastres (10s.) each; 3
cigarettes, 3 piastres (10d.) each; and some dried bread left-
overs for Karamba. The rest of his stock, dried beans, was bought
up by another passer-by. We don't talk about food any more,
though it is never far from our thoughts. Belts tightened and
faces thinner. Ruth has lost 21 lb. in the past two months; I have
lost 15 lb. Water ration irregular; supposed to be daily, but we
get it only once in two days, sometimes once in three.

Saw civilian transport to-day for the first time in weeks: a
mule (the only one I've seen) hitched to a light motor-car

crammed high with household effects—some evacuee family moving from its home.

Off now to broadcast the last programme of the English *Kol Hamegen*.

Night

Felt saddened at closing down our broadcasting service. It went out without any flourish. I didn't even see the Commander —he has sufficient on his mind—I just passed him a chit and he sent back his O.K. Even this finale nearly didn't take place. Both alternative sources of current failed. We sat in Asher's lounge—Laurie, who was to read the news, Minna, the continuity announcer, and I, who was to read the closing-down announcement. Asher's wife brought out some cognac, and we drank a silent farewell to the English *Kol Hamegen*. What a long way it has been for all of us since that evening four months ago when we first went on the air! And for our primitive, makeshift broadcasting service. . . . The darkness, literal and figurative, in which we worked; the blacked-out, dreary "news-room" in the Keren Kayemeth despatch department; the dim candlelight; the incessant rattling of fire; the frantic last-minute assembling of news—without reporters—in a beleaguered city, in an underground H.Q. that itself often seemed cut off from G.H.Q.; the tantalizing doubt every evening whether anyone heard us; the devious ways whereby we sought to get our multigraphed bulletin to the correspondents; the cold question that weighed on us when anyone of the group was late, "Has it got him this time? . . ."

The current seemed off for the night, and Laurie and Minna left. I lingered on, hoping. At 9.40 come on it did, for the *Post's* printing presses nearby. I read the whole bulletin. Even the few battery-set owners probably didn't listen in, not expecting it at that hour. The technician turned off the switch. We said "*Shalom*," and I went home.

10.30. No abatement in the Arab attacks. They say they want 48 hours to consider the Security Council's request. Haganah cease-fire order has just been cancelled.

25 May

FEELING COMPLETELY WASHED out. Dreadful *hamseen*. Is it worse this year, or does it only seem so? People are dried up; their faces drawn with lines of fatigue, anxiety, hunger. Over my own thoughts a kind of grey oppression.

The only spark of animation is induced by the hope of cease-fire; and it isn't much. Everyone speculating about the Arab reply. In the garden I heard Reuvy analysing the situation for the other kids. "Abdullah does what the English say. They hate us like we hate them because they want to come back here and we don't want them. So they want to kill us. They're afraid to do it by themselves. So they send Abdullah, who's a *smartut* ('rag'), and give him Glomp (Glubb) Pasha to see he does what they want." Most older folk share that opinion.

Shells and incendiary mortars fell during most of the night and day, but not as heavily as yesterday. Some of the Legion's guns have been moved to Latrun, where the fighting grows in bitterness. The rumours about an American officer commanding Haganah there are true. Y. confirmed it to me; he is a professional soldier, trained at West Point, fought on most of the main fronts during World War II, and ended up a Chief of Staff to General Clay.

Rehavia had its nightly visitation of shells at 3 this morning. Ruth and I have developed a kind of telegraphic system. When she feels it is getting too thick, she taps me in a certain way and we dash down to the shelter. Sometimes Judy suggests it first. We have dispensed with the wardrobe "partition" in the Bs.' bedroom.

Last night we were in the shelter for over an hour. R. repeated a fantastic yarn that was current yesterday about an Etzel attempt to relieve the Old City. An Etzel unit dressed up as an Arab Legion band, runs the tale, marched down Suleiman's Way gaily playing Arabic marches. At Damascus Gate, which was

thrown wide open for them, they turned in. Crowds of cheering
Arabs marched by their side. Suddenly, off came their disguise
and their trombones turned into machine-guns. Then they swept
all before them. Some people believed it.

Two days ago the Rabbis agreed at last to the recruitment of
Yeshiva students: 17–22 age-group to be trained, but not to be
posted at present for active service; 23–30 age-group for part-
time garrison duties only. Perhaps the peril also helped to move
them; but Haganah had to threaten to arrest the boys as shirkers
before the Rabbis finally agreed. One of their arguments was
that after destruction of the Jewish communities in Eastern
Europe the *Yeshivoth* of Jerusalem are almost the only ones left
of their kind in the world; loss of their students would dry up the
reservoir of traditional religious learning. Another argument was
that the sacred studies and prayers of the *Yeshivoth* are a second
front no less important than the military. About half the 2,000
students will fall away in any case, T. tells me, because they are
medically unfit.

Some of the boys long ago defied the Rabbis' interdict and
changed their knee-length coats, long black stockings and broad-
brimmed black fur hats for Haganah uniform; probably inspired
by the exploits of Rabbi Horonchik, a noted religious scholar and
also one of the most noted snipers in the city.

Saw Myriam G. this afternoon; never seen her look so drawn.
She spoke of conditions in the emergency hospitals. Some days
two people must lie on a single mattress. Food shrinking, several
drugs out of stock, and fuel position getting desperate. She knows
of over 20 civilians killed in the New City yesterday. One, a grave-
digger, killed at his work; another, a woman evacuee recovering
from a wound; and two aged Russian lay nuns. Myriam has been
reading a siege diary of Leningrad. We are still a good way off
from their condition, except for water and the feeling that we
have nothing at all to match the enemy's weapons.

For its men in Jerusalem, Haganah has issued a pamphlet
describing defensive tactics during the siege and battles of
Leningrad and Stalingrad.

Two Oriental evacuee children in tatters, shirtless and sockless, their faces shrivelled and unwashed, came to the door to-day begging for water. Ruth gave them half a glass each. Then they asked if she had any bread. She gave them a bit of our *matza* iron ration. She smiled at them, but they looked as though they had forgotten how to smile. There must be terrible hardship among the poorer people, who never had money to store up food. I hear of people whose only food most days of the week is the bread ration and milkless tea, often cold. And of others who try to cook all kinds of weeds they pluck in the fields.

In spite of the *hamseen*, the gardens in Rehavia are alight with flowers. In the Cs.' garden an unexploded shell (its British origin clearly stamped: I.C.I.) buried its nose in a bed of geraniums and looked uglier than ever in that mass of blazing colour. The florists are closed, of course, but you notice people carrying little posies or single flowers plucked in some garden. Yesterday a lorry-load of weary, unshaven Haganah men, back from an operation, tramped up Ibn Ezra Street carrying bunches of flowers, probably rifled on their way through Katamon. I cannot remember so much interest in flowers in other years. A kind of reassertion that there is still room for beauty in these foul and murderous days.

Returning from the new P.I.O. towards evening, I saw a madman standing in the middle of King David Street, haranguing a non-existent crowd. Shelling started up, and the few people in the street dashed for cover; but he stood rooted. He shouted in a high-pitched voice that the Chief Rabbi was a fool and Ben-Gurion a knave. Suddenly he set up a wail that pierced me like a sharp, icy needle. Even the echo of a crash didn't drown it. "Ben-Gurion sent my daughter to be killed," he cried. "And he wouldn't even let me see how she looked dead." Some of us tried to drag him under cover. But he pulled himself away and started running, screaming, down the middle of the street.

26 May

No cease-fire: that is the upshot of the Arab reply. They are prepared to discuss only a full truce, and on their own terms (which include abandonment of the Jewish State). Nobody had much faith in this cease-fire talk from the beginning; it wasn't more than a half-believing, wistful hope. Yet the disappointment is heavy.

Where does the security Council go from here? It's not the Council, anyway: the real issue is between Bevin and Truman. Bevin determined his Arab allies will win; Truman pledged to support the Jewish State, yet anxious not to antagonize Britain. Over there they spar and fumble, while here the bloody drama deepens.

Was struck to-day once more by the way people are taking the situation. Hunger getting the better of prudence, Ruth and I again braved the midday shells to go to the Ophir for lunch (found it closed, but another restaurant served us soup and dehydrated vegetables). Sheltering behind the Yeshurun wall on the way down, we listened to a woman telling a friend how this morning she saw two men carrying a body on a stretcher with blood dripping over the side "like from a half-open tap." She had to pass it, but tried not to look.

"What use was it to look? Could I do anything? I had to fetch the bread. Last night my little boy burst out crying, 'What sort of a mother are you? What sort of a home is this? Not even a piece of bread when I'm hungry!' So when I passed the stretcher I just didn't look and thought only about the bread."

The shelling flared up again on our way back. We dived into a large building with a "Shelter" sign. It was an ordinary basement, crowded with tired, nervous, unwashed people, with pinched faces of the semi-starved. There were mattresses on the floor, pillows and some bed-clothes, and a few women sat on little stools holding babies. In the gloom some looked like human outcasts. They talked in a desultory way about the obvious things; the shelling, cease-fire, food, the Old City, death, injuries. Not much warlike valour about them, but a tremendous amount of plain courage. One elderly man reflected it for them all:

"The important thing is to keep on."

Somehow, they keep alive, and get through the day. Everyone of them knows how great the danger. Everyone has a husband or son or daughter in the *emdoth* around the city. Many have been bereaved. Not one but knows he may leave this very shelter and not reach his destination. They are full of bitterness, against the Arabs, Britain, U.N.O. Yet in all this not a word that betrays any thought of surrender. Ask myself how much of their endurance is based on resolve and voluntary sacrifice, and how much on resignation. Simple fear of the Arabs as conquerors also doubtless enters into it. But faced with the question, I think most would answer, in their varying ways: "We've run enough in our lifetimes. This is the one place where we belong, and here we stay rooted. Shells aren't going to dislodge us."

I watch the people at the office. Most walk long distances to get there. They know the building is a favourite target of the shells. The work itself to-day is almost fruitless. Yet everyone carries on as though to halt were unthinkable. Confess that sometimes I thought it stupidity or lack of imagination or a form of escapism: that maybe they do it because there is nothing else they can do in these hours. Then I talk to someone like M., who is 46, had three years in Bergen Belsen which broke his health, and whose very manner of talking, gentle and vague, is an admission of being of no great account. The other day he came in late and settled down at the desk to his daily routine. By chance I learnt he had been out the previous night as a carrier for the supplies with a party that tried to relieve the Old City. Their attempt a failure, they returned, under fire, before dawn. He had four hours' rest.

"It's strange how little sleep you really need," he said quietly in reply to my question.

I find myself terribly moved whenever I pause to watch this spectacle of ordinary people, besieged and battered, striving to carry on. Realize the drama of it afresh every time I see the old newspaper "boy" distribute the *Post*, the clerk on his way to office, the stone-dresser chisel stones for buildings that may never go up, or hear the music-teacher around the corner practise scales with her young daughter.

27 May

THE OLD CITY SEEMS to be at its last gasp. Massive relief alone can save it, and it would need a miracle to get it through in time. Their last signal to *Mateh* tells the story in a few words. Ammunition almost gone. About 100 Haganah men dead, 70 seriously injured; 50, some of them wounded, are still resisting. The enemy lines are only 30 yards away. Three times in the past two days the Arabs inched their way into the narrow Jewish strip, but were repulsed. Attacks go on from 5 a.m. until 8 or 9 at night. Then the Arab mobs loot, smash and burn the newly-captured buildings.

Another desperate and abortive attempt last night to breach the wall. Late at night *Mishmar Haam* guards made the rounds of flats and shelters in Rehavia looking for able-bodied men of any age to help. Many volunteered; a few had to be dragooned. I was away on defence works; Ruth volunteered, but they didn't want women.

B.B.C. has just reported that Abdullah visited the Legion in the Old City. He bent his head in prayer before the traditional site of Jesus' entombment. Monks bade him godspeed. "After praying for victory at the Christian Holy Sepulchre and the Moslem Mosque of Omar, he heard the crash of demolition as men shelled the Hurva Synagogue, a few hundred yards away." Yesterday, Bevin told the House of Commons that to the best of his knowledge the Arab Legion was withdrawn from Palestine some months ago. He admitted that 37 Britons are serving with the Legion; official Israel sources claim there are 225.

Shelling of the New City was lighter to-day, but had ghastly effect. One shell killed 8 people collecting their rations, another killed 3 patients in a hospital and wounded 5.

Don has learned from the Red Cross that Tamara is alive and a prisoner of war in Hebron.

"What in the name of God is the Red Cross worth if it can't

rescue these women from the Arabs!" he said bitterly. He has been sent in to town again about his hand, which is giving him trouble. He is frightfully tired and looks ill; says that most of the time he feels he has no sense of acting of his own accord, but as though a spring wound up inside him propels him forward. Just wanted to talk, and we didn't stop him. I had one of the three cigarettes left that Ruth got me, and each of us had a few whiffs at it.

"This isn't war," he said. "It was war in the Pacific. It was hell. But you had guns, planes, transport, food, water. Here we've got Goddam all against their guns and every time we push them back it's a miracle."

He repeated what a friend of his in charge of a mortar told him, that our artillery force in Jerusalem consists of three 3-inch mortars, with a daily supply of 15 shells delivered from Tel-Aviv by air. Davidka shells are made here and taken at once to be fired. And we smiled when somebody cracked a joke last week that the mortarer near us fired only two shells a day because it took him all that time to make them!

"There's no front and no rear; it's all front. Every street and hospital and back garden. And men fighting within earshot of their families. The other night a fellow crawled into our *emda* with a lump of shrapnel in his thigh. He was on duty at Sanhedria and when the shells began falling in Geula he suddenly got obsessed with the idea that one of them must have crashed into his flat, where his wife and two kids were alone. So he stole out to go and see them. He found them O.K. Running back to his post, he got caught by a shell and half lost consciousness. He must have crawled around with his wound for an hour till he got to our *emda*, not knowing where he was. Sometimes I think all of Jerusalem is wandering like that, crawling around wounded and lost."

Don had to report back to camp, but wasn't fit to walk, and we insisted that he remain the night. Fixed him up in the room with the four of us. When he thanked us, Ruth said, "It's all right. You'll do the same for us when we visit the States."

"No," he replied. "I'm here now for keeps."

28 May

THE JEWS IN THE Old City have surrendered. At noon
two Rabbis approached the Arabs with a white flag, and the
Haganah men did nothing to stop them. Faint echoes of the
Arabs' shrieks drifted to the New City. The Legion has taken 290
men between the ages of 14 and 70 as prisoners, including 60
wounded. Twelve hundred old men, women and children will be
passed to the Jewish lines.

A stifled grief permeates the city. No one speaks of it. People
are reacting mainly inside themselves, as in a bereavement in a
family.

We learned of our successes on the Latrun front. For five days
a ruthless battle to relieve Jerusalem has been going on there,
ground changing hands again and again. A crack Legion unit
attacked one of our tactical positions seven times in two days,
the last time engaging us in close combat; but our men clung
furiously to their ground. We are nearer Latrun now than we
have ever been. Whether we in Jerusalem survive depends not
on gains or losses in the city, but on the fate of that narrow
ribbon that runs through Latrun linking us with the coast. The
battle area there extends now over a 20-mile front, the only real
Arab offensive in the country. Everywhere else we have driven
the enemy armies on to the defensive. Legion reinforcements are
pouring in, and there is talk at the *Mateh* of an Egyptian attempt
to make junction with the Legion at Latrun from the south. Our
forces are under the command of the American Colonel, whom
they call "Mickey." They say he has led the commandoes on
some of their most daring raids; his courage has completely won
the men's hearts.

I listened to-night to the B.B.C. on Palestine. They briefly
repeated the news of the fall of Old City and mentioned Latrun.
Then they gave an interview with the Anglican Bishop of

Jerusalem, the Rev. W. H. Stewart; he himself spoke into the microphone, telling of the "little British island sanctuary at St. George's Cathedral" and the difficulties of the 40 people living there. There has been no structural damage and only one stray shot fell there. Thanks to the Bishop's foresight, they have plenty of supplies. Asked whether there were any special problems, the Bishop replied: "We shall have to find a man who can fix stained-glass windows. And that is not easy in Palestine."

I pictured the Bishop, vested in sublime detachment, speaking from his "little British island sanctuary" not a mile from the Old City. Then I went on to the roof and saw the flames from the Old City reddening the eastern sky. For a minute my mind flicked back to London in the Blitz, to the people and their ordeal, to the old streets, churches, bridges, buildings, taverns, and the savage attack unloosed against them. I remembered my elation nightly at the chimes of Big Ben as I heard them in Jerusalem over the B.B.C.: "London still stands!" Never was London dearer to civilized men, never "more touching in its majesty." Then my thoughts returned to the Holy City and the fire that reddened its skies.

29 May

THERE IS A MOTIONLESS haze over the Old City, like a ghastly jelly. Only the nearer skyline is smudged with smoke and shimmering with heat. All the colours have disappeared; the habitual blue, pink, green, all are grey now. A great silence and solitude enwrap it. Out of the haze a single smoke spiral has pushed its way upward, very tall and slender and elegant. I picture the crackling flames below it, the stones turning black.

Hard to think of the Old City without a single Jew. When last was there such a time? Nearly 800 years ago Maimonides found Jews there. The old underground Synagogue of Yohanan ben Zakkai is reputed to have been standing nearly 2,000 years ago; now, like the neighbouring Hurva, it is a shambles. Jews were in the Old City when the Seljuks conquered it, and in the days of the Crusades, and when the Turks took it over. Allenby found them when he conquered it from the Turks. But to-day not one is left.

I watched the refugees arrive at the once elegant Park Lane Hotel in Katamon; from there they will be distributed among the Katamon houses. Some had not seen the sun for weeks, hardly ventured out of their Old City cellars even into the darkness of the night. Only the children seemed to be living in the present. They streamed in by the hundreds, older ones holding younger brothers and sisters by the hand. They sat there in the sunshine, some in speechless misery, others just solemn and quiet, absorbing the relative freedom from terror, their eyes taking in this strange new world of modern houses. Most of the adults were not even sad, just stupefied and exhausted. Their yellow, bloodless faces and lean hands moved in slow motion. But some were utterly broken.

There was one man whose face keeps on floating through my consciousness. I spoke to a girl who was trying to help him. She was a social worker who knew him well. A devout, simple man, unworldly, who barely made a living out of his little shop. He used to speak about the Old City with a depth of feeling that moved her. To live there was not for him, as for some other natives, a birthright taken for granted, nor, as for others, a mark of superior lineage. Old Jerusalem was something whose shadows he felt it a privilege to touch. Until the siege of the Jewish Quarter, he prayed daily at the Wailing Wall. When his father's *Yahrzeit* (death anniversary) came round he was resolved at least to recite the *Kaddish* (memorial prayer for the dead) at the Wall. Through the Jewish and Arab lines he found a way of contacting an Arab friend who smuggled him through the Arab quarter and watched over him while he prayed at the Wall. For the first time in weeks, the social worker saw him again during the evacuation this morning. His cheeks were wet. His feet dragged along the ground; he stumbled, suddenly gone very aged and frail. I watched him now sitting in a corner at the Park Lane Hotel: an empty shell of a man whose soul had died within him. Only stiff, shrunken limbs were left and eyes that saw nothing.

Esther C. is dead, wounded on Thursday by a shell that crashed into her *emda*. She died very early this morning, while evacuation was under way. It was her second injury. A week ago she was wounded in the hip, but left the bed to join in the last desperate defence. "That's where they need me most," I remember the last words she said to me, "in the Old City."

Bertie, wounded, has been brought to hospital in the new city.

The Legion behaved well. After the surrender yesterday they formed a cordon round the remnant of the Jewish Quarter. When the frenzied rabble got out of hand, howling for the Jews to be handed to them, the Legion fired to keep them at bay. Finally, when the fires the mob started threatened the hospital, Legionnaires forced a way out for the patients into the Armenian Quarter. There were only two orderlies, and no stretchers. All but the most gravely injured had to stumble on their feet, one helping the other. When the Jewish relief party arrived at dawn with the Red Cross to remove them to the new city, the 70

patients were lying on the paving stones of an Armenian courtyard. Behind the wall of the Armenian Quarter, a few hundred
yards away, the Jewish hospital had gone up in flames.

Evening

This afternoon went to see Bertie in hospital. Ghastly place;
must write of it later. His wound is not serious.

"I don't fancy being a prisoner of the Arabs, so I put on an
act and make it look worse'n it is," he said.

The same Bertie, still looking like a film star, but now a faded one.

"There was 80 of us in the reinforcement party. What a bunch!
One was half-blind and two lame. Some didn' have more'n three
days training. Dunno where in hell they digged 'em up."

His own group was in the *Palam*, trained for open street fighting.

"Old City wasn't my kind of fighting, that wasn'."

He told how every day they waited for Palmach. "It's bound
to come to-night." When dawn broke, with no sign of Palmach,
they said, "Well, to-night for certain." The only reinforcement
they got was a girl born to a civilian woman in the hospital the day
before the end. The boys named her *Tigboreth* (Reinforcement).

Shelled out of their positions by day, they returned at night,
dug fox-holes in the rubble and put up stones all around it.
When their mortar ammunition gave out, and their Bren guns
choked, and their grenades were finished, they started improvising grenades out of cigarette or jam tins, with bits of enemy
shrapnel, explosives and matches.

"Once we put in bits of bread too. It was as hard as any chunk
of shrapnel. . . ."

"One day my officer says to me, 'Bertie, you come from the
Wild West, so you know all about lassos.' I tell 'im I come from
San Pedro, which is thousands of miles from the Wild West. But
he says, 'All the same, you look right for a lasso.' So I become a
dynamite-thrower. I take explosives in a sack and tie it to a long
rope and when the attack starts I swing hard and away it flies
to the Arabs. And when I hear crash, bang, I say, 'That's for my
emda you smashed up yesterday.' When we had no more explosive

I go back to my tin gun (Sten gun). Mine was O.K.; some was fixed with bits of wire. But so little ammunition, they treat each round like a pearl."

The night before the surrender they knew it was all up. Some of them who had two hours off duty improvised a small party in a cellar.

"We think we'll all be dead to-morrow, so what the hell!"

They finished what remained of a barrel of wine and their iron ration of *matzoth*, and made love to the girls.

After the surrender the Arabs came round asking if any were Etzel men; they wanted to avenge Deir Yassin, they said. There was an Englishman, wearing Arab Legion uniform, who came looking for Americans. Bertie answered him in Spanish.

"When the mob tried to get at us, a Legion officer shouts: 'They are prisoners of King Abdullah. For the King's honour, you must respect 'em.' But the Legion is very angry at us when they fin' only 40 Haganah men left unwounded. 'We'd've covered you with our helmets if we knew you was so few,' they said. They had trucks to take away three or four hundred an' said they wasn' going to return to Amman with only 40. So they take civilian men, anyone they can fin' under 70, to make up 300."

I also saw Dr. L., who was in charge of the hospital in the Old City; his staff consisted of 2 doctors, 2 nurses, 2 orderlies. In the final days they had less than 2 hours' rest in 24. The hospital, with 130 grave cases, had to be evacuated twice. There were 50 or 60 new cases daily towards the end, but they could take only the severest. Operations were carried out at night, in an old kitchen, by torch or candlelight; by day the building shook too much from the shelling and they had their hands full treating new casualties. Most drugs had given out. At night hundreds of civilians herded into the narrow hospital passage, because it was furthest from the enemy. It became harder every morning to move them. The other day the Haganah commander had to force out the solid mass at pistol point. By day the civilians packed the damp, reeking cellars, half-crazed by the shelling, hunger and illness.

30 May

ANOTHER DAY OF merciless shelling. Both the Legion and Egyptians are said to have brought up new guns. The main battle for Jerusalem may be going on at Latrun, but they have decided, it seems, to demolish the city in the meantime. I heard a man say, "Our Jerusalem is melting." Every day it becomes a bit more mutilated.

A city loses its character in war, it becomes a snare; death and survival alone have meaning. But Jerusalem is not just another city. War here is pure madness; obscene, arrogant madness. And as *they* wage it, this is not war. They are not fighting for it, not risking even their precious tanks now. They sit on the hills, pump shells into it, into every street and corner, and mangle it. The city the world calls Holy!

I tell myself I am bored with shells. I have raised a kind of inner protective barrier against them. It works by day, but collapses at night, when I am worn out and crave for rest. The hollow detonations and great tearing sounds have a special quality about them in the darkness. Night, that once was simply a time for relaxation and sleep!

We have given way to the urgings of the neighbours and now sleep downstairs; we in the Ks.' passage, the Bs. in the Rs.' passage. No air, and wide enough for only one mattress, which Ruth and I share. The Ks.' themselves sleep on mattresses on their kitchen floor, the least exposed room. Even down here there is little rest or unbroken sleep. The oncoming screech of every shell overhead still plagues us, but upstairs one almost felt the draught of air they set up as they passed.

In the early morning we drag ourselves upstairs. These first daylight hours are free of shelling. The air is beautifully cool. In the fresh sunlight the city looks like a place of peace. God, what beauty there is in quiet! In our own flat we start another day.

We unroll the carpets, hang up the pictures, replace the ornaments, keep up the pretence that the shells are not likely to strike
the house by day.

"What about a cup of tea?" says Michael cheerfully, and goes
down to light the wood fire.

I shave and wash in my tumblerful of water. Breakfast, as
usual, off lukewarm, milkless, sugarless tea and a slice of bread
and margarine. We cut the bread very carefully to waste as few
crumbs as possible. The daily ration now is down to 160 grams
(5 oz.), black and musty. It occurs to me suddenly that in an
hour's time all this may have been wasted. Some shell in the pile
they are just bringing up to the Legion's guns may be the one
with my name on it. Then I, with my shaving, washing, dressing,
breakfast, will just be snuffed out.

A message to-day to the people of Jerusalem from Ben-Gurion.
"During the last few weeks we have succeeded in substantially
increasing our effective strength on land and in the air in all parts
of the country. It is absolutely essential that Jewish Jerusalem
shall continue to stand fast during these days of trial. Notwithstanding the end of the fighting in the Old City, strenuous efforts
to relieve Jerusalem and its surroundings are in hand and being
pressed. . . . Be strong and of good courage."

Wonder what "substantial increase of strength" amounts to,
and how much of it will get through to Jerusalem?

31 May

AFTER A WEEK'S EFFORTS, got H. to take me down by jeep to the Latrun front. Flew past Kiriath Anavim, which is being heavily shelled from Radar Station Hill that the Legion took from us yesterday. Turned off at Saris into the heart of the hills. From an observation post on a hilltop I could see the grove around the Trappist Monastery and the edge of the police fortress at Latrun. To the south was the Valley of Ayalon where we captured two villages yesterday (and where the moon stood still to help Joshua fight the Canaanites). The battle has been going on almost non-stop for twelve days. We seem unable at present to capture Latrun and hold it. So the strategy now is first to cripple the Legion and cut the line of communication with its base at Ramallah.

An officer told me about the battle last night. For two hours our artillery bombarded the village. Then an armoured tactical unit moved forward. They had the whole force of the Legion's guns hurtling down at them; yet in under three hours they reached the perimeter of the Latrun Police Station. Searchlights were glaring at them, but with a sudden rush one detachment attacked the building with fire and explosives, and others penetrated the village. They withdrew before dawn, after accounting, they said, for about 200 Arab casualties and leaving the village and Police Station half destroyed. All the time, the fighting is going on for height after height (and there are plenty) along the widening front.

Still little news of fighting in other parts of the country. The whole war seems to be marking time for the outcome of the battle for Jerusalem. The Legion is throwing into it every ounce of strength and skill. Both sides are using planes.

The boys were anxious to know how Jerusalem is faring, amazed at its stand. They were dirty and tired. The blast of guns is almost incessant; a few days ago there was hardly a minute in the eighteen hours when they were silent. Sleep is a kind of catch-as-catch-can affair. A small unit of them was encamped in a cave behind the observation post. In the half-light of the gloom within the cave they looked like a group of bandits. Not much talk among them, but little asides to each other, slang of their own and half words which I didn't always understand.

H. tells me that numbers of the men fighting at Latrun are recent immigrants, and five different languages must be used in transmitting orders. The first big attack here was made by a brigade composed mostly of newcomers with little training in local conditions, though many had fought in the World War. They attacked with great courage, penetrated Latrun village, shot up the village and blew up strongpoints. But the enemy's massed heavy artillery was too much for them, and they had to retire. Last night's attack was carried out by a second, more seasoned brigade. When I asked why we launched the big battle with a newly-formed force, H. said, "You should know by now that we never have much choice." I wonder how Haganah's staff work, never intended for such battles or polyglot conditions, is facing up to the test?

Most of the hills around us are terraced. Down our slope, fruit and olive trees. The valley towards Latrun is covered with fields of corn ready for the harvest. A fringe of palms stands stiff against the evening sky. Beyond our hilltop not a human being visible anywhere. In the hour I am there the guns are silent. Looking at the fields and hills I can hardly imagine anything more peaceful.

The strategy H. outlined as we drove back only emphasized the extent of Jerusalem's captivity. There was the city before us, stretching out her hand, as it were, groping in the dark to re-establish contact, somehow, with the world. But the wall of Latrun behind us blocked it at every turn.

When I got home Ruth told me that Shulamith P. was killed yesterday. Heard to-day that in the fortnight since 15 May there are 1,200 civilian Jewish casualties in Jerusalem, about 450 of them dead. One doesn't know who of one's friends is alive or dead. No complete lists are published. From time to time black-bordered posters announce a few names, and sometimes one picks out a name one knows. The death of anyone unknown is beginning to acquire a dreadful negligibleness.

The U.N. Security Council has decided to call for a 28-day cease-fire as from Tuesday night, under threat of direct action. We should be tremendously heartened, but, somehow, are not. Too many tireless moves at Lake Success have neutralized the good intentions of those who want to see peace restored and Israel given a chance to live. Wait and see what comes of this newest resolution.

To-morrow Bernadotte pays his first visit to Israel.

1 June

Everyone speculating about the cease-fire. The Jews have agreed, if the Arabs do. What a miracle of relief it would be! Yet there is some questioning whether it will be to our ultimate advantage.

Shells don't only fall; they seem to steer their own course as well. This morning, about ten minutes after I passed the *Beth Hehalutzoth* (Girls' Hostel), a 25-pounder struck its front steps, passed through the open door into the hall, shot left into the office, then crashed into a waiting-room, killing or injuring someone wherever it passed—six people altogether. *Pagaz* (shell) has come to seem like some ever-present fiend with a malevolent will of its own.

Was invited by the Abyssinian Consul to see the damage caused to the Abyssinian Cathedral. Eighty shells have struck it and the great blue dome looks like an inverted sieve. The simple, likeable monks and nuns, always gaunt, are now all skin and bones. They get the same rations as all of us. Spend most of their time in the shelter in prayer.

Had a stupid squabble with Ruth this evening over the washing of the kitchen dish-cloths, which are permeating the flat with their accumulated smell of bean soup. That on the one hand and the toilet on the other (no disinfectant to be had) are poisoning the house. Fact is, our nerves are bare and we flare up at the slightest provocation. I think of Ruth as she used to be, thoughtless, sailing through life on a sea of cheerfulness, and look at her now, a mass of ragged nerves. I suppose I'm the same. It isn't we alone. Michael, who has been the soul of consideration towards Judy, gets irritable in a way quite foreign to his real temperament; for the first time the other day I saw Judy in tears. Behind closed doors the same must be happening in most families.

Erwin came in asking what the date is. We didn't know and

didn't care. In his dry, quiet way, Erwin tirelessly enumerates
the calamities he sees lying in wait for us. He admits that he has
the jitters; claims that anyone who hasn't is either unimaginative
or a moron. A relief when Dick dropped in. Talked about our
cable despatches, which are getting out now, but still with
delays. Some of the correspondents have crossed over to the Arab
lines, giving as their reason the lack of proper communication
here. Dick went on to tell us about his experiment in sowing
dried peas in a dampened handkerchief. After some days the
peas sprout, he says, and you have the sprouts to cook as well as
the peas. Then he went riding his hobby-horse of watches, all
enthusiasm about Breguets, repeaters, stem-winders, etc. Erwin's
look said plainly, "I always knew the English were crazy."

We waited up last night until 11 in the hope that the water
lorry would come. Second day without water, and *hamseen*
burning us up. When the shelling started we gave up hope. Were
discussing whether we could ask the Ks. to lend us a few cupfuls
in the morning, when I heard the rumble of a lorry. Then down
the street came the shrill echo, "*Mayim! Mayim!*" ("Water"). In
a few minutes the lorry drew up at the corner. Men, women,
children poured out of the houses with the usual assortment of
vessels, from kettles to baby baths. All the neighbours were there:
the bookkeeper, professors, doctors, judge, dressmaker, plumber,
economist and the rest, most in pyjamas.

The Mishmar Haam man on duty, worn out though he must
have been, was still in good form: "Ho, everyone that thirsteth
come ye to the waters," he called out with a gesture of royal
generosity. (How well we understood Isaiah!) Somebody tapped
on the tanks, the water seemed to be low; would there be enough
to go round? The shells started coming nearer. Two whistled
overhead. Some people dashed into their homes; other stood their
ground, crouching low. Suddenly a loud, tearing boom. Someone
shouts, "It's all right, it's ours!" Slowly the queue reforms, and
they go back to the subject of water. "We haven't had any for
four days," "We had only half a ration"; and the man with the
hose, electric torch in hand, patiently goes on pouring the

precious fluid which flashes silver in the torchlight. In the darkness an elderly man, carrying away his load, stumbles over a
stone thrown up by an earlier shelling; half his water spills on
to the ground.

In ten minutes the lorry has rumbled away. The street is
empty. No other sound to disturb the shells and shots.

2 June

THE ARABS HAVE ACCEPTED the cease-fire, conditionally; conditions to be announced later. If they are similar to previous conditions, the cease-fire is as good as still-born. The broadcast of the news of Arab acceptance was almost drowned by cannon fire, earlier this morning than usual. The Jews understood that the order came into force at 3 a.m. and stopped firing at that hour. But by midday the Arabs had shelled eleven sectors of the city. So our mortars started up again. All as it was, except the general mood, somewhat dashed, but still cautiously hopeful.

Odd thing is the number of people who doubt the wisdom of a cease-fire now. The argument is that it will only give the Arabs the opportunity (denied to us) of adding to their strength. Now that we have them on the run everywhere except in Jerusalem, we must defeat them once and for all; if not, we shall never have peace from them. Admirable the way they can rise above the danger to Jerusalem and themselves and view the situation as a whole. Y. tells me, on the best authority, that the Government's main consideration in accepting the truce is precisely to save Jerusalem.

To-day the Pope has withdrawn from his silence and welcomed the efforts for truce in the Holy Land "with a sigh of relief, as a dawn of hope. How could the blood of men continue to flow in torrents," he says, "on the land which the blood of the Saviour reddened to bring all men redemption and salvation? How could the Christian world gaze indifferently or with sterile imagination as the Holy Land, which all approach with deepest respect to worship it with most ardent love, was trampled on by troops and struck with aerial bombardments?"

Where has His Holiness been all the time? The blood has been flowing since December.

Great jubilation at the news that Israeli planes bombed

Amman yesterday, the first time they have been in action over an Arab capital. At last we are beginning to strike at the enemy on his own ground. What a grand feeling to be able to stretch out and hit back! The people of Amman, according to the B.B.C., are "very indignant," and the Egyptian Premier calls it "a horrid crime."

To-night the daily Bible reading over the wireless had this passage from Jeremiah (pure chance, as the order of the readings are fixed long in advance): "For thus saith the Lord, the God of Israel, to me: Take the cup of the wine of this fury at my hand, and cause all the nations to whom I send thee to drink it. And they shall drink, and reel to and fro, and be mad, because of the sword that I will send among them. . . . Egypt . . . Edom and Moab and the children of Ammon . . . and all kings of the mingled people that dwell in the wilderness."

3 June

Bᴇʀɴᴀᴅᴏᴛᴛᴇ ʜᴀs ʙᴇᴇɴ asked by the Security Council to fix the cease-fire date. This has been the signal for a renewal of hard fighting on all fronts. We are on the offensive everywhere. It is balm to hear of Jewish planes bombing Arab troop concentrations, of our fighter aircraft engaging their bombers over Tel-Aviv, artillery shelling their positions, infantry pushing back the Egyptians, and knocking at the gates of the Arab Triangle.

Elsewhere in the country our armament seems to be growing, despite the American embargo. They say most of it comes from Czechoslovakia, with bits and pieces from wherever else we can get it. The fellows who smuggled refugees out of the D.P. camps and got them past the watchdogs of the Royal Navy and R.A.F. into Palestine must know a few things about underground routes.

Only in Jerusalem our arms remain grotesque.

Nothing at all reaches, nothing leaves us. Detached from space and time alike.

For months there was the obsession of losing contact. Then one day the last link was cut. But so long drawn out the process that I didn't realize it was completed until well after the climax. Quite suddenly it burst on me: we are cut off, absolutely. Except for our shrunken newspapers, with their headline news of the biggest events, no word comes from the outside. And they from us? A few delayed stories, like the disjointed phrases that came through the earphones in the pioneer days of wireless. "Jerusalem —what a story!" says the news editor! "Blasphemy!" cries the churchman. And they don't know the half.

Hundreds of thousands of our letters, with the bright new stamps that gave us such a thrill, have accumulated in the post; the plane service didn't even start working. The wireless service relays a few messages from people in Jerusalem to their families outside: "Jonathan X. to his mother in Haifa. Keeping well; don't worry." But not an echo of an answer.

I sit here by the pin-point light of a small candle, that seems designed to throw up dark shadows rather than illumine, and think of us, buried in night, and the world there, vast and self-absorbed. Out there people walk across fields, saunter home in the evening shadows. Lights are lit in homes and halls. Music played, books read; a crowded, pulsing life. . . . People go to their appointed work, are busy with it, know the purpose it serves. They eat a square meal and don't give a thought to what there'll be to-morrow. In some places they are even feeding corn to the cattle; use milk to fatten pigs, having no other use for it. They stay at home or go out, as they wish. They talk about all things under the sun. They sleep in a bed and take a shower. Their children play in the parks. They find men and women and objects where they belong. They find it the most natural thing in the world for people to be alive, and are terribly shocked by death. Everything has its meaning, its place, its value, fits into the whole.

But here it seems to me sometimes that I move in a sort of supplement to life, that life itself has been drained from me because it belongs only over there, beyond the great wall. . . . The whine of a shell stabs me into life. And then everything changes. I feel it is the world that is drained away. There is no other city, no other people, no other sky, no other light, but these I know here.

4 June

THE ARAB TONE IS stiffening. Recurring theme in all the Arab capitals is: no cease-fire without cancellation of the State of Israel and restriction of Jewish immigration to a permanent minority. (How can a State be "cancelled"? Like pushing a chicken back into an egg.) U.N.O. officials estimate at least a week or ten days of negotiations with the Arabs to put cease-fire into effect.

Etzel, which has managed to get a single-sheet daily newspaper started in Jerusalem, is raging against the "defeatist" Jewish leaders for accepting cease-fire: "A scandal," they write, "the like of which has not occurred among any other people, that has made us the laughing-stock of the world. . . . And it is in their hands that the fate of the war is entrusted! Will the public keep silent? Will it continue to bear its suffering? . . ."

Unhappily, the Dissidents don't merely talk irresponsibly. Who knows what mischief they will be up to next? Under the new agreement, their forces are to be absorbed as special units in the Israel Army, except in Jerusalem; here they continue as separate groups.

Haganah has become the official Army of Independence of Israel, with land, sea and air forces. Ben-Gurion, as Minister of Defence, yesterday issued the first Order of the Day. ". . . The Army of Israel will be built on a basis of social equality and freedom of religion and conscience, faithful to the principles of the Prophets of Israel that 'Nation shall not lift up sword against nation.' " Needs an effort to think of the old underground as "Army," and of Haganah men as formal soldiers.

Shelling a little easier in Jerusalem to-day, with plenty of duds. More casualties caused by snipers and stray bullets. Some fantastic stories of lucky escapes. (Mrs. C's. old mother, who has decided that the space under her son's writing desk is the safest

spot in their house, finds a dud 6-pounder in one of its drawers;
K. gets a sniper's shot through the cushion under his head.)

F.'s rockery, full of the rare specimens he has collected all over
the Middle East, knocked to pieces by two direct hits.

At Latrun the indecisive struggle goes on and on. But in the
rest of the country the mounting fighting seems everywhere to
our advantage.

Coming home this afternoon, Ruth met the Mea Shearim
beadle, who gave her some synagogue candles from his stock last
month. She was appalled by his appearance: a shadow of a man,
broken, with stricken eyes she could hardly look into. He didn't
recognize her at first; then he started weeping and told her that
his wife and two children were killed and a third child injured
by a shell that fell on their house ten days ago. He kept on
repeating, "Why was I saved?" He has been evacuated to
Katamon, to "another box in which men place their lives for
safe-keeping."

Calling-up notices posted up for men under 50 not already
doing essential work. How many can there still be? Whether all
serving already are being best employed is another matter. There
is enough inefficiency and disorder. We pay for it, far more than
usually, by tremendous expenditure of zeal, energy and all our
other virtues.

Growing criticism of David Shaltiel, the Haganah Commander
in Jerusalem. There is a feeling that the Old City might have
been saved, and even captured in its entirety, if only a few
hundred men were provided at the right time. He is blamed for
not checking the looting, which has begun to spread, meanwhile,
also to Jewish property. The public feels he is too ruthless with
civilians, has no interest in them. I don't think many people
have any idea, even now, of his problems. Incidentally, he's an
unusual type for a senior Haganah officer. Many of the others are
essentially products of the underground; he is a military man by
instinct and training. At 21 he joined the French Foreign Legion
because he wanted to learn how to fight under harsh conditions.

The other man at the head of Jewish affairs in Jerusalem is

Bernard Joseph. As Chairman of the Emergency Committee, he also has impossible tasks. A man of great abilities, tremendous devotion and no charm. One of the Consuls said of him the other day that on the rare occasions when he smiles he immediately regrets it. But if it had not been for him the situation in Jerusalem would probably be even worse.

There was a ration of meat yesterday—real, fresh meat, $\frac{1}{2}$ lb. per person. Whose cows now? Ruth waited in the queue for two hours to get it.

To-day Judy told Ruth that when the cease-fire comes she and Michael are thinking of returning to the States for a long, comfortable rest. She spoke hesitantly, and her eyes were full of sadness. Ruth is shocked at the suggestion.

Night

In a state of indescribable excitement all evening, since A. told me the stupendous news: We have a secret route to the coast, by-passing Latrun! Most of it just a jeep and mule-track, but he says stuff has been coming in by it for over a week. Light arms, ammunition and food! But for this track Jerusalem would have been without bread several days ago. He says they're widening it and that trucks already travel part of the way. I couldn't believe it at first. But why not? And A. must know. This means we shall be independent of the old road. Truce or no truce, the siege will be broken; we shall have arms, real arms!

5 June

CANNOT GET MY THOUGHTS off the secret road. Whatever happens to occupy the forefront of my mind, the background keeps on dispelling it with new flashes of that track—lines of jeeps, mule-packs, toiling towards Jerusalem.

Masses of rumours about cease-fire prospects. Awaiting Bernadotte's clarification of the Security Council's resolution: ". . . to bring about the cessation of hostilities and to ensure that no military advantage shall accrue to either side during a truce." The Arabs say it means complete cessation of immigration. The Jews say they cannot accept orders as to the numbers of civilian immigrants who may enter into their territory. But nobody seems to have heard about the road, which promises to make a mockery of the Legion's stranglehold of Latrun. And, without that, what have the Arab armies achieved that gives them the power to impose demands?

I challenged Y. about the road. Reluctant even to confirm it, but then told me it all began on 18 May, when three picked men were assigned to try, on foot, to find a new route to the coast by skirting the Latrun battlefield. They moved down through the Judean hills in the darkness, to the thunder of the Legion's cannons and machine-guns in Latrun. They threaded their way between boulders and huge brambles, across gulleys, part of the course along a goat's trail. At one stage they found themselves within easy rifle shot of Latrun. The moon was at its height then, and they hid behind boulders or crawled along the stony floors of the *wadi* until a passing cloud blacked out the moonlight; then they ran. One of their main dangers was from our own patrols.

Before dawn, with the Legion's guns just starting up again, a wireless message came through from Hulda to field H.Q. in the Judean hills: the scouts had got through. They had found a route to the coast. As Y. spoke, I could picture the excitement that ran through the mountain base when that wireless came to life. The following night the scouts returned, and with them, a first reinforcement of 30 men for Palmach in Jerusalem. Next night, three jeeps made the trip. Now, says Y., convoys of jeeps and mules jolt along the path every night, and already trucks go part of the way. Combat engineers and workers are roughing out and widening it, and it takes more traffic every night. . . . Our own life-line to the world! Must get out, somehow, to see it for myself.

Shelling of the city continues; 9 killed within a few hours in the heart of the city this morning. Among them Sylvia B., caught on the way to collect her bread ration; almost two years to the day since she arrived from London. Consulates have also had a bad day. Fourteenth casualty in the French, and second in the Swiss. British, Turkish and Yugoslav Consulates hit as well, and a car of the Truce Commission, on its way to a cease-fire meeting. I hear that N., the French Consul-General, and part of his staff sleep in the cellar.

We attacked Sheikh Jarrah during the night, but it petered out. Some of the arms to be brought from another part of the city apparently didn't arrive. News from the north: our people attacking Jenin, right up in the Triangle.

Got our rations to-day, first in nine days, apart from the meat: a few ounces each of five items, all of it together under 1 lb. Not enough has come in by the road yet, I suppose, materially to affect the rations. But the Emergency Committee has opened several emergency restaurants; a meal consists of a bowl of soup, a slice of bread and a small plate of custard.

Ruth is very worried by our own supply position. We have 11 tins left, four of them asparagus soup and one caviare; some oil, odds and ends of dried peas, lentils, etc. To-day she got a tin of jam and a tin of D.D.T. (for fuel) in exchange for a tin of cooking oil. Quite a bit of bartering going on, but we haven't much to barter. Thank God for Dr. B.! Every day, going across to collect our bowl of soup, we hold our breath lest he says he cannot continue.

A new vitamin tablet on the market. The very improvised

wrapping claims that it "substitutes for many normal articles of diet." What are we going to do if the cease-fire doesn't come off? Ruth keeps asking. Shall I tell her about the road? Remembering the spy talk, I decide to keep it to myself, but I say airily that I am certain of the cease-fire.

Karamba, wise old dog, has decided to sleep off the siege. She doesn't bat an eyelid at the shelling, just lies curled up in the passage corner, her puckered forehead proclaiming hunger. In her waking hours she prowls disconsolately about the kitchen, sniffing deep breaths at the dish-cloth with its smell of bean soup.

The schools, which have been shut for over a month, are trying to conduct classes through the newspaper, briefly setting lessons day by day.

More rumours of spies. What is a fact is that nine Jewish girls are being held by the Army under suspicion of contacts with the enemy. Against two there is said to be definite evidence of guilt; both had Arab lovers, one of them, I hear, Abdul Khader Husseini.

6 June

BAD NIGHT. Some of the shells seemed to be of heavier calibre than usual, and K.'s snores from the kitchen also of heavier calibre. Very little sleep, yet only moderately tired to-day. Radiant weather; and more hopefulness in the air, at least, for me.

Don phoned in wild excitement to tell us what I had already heard; that the Etzion women are to be released in two days' time. Haven't heard such joy in anybody's voice for ages—except in my own inner voice when I heard about the road. Don is in hospital; the injury to his hand has spread and appears to be serious, although he says it's nothing. He is trying to get leave to get up for a few hours when Tamara returns.

Haganah Intelligence reports at *Mateh* say that most Arab states have had enough of the war and are ready for a real truce if they can honourably extricate themselves. Diplomatic sources confirm, and add that the Arabs seem to have measured the Jews' strength and know that they cannot drive them out. The Syrians and Lebanese are said to claim that, in any case, they would have been ready for this war only in three months' time. Abdullah is disappointed and bewildered. He told correspondents in Amman the other day: "The Jews have made up their minds to turn every house in Jerusalem into a fortification. The battle for Jerusalem will be a second Stalingrad." (Seems to have forgotten what happened to the attacking army at Stalingrad.)

There is a palpable change also among the people of Jerusalem. Although the systematic shelling does not stop, they are beginning to feel that the bubble of the Legion's power has burst. When it started in earnest, the siege of Jerusalem was like a game in which the Jews held all the low cards, the Legion the trumps and U.N.O. the joker. The Legion's cards don't seem so high now, nor ours quite so low. True, the Latrun battle is as fierce as ever, the Arab fortress still holds, the main road is still closed; and the outcome of Latrun, everyone knows, is far more important than the shells in the city, or our hunger. But here stand the Legion impotently on the fringes of Jerusalem, lobbing their shells only to mutilate it and terrorize the inhabitants. Their attack has reached stalemate. The feeling grows that if only we can hold out until Latrun falls, not only will Jerusalem be saved, but we shall also drive the Legion back whence they came. . . . And our people don't know about the other road!

Strange how little hatred there is of the Arabs, for all the suffering they cause us. Desperately, we want to pay them back in kind! But there is no loathing, singularly little venom in the way most people speak of them, except perhaps of the Iraqis. Maybe because *we* know they're only stooges, the great mass of them political babes, immature and unformed, and their rulers thinking they are kings when they are only pawns.

U.S.S.R. announced its readiness to send military observers for Bernadotte's truce team—the one thing the Western Powers will act quickly to avoid. I can even see some English churchmen writing to the newspapers from their comfortable, scholarly studies to warn the world that the Crimean War started because Russia got a foothold in the Holy City.

Hear that some hundreds of Arab families are still living in Bakaa Quarter under Haganah authority. A little while ago Haganah offered to exchange unattached women among them for the Jewish women from Etzion; but the women at Bakaa said they preferred to remain where they are. On the other hand, many of the Jewish refugees in Katamon from the Old City are becoming difficult: not only about the food and water situation, but also about their quarters: complain they are too big, too empty, too much light and air. One old woman in a sumptuous Katamon villa told Rosa G., "Darkness comes over me every time I look at these big windows."

"Who wanted a state?" said another. "I lived fifty years with the Arabs. . . . Why did we have to leave the Old City?"

Was it only a fortnight ago, less, that they were living through "all the torments and agonies wrought on scaffolds in torture chambers, mad-houses, operating theatres"?

The Old City, meanwhile, seems to have gone to sleep in a cloud. The Jewish Quarter, including its 27 synagogues (report the correspondents with the Arabs), is a mass of debris, shoulder-high.

Sunday to-day. Don't know how I came to think of it. Who bothers about what day of the week it is? But recalling Sunday, it suddenly occurs to me that (besides the little Ratisbon chapel bell) I haven't heard church bells for months, it seems. No church bells and no clocks. What happened to them? Stopped? Blotted out? Deadened by the shells? Who would ever have thought a Sunday would dawn without church bells pealing through Jerusalem?

7 June

I WON'T FORGET LAST night. I saw the road, and the men who are making it, the stream of supplies and arms flowing to the city. I travelled along it. The ride itself was an epic. The knowledge of the strategic victory in the making filled me with exaltation. But most of all I was moved by the ingenuity, determination and devotion of the men.

A. himself took me down to the last loading base in the Judean hills. A starry night, cool and clear, and my eyes quickly grew accustomed to the darkness. It was a fantastic picture, like a scene out of purgatory. A turmoil of trucks, jeeps, mules and men under the starlit sky, the men bowed, twisting, writhing like slaves under cases of all sizes. The dark masses of hills looming up all around. The flash from shells and shots from the Latrun battlefield a few miles away.

From the base I went down with a train of empty jeeps that had come up full. The start of "the road" proper is a dusty track. "Road" is a euphemism; so is "track." It is an uneven lake of dust, churned up by the jeeps into endless swirling pillars. But that didn't last long. We came soon to the bed of a *wadi*, hastily rough-hewn, full of sharp twists and turns, with half the rocks of the world, it seemed, deposited there, and dust between them. We jolted along without lights, not even the light of a cigarette. No conversation, except the driver's whispered cursing heard through the muffled whirr of the jeep's engine. In the distance the boom of cannons and drumming fire from Latrun. The only light was from stars, fireflies, the yellow flares that rose from Latrun, and the probing fingers of searchlights that flickered occasionally over the single low ridge that stood between us and the battlefield.

We pitched and tumbled and jolted, the jeep creaking in every joint. We ricocheted from side to side. Sometimes the jeep could

move no further and we jumped off to coax it between the rocks
with our shoulders. I hardly knew whether we were travelling
uphill, on a hilltop or in the bed of a *wadi*. It was a clambering
over rocks all the time.

We passed squads of men clearing away rocks, and engineers
improvising surveys and planning in the dark. It was too close to
the enemy for blasting; further along, A. had told me, they were
using dynamite. We stopped to make way for oncoming traffic,
jeeps and mules, carrying supplies for Jerusalem. Once it was a
herd of cattle stumbling along beneath heavily-laden saddlebags,
doing double duty as pack animals and as meat for Jerusalem. We
passed men waiting to instruct the drivers or to pass on messages.

Then we came to Jeep Junction. For a few miles beyond here
the route runs close to the battlefield; the noise of the jeeps would
give them away at once. A loop over the hills lower south, now
being rough-hewn, will be usable in a day or two. Until that
is ready a human mule-train carries the loads across this stretch.
240 men, most of them immigrants a few weeks from the deten-
tion camps at Cyprus, volunteered for the task. Twice nightly, an
hour and a half each way, they stumble and slip across the rocky
defile, each carrying a 60-lb. load in a jungle-pack on his back.

I watched them come up in single file out of the darkness, a
long line of phantom shapes, bowed under their loads, each man
with a gun over his shoulder. I saw them drop their loads, flop
on to the earth to rest from their gruelling march before turning
back. After a while I spoke to them, in low tones. They had
brought flour. Panting still, they answered in brief, disjointed
phrases; in Yiddish, for they know no Hebrew yet. "Bread for
Jerusalem . . . for the children," one said. A group that had
come in earlier assembled for the return trip and to bring the
second load. They lifted their empty packs and rifles, fell into
line and moved like wraiths down the tortuous path. Then darkness and silence consumed them. I was stirred, and very proud.

I could have gone on, to Hulda, to Tel-Aviv. How I longed
to do so! But I couldn't get back the same night, and Ruth—
whom I told I was going out on defence works—would go mad

with worry. I stopped awhile, watched a mule-train come in, saw the precious sacks and cases being loaded on to jeeps, spoke to some of the men. One told me that camel trains had been tried, each animal carrying a quarter of a ton, until one of the animals bolted. They caught it before it could reach the Arabs and give away the secret, but they gave up using camels.

An engineer mentioned some of their problems. Altitude isn't the most serious; the highest hill is not more than 600 feet. The big problem is the rockiness of the route. Higher up they are using two bulldozers. He told me that a petrol pipeline is being laid alongside part of the route; tanker trucks do the job over the rest of the route. Over one gulley that no tanker can ford, they syphon the fuel from the tanker on one side to empty tanks on the other. Up some slopes the tankers are drawn by tractors; one such slope lay just ahead, a 50-degree climb. In this area, where the Legion might make a sortie at any moment, we have units lying in the shadows on the hilltops. Elsewhere, the route is unprotected.

I asked the engineer about himself. By day he lays and removes mines and does other combat work around Bab-el-Wad. Rest? He laughed. The road was a tonic, he said; he didn't need rest.

Back again the way I came, this time in a convoy of loaded jeeps, each carrying one quarter of a ton. It was slower now, but I felt just as beaten and pummelled at every twist. Around Latrun the shelling went on intermittently. The irony of it! There they were fighting to keep us besieged, and here our supplies were slipping through, just out of their sight.

A. was still at the mountain base. I learnt from him that our flour in Jerusalem is practically exhausted, that for days we have depended on these nightly supplies. Twelve tons a night are getting through; Jerusalem needs 17 tons daily. In three or four days we shall be getting 20.

I don't think I ever enjoyed a stranger emotion than on entering the city last night. Shells were falling in different parts, but I hardly heard them. When I reached home the sky was growing grey with the first hint of dawn.

8 June

A DAY OF FRIGHTFUL shelling; some claim the worst we have had yet. The Legion Commander in the Old City told correspondents that he is firing ten cannon shells for every mortar shell of ours. Michael says about 60 shells were counted in the centre of the city in two hours this morning. Five fell in our street during the afternoon, and lots more around us. I kept uttering a silent prayer that our own guns, coming in their parts along the road, would soon re-pay the enemy in full measure.

To-day's shelling has cast people's spirits down to the trough. I heard a woman half-sobbing, say something indistinct, in a thick and trembling voice, then: "God! How long must we bear this?" Mrs. R. in a desperate tone in the shelter this evening: "When are we going to answer back? All the time, all the time, it's against us."

I notice, nevertheless, many people greeting each other now with *Yihye tov* (It will be all right) in place of the usual *Shalom*. Bernard Joseph broadcast a "Be strong" message to the people; few heard it. (Our own wireless set is hardly working now, and no battery replacements to be had.) A new poster appeared on the hoardings: "In that day it shall be said to Jerusalem, Fear thou not; and to Zion, Let not thine hands be slack" (Zephaniah).

I feel such a powerful bond with these people. Nothing, it seems, can ever be stronger than this community of feeling between us which is reflected when one thinks, "We are the people of Jerusalem. We are living through this together." Strange that I am moved more by this feeling than by the sorrow which death arouses. I am stirred the more, somehow, because I know, and they don't, about the road and how near deliverance lies.

Victor C. killed to-day, and yesterday Yitzhak B.-D. died of his wounds. Victor went through World War II; all the way with the Eighth Army; fought in the hills for months—and must be killed walking up a street in Jerusalem! A few months ago I would have said it seemed impossible that someone I liked so well, who was so whole and full of vitality, whose teeth flashed in such a warm smile when I saw him walking into the *Mateh* yesterday, could be blotted out just like that to-day. Now, here I am, only slightly shaken by the news. That seems more horrible than anything.

The Etzion women have come home, to the State of Israel whose existence they know nothing about. First held in Bethlehem, then in Hebron, then sent—part of the way on foot—to the Transjordan P.O.W. camp at Mafrak. I think of the reunion of Don and Tamara, and of 80 other women with their families; and of all the families who will be reminded again to-day that there will be no such reunion for them.

Bernadotte is still mediating for the cease-fire, but people aren't talking much about it (except Etzel). The Israel Government agrees to segregate immigrants of military age during the cease-fire. No word yet of progress with the Arabs.

To-day I passed the only professional prostitute I know of in Jerusalem. She was hurrying along, much thinner than usual and more worn, wearing a short, untidy frock and high-heeled shoes. Dilapidated, grey-faced. In the past she stood out, her profession proclaiming itself in every gesture and every look. Now, nothing unusual or distinctive about her, just part of the battered scene.

Stirrings in Rome: a report that a Prince Gianfranco Alliator, a monarchist Member of the House of Deputies, is organizing a group of 500 noblemen for a "twentieth-century Crusade to defend the Holy Places." Another despatch about a world-wide appeal by a group of Franciscan friars for Christian volunteers for "a Holy Land Legion" to guard shrines in Palestine; their banner to be the white flag with the Cross of Jerusalem.

9 June

BERNADOTTE HAS FIXED the cease-fire for Friday, 10 a.m. Two more days—if it comes off. One is full of doubt. There have been announcements before, and cease-fires before, and always something went wrong. But it looks rather different now. Bernadotte strikes one as clever and cautious. In him, U.N.O., for the first time, seems real.

The Arabs have climbed down a long way from their previous minimum terms. How different life here would have been had Whitehall's experts not allowed Arab bluster to work its magic on them! But the siege of Jerusalem is not to be lifted, as far as the truce conditions are concerned. The main road is to be kept closed; we are to get food, through the Red Cross, measured out for 28 days only; no fuel or other supplies; no traffic with the outside world; even strangers caught here by the siege cannot, apparently, return home. On the general immigration issue, Jewish immigrants of military age are to be held in camps under U.N. surveillance.

Cease-fire prospects have spurred both sides to go all out in the remaining few days. Yesterday evening we attacked Musrara Quarter in two columns. The battle lasted all night and we drove them from house to house. By this morning a large part of the Quarter was in our hands. The roar of Arab shells, for their part, has enveloped us even more than before. Strange how little the Arab troops are ready to fight. A few hundred Arabs ready to die for their cause in those first days, and Abdullah might have been King of Jerusalem to-day.

Decided to forage for lunch in town, as both Ruth and I had to be there towards midday. Found Ophir open again, and meat once more on the menu; microscopic portions. The waitress (in uniform—off duty from the Army) said she thought it was the last of the Kiriath Anavim cows. Those much-consumed cows! I thought I knew better, but hugged my secret to myself. What Ruth calls a "new, new look" has invaded the tables; no cloths or full sheets of tissue paper now, but only carefully cut paper squares. I notice people leaving the restaurant taking with them their half-finished slices of bread.

An acquaintance of Ruth's who sat at our table told us of this incident: he was in a group putting up an anti-tank block last Saturday when an Orthodox young man from Mea Shearim passed by on his way from Synagogue. He stood watching them, then suddenly asked if he might help. They thought he was joking; such open and voluntary desecration of the Sabbath is unheard of, even in these days, among the ultra-pietists. But he was in deadly earnest.

"If the enemy chooses a Sabbath to violate the Holy City, is there a greater *mitzva* (righteous deed) than to help frustrate them?" he asked.

He placed his neatly-folded Sabbath *kaftan*, *shtreimel*, prayer-book and velvet embroidered *tallith* bag on a rock, and set to work. The sweat poured from his red face down his curly beard and side-locks and on to his white Sabbath shirt. He puffed and coughed under the weight of the rocks. But he stuck it for over two hours. Then he went to the side of the road, murmured a short prayer, and staggered home.

The *Palestine Post* (multigraphed again to-day) reports an extraordinary statement by Bevin to the House of Commons yesterday: "I say that the Arab Legion did not start the battle in Jerusalem. The attack was made on the holy places of the Arabs. I hope the House will pay some regard to the holy places of others, as well as their own." Even more than by Bevin, one is staggered by the gullibility of the House of Commons.

Night

I went this evening to see Don, who is temporarily at Hadassah's emergency hospital at the Convent of St. Joseph. He is in bad shape, but filled with happiness at Tamara's return. They would not let him get up to meet her, but she has already been to see him. He was almost apologetic about his personal joy when there is so much suffering around him. He will not stay long, as there is no room at Hadassah and, I suspect, little that they can do for him at present. He was lying on a palliasse on the stone floor of a small cellar.

His ward was bad, but when I visited the others after leaving him, I felt sick in the pit of my stomach. Men, women and children, with bodies crushed, torn, mutilated beneath the bandages; eyes blinded; teeth knocked from their jaws. I wondered how Edward, who walked around with me, could examine these bodies day after day and retain his equilibrium. Most were civilians, many of them children and old people unable to understand what had happened to them.

"A clean gunshot is child's play to treat compared with these," Edward said with a helpless gesture.

He told me they are short of some essential drugs, cannot sterilize their instruments properly, and must count each drop of fuel. The position has improved slightly in the last few days, but is still appalling. I saw some patients lying two in one bed. Strangely little moaning. Most lay docile; some looked dead already. Edward was called away to a truck-load of 28 more wounded just brought in.

A nurse told me: "From here we bury about 30 people every day. We can take only the very badly wounded. There is no room for the others."

The convent was taken over as an emergency hospital when the Arabs cut the road to Mount Scopus. The French nuns previously conducted a school here for 600 Arab girls from the neighbouring countries. Most of the girls managed to return to their homes. A few remained, and are still here. The nuns also remained, and everyone spoke with deep gratitude and respect of their help and devotion. I saw the nuns in their black robes and white coifs moving quickly and silently about their tasks, some even speaking a little Hebrew. The top floor of the main building was first turned into the principal ward, but six direct shell hits on the roof and 50 in the courtyard made them transfer the wards to the store-rooms, in the basement. The dark, dirty cellars were renovated, shelves turned into bunks, and the windows bricked up.

Have just heard faintly on the wireless that as a gesture to de R. of the Red Cross, who is leaving Jerusalem to-morrow for Amman, the Arabs have offered to observe a cease-fire from 8 a.m. to 2 p.m. to enable him to leave the city without danger. The Jews have accepted the offer.

10 June

LAST DAY BEFORE cease-fire; 27th day of consecutive shelling, and the bitterest. For the first time they are firing hundred-pounders.

The six-hour "Red Cross Truce" was a farce. Thinking that *this* little truce, which the Arabs themselves proposed, would be respected, many people went into town. A sense of almost cheerful expectancy. Shops that had wares to sell were open and people crowded them, spending money for the pleasure of it. Ruth went, too. Housewives, chafing for normal life again, were buying crockery, household articles, even dress materials and ribbons; parents queued up to buy toys. Shop-owners said people were hungry to buy, vying with each other to get served first. Judy was with Ruth and felt uneasy all the time. "Something phoney about this truce," she said. Suddenly, the familiar shrieking tore the air. People were indignant even more than frightened.

"It isn't 2 yet. What do they mean by it!"

Shutters came banging down, everyone dashed into shelters, and in a few seconds the streets were empty. De R.'s party, caught in the thick of it, also had to take shelter. Eventually, a 2-hour stoppage was arranged, during which the Red Cross cars got away and the shoppers ran home. Then it started up again in howling earnest.

Depressed by a talk I had with L. K. I met him wistfully trying to buy something for the *Shevuoth* festival, "a tin of sardines or some other luxury, even at the blackest black-market price"; all he got was a bottle of sweet wine. He tells me the situation in Jerusalem, in spite of our road, is perilous. Little over a week ago soldiers in some parts were being fed only on bread and synthetic chocolate spread. The fuel position was catastrophic and the last remnants of oil in central-heating systems throughout the city were requisitioned as fuel for the bakeries.

"Our supplies are down to rock bottom. They would starve us out if we didn't have a cease-fire."

I was shocked to learn that we cannot get sufficient supplies to keep us going by the new road until it is vastly improved, and that will take some time. Nor does he believe that we could continue much longer fighting as we are doing. The same handful of men carry out all the major operations, one day on the northern front, a few days later on the southern; and they are nearly done in. Without real armour, we cannot, he thinks, hope to beat them, for all the extraordinary courage and mobility of our men. Nevertheless, but for the situation in Jerusalem, the Government would not have agreed to the cease-fire, he says. Some equipment *is* coming in and new men are being trained. In spite of our plight, our leaders consider the Arabs beaten morally, and believe that a supreme effort would soon defeat them also militarily.

Intense fighting all over the country. We have pierced the outskirts of Jenin in the Triangle; Arab villagers who took refuge there have fled again, with the rest of the civilian population. Air attacks against our settlements all over the country. The little settlement of Nitzanim in the Negev fell yesterday before overwhelming Egyptian aircraft, tank and infantry attacks. But everywhere else in the Negev the Egyptians are on the defensive. One of their forces is besieged, and we have cut their main line of communications. Egyptian communiqués are full of ghost victories at unidentified places; also a report that a woman settler of Nitzanim is to be court-martialled for mutiny: found in a dug-out after the place was taken, she shot three Egyptian officers dead before being removed.

The cease-fire is on everybody's tongue. They ask each other what is the first thing they want. "Food and a bath" is the general reply. Ruth wants a quiet week-end, "with not even the sound of a falling leaf." Only the Etzel continue to regard the cease-fire as a calamity, their paper raving hysterically against the Jewish leaders, "slaves by their very nature, who never raised a finger to bring freedom to the people in Jerusalem."

Three shells exploded in quick succession somewhere near us. I was thinking how stupid it would be to get killed now, a few hours before the truce, and imagined my death being announced just as everything was quiet again. Suddenly, in the brief lull that followed, a boy's shout split the silence. It came from about a block away. The cry was more terrible even than the shells: "*Ima* (Mother). . . . *Ima*. . . . *Ima* . . ." each call louder and more horror-stricken than the last, and the third broke down in sobs.

An abominable day. I feel nervous, restless, like an animal when the wind is changing. Will it really be cease-fire to-morrow?

11 June

IT IS FRIDAY AFTERNOON, first day of the cease-fire. Not a shot in 7 hours. A strange feeling to sit before the open window without having to keep an ear cocked for the sounds outside. "This is one of the great days in the history of the United Nations," says Trygve Lie, its Secretary-General.

From midnight until 7 this morning they plastered Jerusalem as they have never done before; seemed determined to shoot off before cease-fire all that remains of the stock pile of shells they have been hoarding for years. It sounded like the end of the world. We sat in the shelter, not even trying to talk. On the dot of 7 it stopped. I had to shake myself to get the noise out of my head. At 9 it started up again. The last shells fell at 5 minutes past 10. I don't know the extent of the casualties. M. tells me of four men killed in a house near hers at 3 minutes to 10.

At 10.30 the streets began to fill. People walked warily, close to walls, running past open spaces. Later they appeared on roofs, for the first time in weeks. Through glasses I saw Arabs on the walls and roofs of the Old City.

The streets grew fuller as the hours passed. No gladness on people's faces, only a kind of dazed relief. I saw some of them crying and embracing each other. Children came out again into the city's streets. Shops opened, but not many. "I've a spending fever," I heard one woman say. I met L. wearing a spotless white shirt; said it was his last clean one; he had kept it for just this occasion. He had just been to collect some laundry handed in six weeks ago. But the laundryman didn't believe in the cease-fire, or perhaps he was away on duty, or dead; anyway, his shop was not open.

Went into a café; all they could offer me was some foul coffee and a thin slice of bread coated with glutinous mixture they called jam. The place was full, buzzed with talk and an under-current of exhilaration. Everybody asking the same questions: Will it last? Will food be freely available? And water? Kerosene? Electricity? Buses? Will they let us visit Tel-Aviv? What does the State look like? And if the cease-fire lasts the full four weeks, what then?

As we walked up Ben Yehuda Street we heard the edgy, tinkling, scraping sound of glass being swept up in the street. We looked around, slowly taking in all we saw. Disfigurement, wretchedness, desolation. Piles of debris. A few scraggy, hungry cats scratching fruitlessly among the garbage for scraps that weren't there.

Ruth has set out the pictures, carpets, ornaments, valuable books in their old places. On the water-tank in the kitchen she has painted bright patches of flowers and the legend "HAPPY TRUCE."

"And to-night we'll sleep in our own room, in our own beds," she says. "No more passage floor at Ks.'. . . . No more shells. Is it possible?"

Bad news: Just learnt that Colonel David ("Mickey") Marcus, "the American Colonel," was killed last night on the Latrun front—and by one of his own men! A strange and tragic accident. The sentry challenged him during the night. His response was not clear and the sentry shot him dead. Discovering whom he had killed, the soldier tried to shoot himself, but was disarmed.

12 June

A precarious peace, like an ominous waiting stillness. Ruth dreamed all night of shelling. Others say the same. I looked around for signs of real cheerfulness, but there isn't any. Perhaps people are over-weary.

Shabbath to-day, and the streets are full. Friends meet or seek each other out and are grateful that they are alive. Some look with a shocked air at shattered houses and broken roofs and seem unaccustomed to the glaring sunshine. Others go about saying "Good day" to perfect strangers.

I go into the little park; only a few people there, sitting in the shade of the trees or standing about, savouring the quiet, the sensation of safeness in just being in the open. I, too, stand there and feel as though I have plunged into a bath of silence. I notice a pretty frock, and some children with toys. Karamba stiffens and pricks up her ears; another dog has ambled in.

Went visiting this afternoon. The same cycle of talk. The news of the road is out; enormous excitement as people pass it on. Can we use it during the cease-fire? If fighting is resumed, will we be able to hold it?

We have just had supper, opened the tin of caviare, carefully cut the remaining bread of to-day's ration into one slice for each, spread the shred of margarine, distributed the balance of the soup from lunch. In the dim light (made out of oil and a cork) we sat and talked, listening unconsciously for "the sounds." All we hear is the crickets. What long ages since we last heard that! I feel painfully hungry, more than ever before.

Evening

Into town this evening. Streets filled with people strolling—how quickly they have learned to stroll again!—by the light of the moon. At one street corner a group of boys and girls have joined hands to dance the *hora*. Cafés, lit by candles or small kerosene lamps, are packed. Some have stopped serving because their water ration has given out. But the people sit on for the pleasure of being in a crowd.

18 June

T HE FIRST WEEK OF the truce is gone. The same strange, uneasy feeling all the time, suspension between war and . . . we don't know what. At the back of your mind the thought recurs: Don't relax too much; nor let the narcotic of quiet delude you. Keep ready. All around, the guns still point at you. This isn't peace. . . .

But it's quiet. The dead are buried, and the maimed and wounded are still out of sight. How quickly the dead of yesterday are forgotten—unless they be your very own. Life strives to take shape again, closing up its gaps.

We watch the moon rise quietly, silvering the old stones. A few nights ago there was conscious rest and peace in that sight. Now we are impatient. We are hungry. There are a thousand things we want daily and can't get, a match, a cigarette, a book, a Tel-Aviv newspaper, a sound of music, a bath, contact with the world. But the main road has been cut by the Arabs in five places and is still mined, and most of what comes by our own road goes to replenish our empty warehouses. Still no water except the ration. Nor electricity, except for a few rare hours a week.

The Mediator and Bernard Joseph are still arguing about the quantity of food we should get. Our people ask for 4,200 calories a day, to make up for the 800–1,000 daily average we have had in the last few months. Bernadotte thinks 2,400 enough. Whatever it is, *when* are we going to get it? Yesterday a crowd from the poorer quarters demonstrated before the Jewish Agency buildings.

With the quiet has come the after-effects of tension. People are irritable, full of bitter retrospects. You feel the sagging of their will. Ruth says:

"Everything is angular; people and their tempers. Nothing is round or smooth any more."

It is hot, and bodies smell, and the toilet is more horrible than ever.

We had not bargained for this kind of quiet. The city is almost dead. Business life paralysed. Many people without work or money; I wonder how they will pay for the food when it comes.

Everybody is trying to get to Tel-Aviv, but only a few of the privileged have been taken by jeep along the new road—the "Burma Road," someone has called it, and the name has stuck. Tel-Aviv is everything normal, vital and desirable. Tel-Aviv is the capital of our young State, leaping into shape. It is life, vigour, energy, activity, all the qualities that have been battered into quiescence here. From Tel-Aviv two days after the cease-fire they went out and established three new settlements on the land. Here, attention is riveted on destruction; there, on building, growth.

By the same route a few Tel-Avivians have come to us. Saw L. to-day, looking very sad and shocked. "I am weeping for Jerusalem," he said in his dramatic way. His grief was real, but I was impatient with him.

The Bs. are returning to America, heavy-hearted, and a little conscience-stricken. They came to stay. They say they will return when Judy gets her strength back. Just as those who left at the start of the siege can never be in quite the same world as we who remained, will always, in some sort, be exiles when they return, so those who lived through the siege have won a new bond with Jerusalem, and I think it will persist.

Reports come in of Arabs and Jews fraternizing across no-man's-land from the first day of the cease-fire. "Friends, friends, come along," shouted Legion troopers coming up from Damascus Gate towards the Jewish positions in Suleiman's Way. "What do you need? What are you short of? We will buy it for you."

"Give us bread and we give you cigarettes," another group of Arabs called out, approaching the Jewish lines at Deir Abu Tor. Told they must leave their guns behind, they hurried back and returned, with a white flag.

Near Ramat Rahel, Arabs suggested to Jews: "Come, let's

have coffee." Three Jews were given leave and went with the
Arabs to their post in the nearby Arab village. Then they were
invited to Bethlehem to lunch.

These are the small people of the country, but without whom,
as Ecclesiastes said, "cannot a city be inhabited, and they will
maintain the state of the world." They go on their way from birth
to death wanting only the simplest necessities of living, to feed
themselves and rear their children. And, left to themselves, what
do they do? Call out to each other: "Let's have coffee." "Friends,
friends, what are you short of? We will buy it for you."

How little have these ordinary people ever been left to
themselves!

Bernadotte has arrived in his white plane—"like a dove of
peace over the skies of the Holy City" is how N., the Belgian
Consul-General, describes it.

25 June

LESS THAN TWO WEEKS of the truce to go, and Bernadotte still trying to prevail on the Arabs to let water flow through the pipe to Jerusalem. They have not stopped raging about the "Burma Road": threatened to bombard it out of action if we continued using it. We replied that we are entitled to keep on using any route which we were using before the cease-fire. The Mediator agreed, but finally prohibited us from using it for bringing in arms. The main road has been opened to food convoys under U.N.O. supervision. Food is coming in, about 200 lorry-loads daily, but our rations became reasonable only to-day. Still no agreement on the number of calories. Anyway, a good deal of what is coming in, especially by our own route, is finding its way to the warehouses against the probable resumption of the siege.

Got our first fresh vegetables a week ago: a ration of 3 oz. of onions. Odd thing on which to break our fast; yet I counted 128 people in an onion queue. Yesterday our greengrocer somehow got hold of a few oranges, and I watched him distributing a slice to every customer. Carefully dividing it to ensure the waste of not a single drop of juice, he handed out each portion like a priest bestowing a benediction. Electricity still comes on for tantalizingly few hours once in so many days, and only a miserable ration of kerosene has been distributed.

Bernadotte must work fast if he hopes to find a permanent solution in the short time left. The Arabs already say they will refuse to extend the cease-fire. Most new suggestions, especially from London, have the same old end in view: a pocket Jewish State, or a scheme of federalism, the Jewish State firmly under Anglo-Arab control, either way. L. writes from London that British Middle East experts had forecast a war of attrition between Jews and Arabs which would suck the strength from both sides. It would end, they thought, with Britain as mediator and a special status for her in the final settlement. That still appears to be their idea, and even now they seem to think they can force it on us through some side-door.

More than ever we feel that the cease-fire is nothing more than a breather in which both sides are re-grouping and preparing for the final show-down.

Few Jews take seriously now the talk of an international régime for Jerusalem, at least for the New City. The Arabs ran away, the Arab States turned their guns on it, and the Jews alone have defended it. These months have given it added holiness in Jewish eyes. What did the nations do to save it? Even the special Mayor whom U.N.O. appointed never took office. And what a scene communal strife and international intrigue Jerusalem would become under international administration! After a great rumpus (inspired in the main by the Vatican), the Nations will probably agree finally on some kind of international authority (bound to be uneasy) over the Holy Places alone; and include the New City in Israel, linked by a corridor.

Ben-Gurion is in town, on his first visit since *Pesach*. Saw him in the street to-day, greyer than before, graver, unsmiling, striding along as though his eyes were fixed just above ground. But you know that his quick glance takes in everything around him. A bodyguard of two armed men walk some distance behind him. Talk is that Etzel, embittered by the Government's shelling of their secret arms ship near Tel-Aviv last week, may try to kidnap him.

Mail is beginning to dribble in to the city by plane; a few Hebrew newspapers also found their way up from Tel-Aviv. Everyone posting letters and hoping for the best. Fifty telegrams, of not more than 10 words each, are accepted at the post office daily, but the queue is full long before the Post Office opens.

The Bs. are putting the final touches to their packing. To-morrow they leave for America.

26 June

THE Bs. HAVE LEFT. There were three armoured busloads of
Americans travelling to Haifa by authority of the Mediator and
under protection of the American Consulate. As we stood by the
bus, no one said much. Probably the same thoughts were in the
minds of the four of us, the same flashes of days and moments
we lived through together. Whatever we said, it wasn't what we
felt. Judy stood silent, tears in her eyes. Michael busied himself
with the luggage. A man from the crowd came up with a little
girl and drew Michael aside: Would he take the child to her
mother in Haifa? He and his wife had been separated by the
siege. He would never forget the kindness. Michael couldn't do
it. The American Consul was standing by to see that only the
registered Americans boarded. Ruth recalled that it was just
three months since we were last at the Egged bus terminal,
when we came up in the convoy. It had just been snowing in
Jerusalem then; it is high summer now.

Many of the departing Americans were elderly, Orthodox
people who had come to the Holy City to spend their last days
here. "I suppose they don't want to die too soon," someone
remarked. A woman sat quietly in the bus, her lips moving
hardly perceptibly. The buses moved off abruptly. Ruth and I,
sad and quiet, walked back through Ben Yehuda Street.

29 June

We are going to-night to Tel-Aviv. The mere thought of it sends a thrill through me, and Ruth!—she has been in a continuous ferment of excitement since we got our permits yesterday. We are travelling by army bus along the "Burma Road."

Yesterday I was taken out to Ramat Rahel. A haunting desolation; masses of debris; communal buildings, dwelling-houses, byres, sheds, wrecked and burned. Everywhere the stench of death. The blackened corpse of a burned Egyptian soldier lies on the wreckage of a hillock, and a cow's tail peers stiffly from the rubble of a byre. Relics of toys among the wreckage of the children's nursery. A half-burnt Passover *Hagadah* buried in the debris of the dining-hall. Snapdragons and geraniums still growing before one of the shattered houses, beneath twisted coils of barbed wire.

Amidst the ruins one sensed the elation of a triumphant stand in a vital spot. Six times it changed hands during the most critical stages in the fighting for the city. The settlers were evacuated, and only soldiers are guarding it now. Bethlehem lies about two miles away; through glasses I saw Egyptians working on their fortifications.

One of the settlers was with us.

"Twenty-five years of our strength and energies lie buried here," he said.

Last night we met Tamara. Don, up and about now, with his hand in a sling, brought her up to us. She is very striking; Ruth thinks her beautiful. Her face is full of character and intelligence. Dark, strong, high cheek-bones, and out of her khaki shirt her neck rises to the undaunted bone of her chin. But it is her eyes, grey and bright, that are entrancing. She did not say much about her own ordeals. She spoke mostly of "Mosh," the Haganah

Commander of the Etzion Bloc, told us of one of his last Orders
of the Day: "I do not believe we can get reinforcements and our
position is precarious. But we are the advance post of Jerusalem.
We shall hold it whatever the cost."

Don is his old laughing self again. There is a great tenderness,
hardly veiled, between him and Tamara. He speaks of their
settling in Jerusalem.

30 June

I AM WRITING THESE lines seated on the terrace at Mark's in Ramat Gan. It is 7 a.m. and we have been in Tel-Aviv since 1 a.m. I am exhausted and could sleep all day. But how can one sleep now in Tel-Aviv? Will leave that for Jerusalem. I begrudge the time even to jot down these notes.

We left in a convoy of Army buses at 6 yesterday afternoon.

"I am alive, and travelling to Tel-Aviv," Ruth exclaimed, as if hardly able to fathom it.

We look at the hills around Jerusalem, like parts of a great living body sunk in sleep. We drink in everything: the glowing sunset over the Judean mountains; the Arabs of Abu Ghosh, strolling normally through the village; their roadside coffee-house, where Jews and Arabs sit side by side; the hilltops, scenes of so many bloody encounters; the blackened wreckage of the food trucks strewn in the ditches.

It is dark when we pass Bab-el-Wad. A Jewish soldier examines our papers at the check-post, a uniformed U.N.O. observer looks in and gives a cursory nod. . . . We turn into the Burma Road. Wider and far less rocky than when I travelled on it three weeks ago, but is still excruciating.

This time our head-lamps are on. They light up the great pall of dust that rises from the wheels of the bus ahead. It is so thick that our lights barely pierce it. Shrubs on either side show up enveloped in white dust, like the edge of a snow landscape. Great boulders, all in the prevailing white, jut sharply into the road. The stones and corrugations toss and bump us without end. I recall my previous journey here, but Ruth cannot imagine anything worse than it is now. Even so, one barely recognizes when the bus is on a rise or in a trough; it's a perpetual up-and-down. Men are working all along the road; some direct the traffic at the more dangerous twists. Iron mesh has been laid down at the

sharper turns as a grip for the wheels. Sections of a water pipe-
line lie by the roadside: our new water pipeline that will make
us independent of the old one through Latrun. A fellow passenger,
an Army engineer, tells us the story of the pipes. A few years ago
they were held in readiness to provide an emergency water service for London during the Battle of Britain. The *Keren Kayemeth*
bought them for its water pipeline to the Negev.

In the distance, long, uneven lines of headlights move towards
us, up and down, up and down, like a line of warships in a stormy
sea: a supply convoy to Jerusalem.

Most of our passengers are Army men and the snatches of conversation are mostly military. I hear two officers behind me
remarking on the physical condition of some of their men. They
talk already in that professional tone which does not exclude
sympathy but seldom expresses it. They discuss the fighting in
the Negev, the extraordinary bravery of a unit I have never
heard of, "Samson's Foxes." One tells of the Sudanese who are
fighting in the Egyptian Army: they walk straight into the line
of fire like toy soldiers.

Most passengers wear handkerchiefs over their noses and
mouths, against the dust. Everyone is coated in dust from top to
toe; those who haven't hats are completely white-haired.

. Dead-beat, we reach Tel-Aviv at midnight. It is blacked out,
but there is movement in the streets. The family overjoyed to see
us. The question we had asked ourselves, What shall we do first?,
answers itself. A hot bath is waiting, and a real meal. Gratefully,
we eat apples while having a bath. We let the water run, and
splash in it like children on their first day at the sea. Then
a meal. . . .

Have been munching fruit since I got up. Breakfast now—a
real breakfast, eggs, toast, coffee, cheese. Then into town.

2 July

Two days in Tel-Aviv. After Jerusalem, it is like emerging from a nightmare into the brilliant light of the sun. Everywhere delirious enthusiasm for the State, immense assurance. Incessant, surging movement.

If Tel-Aviv, too, has been at war, you can tell it only by the omnipresent khaki, the military traffic and the black-out. The streets are crowded, people eat well, sit at ease in the packed cafés, patronize beauty parlours, cake-shops, gift-shops, stand window-shopping amidst the endless clatter of traffic, queue up for seats at concerts, theatres, opera, cinemas, lectures. They jump on buses, order taxis, switch on lights, turn on the water without giving it a thought.

They are full of sympathy for Jerusalem, go out of their way to be helpful to offer you courtesies. In the restaurants they give you "special portions for a Jerusalemite." Strangers come up, shake you by the hand, ask questions, are gratified to learn that anything of Jerusalem still stands.

They exult in the State, and are tremendously proud of the infant Army and its victories. The future is uncertain, but Tel-Aviv doesn't doubt that if the Arabs resume the war they will be beaten. Just how it will be done they have no idea, but everyone believes now in miracles.

"Isn't it *all* a miracle? The State itself? The way we have held the Arabs?"

They take unashamed delight in every new feature and trapping of independence. *Our own* Cabinet Ministers, diplomats, officials, police; our own stamps, *Official Gazette*, ration books. They remember to tell you that the Prime Minister still wears an open-necked shirt (his formal wear he calls his "working clothes").

The State is a visible fact. It is confused, but feels its way forward all the time. Nourishes itself from its own flesh and faith. Plenty of muddle and self-criticism, and the red tape will doubtless come. But the dominant spirit is the vast enthusiasm. Everybody ready to accept new responsibilities without hesitation.

Small men who were "native" clerks or policemen or mechanics under the Mandatory Administration now have their chance. Without a tremor (that the outsider can see), they occupy the new seats of authority. One is dubious about how some of them will shape. There will be mistakes galore. "Of course. That's how we'll learn."

Shiploads of immigrants come in almost daily, all penniless refugees from Europe. There are plans for great new housing schemes, settlements, enterprises of all kinds; but already some are bogging down in face of the preparations for war and shortages of essential requirements. Many immigrants are broken in body, and even more broken in spirit. They need social and health services on a vast scale. They must be educated in the duties and responsibilities of nationhood, and in the needs of this land, so different from Europe. Where are the experienced people and resources to carry all this out?

War damage is slight. There are buildings wrecked by Egyptian raiders, but you have to look for them. Few people believe in the truce, and everyone bitter with U.N.O. Strikingly designed posters demand sacrifices, proclaim: "The whole country is the front. The whole people is the Army."

For hours yesterday Ruth and I just walked, allowing ourselves to be carried away by the dream come true. We looked at all the signs of Israel re-born, at the people. We looked at the food-shops stacked high with provisions, at the fruiterers' crates overflowing with abundance, at the smart clothes in the windows. Suddenly Ruth, bethinking herself that she looked thin, pale and ugly, made straight for a hairdresser. It didn't help her much, because her hair, the hairdresser said, was brittle; she could not, he thought, be having enough vitamins.

We walked into a confectioner's, but Ruth found the display

overpowering; not knowing what to choose, in the end she chose nothing.

Last night we went to the theatre and found the tickets sold out; but hearing we were from Jerusalem, they found us seats. Saw *He Walked Through the Fields*, a new Palmach piece. Not great, but a sincere and moving story, well-acted. Uri might be any one of the hundreds of Palmach boys we know; Mika, any of the young girl refugees with a Nazi-scarred past; Willy and Avraham and Rutke, almost any *kibbutzniks*. The pattern is the pattern of life all around us, a people hungry for normality and equality, for status; struggling with one hand to build itself up and with the other to hold off its enemies. . . .

We are sitting on a café terrace by the sea. This evening are going to hear the Symphony Orchestra; Izler Solomon, the American, will be guest conductor. The Mediterranean is indescribably beautiful in the last rays of the sun. Laughing children, brown as nuts, are still playing in the sand. Joy fills me at being alive, at being in the front row of the building up of Israel. I try to analyse it all, but it's hard. Perhaps I am weary. The outlines remain fuzzy in my thoughts. So I give it up, just sit and feel and drink in the sounds and sights, and the brine of the sea.

A little while ago I heard an immigrant, speaking in Yiddish, at the table behind us, tell his companion that before he came he dreamed only of Tel-Aviv; but now he wanted to go on the land.

"I was a book-keeper in Budapest," he said, "but in the camps they taught me what labour is. I want to start life anew, like Israel, for myself now. I want to dig my hands into the earth and know that it is mine and that I'll never have to leave it."

4 July

I HAVE SEEN ISRAEL, not only Tel-Aviv. For two glorious days we travelled up to Galilee. We saw enthusiasm and disorder, and old wine with new labels and new wine in old bottles. We saw the land, horribly disfigured sometimes, but mostly following its own ways. We saw and heard so much in these crowded hours that I cannot here put down more than the briefest notes of some of it. Now I know how painfully little came through to us in Jerusalem; and even so I have only touched the fringe.

Our furthest destination was a little Arab village, Tubeh, midway between Rosh Pina and the Syrian frontier in Upper Galilee. A group of us, all newspapermen except Ruth (and she, for the occasion, found herself accredited), were taken there to meet Sheikh Husein Mahommed Ali Abu Yussuf, of the tribe of El-Herb—of the Army of Israel! But almost every inch of the way held its own story.

We travelled in an Army car up the coastal road to Haifa. It hummed with traffic, mostly military, all in their mud-brown camouflage. Soldiers, more affable than formal, stopped us to check our papers. We sped through the Sharon settlements, their white, red-roofed buildings glowing in the deep green sea of orange groves. Only soldiers and barbed wire spoke here in accents of war. But near the edge of the Triangle were scattered marks of Transjordan and Iraqi guns. Yet it remained incredibly peaceful to the naked eye. The clusters of houses around the high water-towers, the cool avenues of trees, the signs of careful cultivation—how could this be a land at war? Yet a bare three miles to the east stood enemy guns, and somewhere on the quiet blue sea, a mile or two to the west, Egyptian warships were on the prowl.

Beyond Athlit we passed the first Arab villages, heaps of ruins, bereft of all sign of life. But a little way further was Fureidis village, with Arab *fellaheen* harvesting their crops: the old familiar scenes of donkeys and camels laden with sheaves, and muzzled oxen patiently circling round and round to tread out the grain on the threshing floor. The villagers of Fureidis, who had submitted to Israel troops before the war engulfed them, were to continue their regular life, unmolested.

Haifa. Massive damage where the fighting had been. The ghost town of the Arab quarters, all except one quarter completely deserted. The white-and-blue Israel flag over the port, evacuated a few days ago by the last British troops. At the docks one of the "illegal immigrant" ships, seized by the British, but now back in use.

Freshly painted signposts in Hebrew, and old signs of the Mandatory Administration in the former three official languages. Immigrants in the streets asking directions in a score of different languages. The factories working at high pitch for the war. Jewish policemen in the former uniforms of British constables. The primitive airport, with its Jewish immigration and Customs officials, all in a single uniform, worn by soldiers and most civilians alike: khaki shirt and shorts. And the big thing: It all works! How much we feared the hiatus between the chaos left by the departing British and the smooth functioning of our own Administration!

Then on through Emek Jezreel, historic old Esdraelon. In ancient days it was the granary of the land, and in peaceful days it still is. A commonwealth of settlements of men and women who work the nationally-owned land and employ no labour, a peasantry of a single generation that looks as though its ancestors were never separated from the soil. . . .

Past the Balfour Forest, an evergreen memorial to a man who spoke for the bigness of England. High up in the mountain, cupped in a hollow, lay Nazareth, where Kaukji's men are regrouping. Then straight across the floor of the valley to Ain Harod. Nothing but fields all around, and the occasional music of tractors going out to reap, and women and children, and some men, harvesting their crops.

On the tip of the Gilboa range that closes in the broad valley plain to the south stands Zere'in, once the site where Israel crowned its kings. Barely a month ago it was a forward post for the Arab Triangle. From its height, fire poured steadily down on to the Emek, whose settlers had to work their fields under armed escort. Traffic between settlement and settlement also ran the gauntlet of fire that poured down from the hilltop. (Once Zere'in was the best of neighbours with the Emek.) Haganah set out to clean it up, but found a virtual fortress, and were repulsed. They came again; this time Zere'in fell, its Syrian band and the villagers augmenting the rising tide of refugees flowing into Jenin.

We stopped at Ain Harod, the largest settlement in these parts. Their main task to-day is to gather in the crops. Closer at hand, you see how some of the fields are choked with thistles. Like every settlement, Ain Harod has a heavy quota of men in the Army, and the few who remain do guard duty as well as work. No one is too old or too young to lend a hand.

They tell how at nights the Emek looks like an illuminated map with cords of light from the searchlights of the settlements and signals flashing back and forth. In the mornings the *Tnuva* (co-operative marketing organization) trucks are on the roads collecting the milk from village to village; the output has dropped, but not a morning has been missed. A simple thing, but to the people of the Emek a signal that another night has passed and all is well. The Emek isn't secure yet. When the cease-fire started, its men were denting the sides of the Triangle in the south. But in the north Kaukja's reorganized force is vigorously preparing, by all accounts, to resume the fight.

I looked for the State in the Emek. But there was nothing new to see; it has been there all the time, since the first settlers drained its swamps a quarter of a century ago. Only at Ain Harod we remembered Zisling, who serves all week as Minister of Agriculture in the Government, but resumes his normal duties when he comes home to Ain Harod for week-ends; for the present, it's his turn to help distribute food to his thousand comrades at mealtimes.

On to the old Crusader fortress of Belvoir at Kaukab-al-Hawa
—the Wind Star—magnificently situated, and still a valuable
fortification. An Arab band held it, but we captured and retained
it in face of repeated attacks by Iraqi land and air forces. Had
coffee with the fortress commander in his dungeon H.Q., which
one enters through a window. . . .

Eastward into the Jordan Valley, Kinnereth, Dagania, Beth
Zera. Not much farming here; no voices of women and children;
buildings crashed in by bombs; lawns seared; barbed wire and
double trenches; only figures (some young women among them)
carrying rifles. A disabled Iraqi tank, which reached the front
garden of Dagania before the men in the trenches, a foot away,
could halt it.

A few miles away at the other side of the Jordan Valley,
Massada and Shaar Hagolan, right on the enemy border, both
of them evacuated by the settlers after heavy attacks, then
occupied and razed by the enemy. Some shaking of the head at
Dagania about the evacuation: "They were in a tight spot, but
so were we all. They should have held on."

They told us about Ashdod Yaacov, lower down the Valley.
The neighbouring fields of Beth Zera had been completely destroyed by Syrian incendiaries, and the settlers of Ashdod were
not going to let that happen to theirs. So they harvested after
midnight, going out armed with a Bren gun and machine-guns,
and camouflaging their tractors and combines. One of their best
fields was on the Gilead slopes, within easy range of Syrian guns.
They called it Narvik Field, having reclaimed it from desolation
and sown it at the time of the Battle of Narvik. Here, too, they
went out at midnight. A dark night, but the Syrians detected
them, and their heavy guns started blazing down. The settlers
flopped into the furrows; when a lull descended, they resumed.
At dawn Syrian planes came over, but the Narvik crop had been
harvested.

Everywhere I find excitement at meeting a traveller from
Jerusalem. Some seem disappointed that you are not a bag of
bones. They ask about Jerusalem even before they know you

come from there. Once we passed an armoured car that seemed to be having engine trouble. (It was really a steel-plated tender, but pretended to be an armoured car.) We stopped to ask if we could help. "Everything's fine," they said. "What's the news from Jerusalem?"

Tiberias, Galilee, Abu Yussuf—further notes must wait. This is our last day in Tel-Aviv before returning to Jerusalem, and we have other use for it than writing notes.

6 July

Back in Jerusalem, sombre, brooding and still half-numb. After Tel-Aviv, what a lesson in contrast!

The Arab League has rejected Bernadotte's proposed solution, and declines to send representatives for further talks at his Rhodes headquarters. The Jews will also certainly reject the proposal, which is a sharp revision of U.N.O.'s Partition Resolution. Under the new plan, Jerusalem would go to Abdullah. (Bernadotte doesn't believe in internationalization; compares the prospect with Berlin's position to-day.) More startling still: Israel's defence and foreign policy would be ingeniously "co-ordinated" with Transjordan's. One of the Hebrew papers calls it an attempt "to harness our defence and foreign policy to the chariot of Abdullah's master, Britain." Bernadotte's shares have slumped.

Still light during part of our journey back from Tel-Aviv. The road looks as fantastic as it feels. Nothing stirs in the hills or grey-brown land, and Arab villages lie dead among fields that are still half-alive. . . . An overturned oil tanker; two wrecked food lorries over a precipice; a saloon car that boldly tried to negotiate the road but failed, bulldozers, men (most stripped to the waist), machines, working on the road and laying the pipe-line. The road plunging this way and that, but irrepressibly forward. We get caked with dirt, and have to use half the day's water ration to wash it off.

The soldiers in the bus were something of an international unit in themselves. We spoke to them during a halt. A Hollander; a Dane (Gentile) who fought with the R.A.F. during the war; a murderous-looking Moroccan who was with the Free French. A small, thin dark lad, whose shirt was too wide for his scraggy body and his khaki shorts too long, came from Hadhramaut in Arabia.

There was a Canadian who had fought on the beaches of Normandy. The fellow who interested me most was my neighbour. Tall and lean, everything about him was wiry. During most of the journey he looked steadily and silently through the window. Suddenly he turned and asked me in German:

"Who worked this land?"

"Arabs," I said.

"They till the soil badly."

He spoke in a deep, sonorous voice, his speech almost clipped in its sharpness. He told me that he arrived in the country three weeks ago.

"Were you a farmer?"

"No; a soldier."

"Before you were a soldier?"

"I have been a soldier from the age of 16."

He was born in Poland. During the war he fled eastward before the Nazis, finding refuge in the Soviet area. They placed him in the Red Army. He fought subsequently on many fronts, Stalingrad among them. Then they transferred him, as a Pole, to the Polish Army. Demobilized two months ago, he was permitted to go to relatives in America. But news of the fighting in Palestine roused his dormant Zionist sentiments, and he came here instead. His family in Warsaw was wiped out. He showed me photographs of them, and another of himself as a captain in the Polish *Panzer*. He thinks our armoured equipment ludicrous, but the men fine. He asked me about Jerusalem, and I asked him about Stalingrad. He learnt there how an infantryman fights against tanks, and some other useful bits of knowledge.

During a halt some of the soldiers in the bus started singing Army songs. The Pole joined in, singing the words in Russian. He smiled when I asked him how he knew them. "They are Russian songs," he said, "translated into Hebrew."

Most of the other soldiers seemed Israelis. Two, wearing the new Israeli Air Force badge, looked as if they might have been in the British Army or R.A.F. Their chaffing was full of Hebrew translations of British Army slang. "Why don't you go and die!"

one of them remarked in exasperation during an exchange with the driver. . . .

Feel less gloomy coming back to Jerusalem from Tel-Aviv than we feared. Torn, warped, contaminated, embittered—Jerusalem is still in your veins.

Rations improving: to-day's included 1½ oz. of sweets and 2 boxes of matches. We have brought a suitcase full of provisions back from Tel-Aviv. But no running water or electricity yet.

Everyone eager to hear about Tel-Aviv and the progress of the State. They listen like Rip van Winkles, in wonderment and with envy. Some indignation, too; they feel that Jerusalem is honoured, but neglected none the less.

7 July

THE STORY OF Abu Yussuf.

Was sceptical when I heard of an Arab tribe fighting with Palmach; now I know that it's true. The Jews of the district were friends of his youth. Later, he ran a profitable smuggling partnership with some of them between Syria and Palestine. He never thought much of the Arabs political "bosses" of Safed and wouldn't toe their line. When Arab bands tried to enrol his help against the Jews, he threw them out. One of his sons went over to the bands. But Abu Yussuf continued his friendship with the Jews. When the Syrians began shelling Galilee from across the frontier, his village, Tubeh, was one of their targets.

The Palmach victories on the Lebanese frontier made the first deep impression on Abu Yussuf. And when they took Safed, he decided that his place was with them. He offered himself and his tribe, and they were accepted. Two Palmach officers were detailed to train and lead them. They have seen quite a bit of action. Are fine marksmen and know every inch of Galilee; but sometimes have to be restrained. The old Bedouin habit of looting dies hard; so does their desire to pursue the enemy to the end. Once they helped carry out a raid into Lebanese territory.

"But the job done, they wanted to go on and drive the enemy right up to Beirut," said one of their Palmach officers.

Only a primitive camel track between basalt boulders joins Tubeh to the Upper Galilean highway. The village is a wretched, shapeless place: about half a dozen stone houses, some double-storied, and a few scores of black camel-hair tents (marks of Abu Yussuf's Bedouin origin) sprawl like the skins of wild cats pegged out among the rocks. The characteristic Arab village smell of charred wood, grain, smoke and camel dung. The wistful notes of a shepherd pipe. A few women watching our approach from behind the tent flaps. But no sign of men.

Turning into the centre of the village, we found the reason. Headed by Abu Yussuf and his sons, about 100 men of Tubeh lined the path waiting for us. Some clad in a motley mixture of khaki uniforms, others in native costume, and all heavily armed. Over his black traditional Arab dress and black *kaffiya* (kerchief), Abu Yussuf himself wore the tunic of a lieutenant of the French Army. A pistol and jade-handled dagger were stuck in the cartridge bandolier around his waist. The old man's face, brown-black as his native basalt, full of dignity and charm. His eyes lively and dashing, and black-pencilled with antimony. A Vandyck beard trimmed off his sinewy face.

The reception room of the guest-house was half European, with torn sofas and chairs of startling design; stone floor carpeted from corner to corner. The walls were pinned with pictures of Arab rulers, including King Farouk of Egypt and President Kuwatly of Syria, now enemies of Israel. Abu Yussuf of the Palmach apparently forgot to take them down.

Lunch was a feast: large bowls of *lebben*, platters piled high with boiled and grilled mutton, and an enormous tray of *cali*, the ancient dish of roasted young corn that Boaz once tendered to Ruth. The Sheikh and his twelve sons stood behind us caring for our wants. Abu Yussuf himself handed round bowls of fruit. His handsome eldest son, with eyes fixed on Ruth (and Ruth discreetly responding), held a jar of water, waiting to fill our glasses.

One of our party asked Abu Yussuf what made him fight with the Jews.

"When I make friends I cherish them," he replied. "Is it not written in the Koran that the ties of neighbours are as dear as those of kin? Our friendship with the Jews goes back for many years. We learned from them and they learned from us. We felt we could trust them. Then a time came when they helped me, after I had been betrayed by my own people. . . . This is not a religious war. The city *effendis* started it. Our Moslem Prophet told us to follow the right, and I believe the Jewish cause is right."

Abu Yussuf bade us farewell as he welcomed us, hand to his heart, then to his head, and a slow bow.

"We have honoured ourselves," he acknowledged our thanks.

H., the Military Governor of Safed, and N., of Tiberias, who came with us to Abu Yussuf, kept us enthralled all the way with their talk. H. told us that "Mickey" Marcus, the American Colonel who had inspected Safed from the air a few months ago, said that 10,000 men would be needed to take it, and he described to us how, in the event, 400 Palmach men took it in under 24 hours. Told us how the Lebanese Army ran almost before they got into action; how Druses were slipping across the Syrian frontier to join the Jews in the fight against the Syrians: how Christian Arab priests went out into the roads in Galilee trying to stop Christian Arabs from fleeing, saying no harm would come to them (numbers of Christian Arabs did remain, some even in Safed).

N. told about an Arab friend of his from Safed whom he saw in Haifa the other day. The Jews had two good allies, the Arab said; Arab fear and the lies of the Arab leaders.

'When fear attacks you, my friend," he said to N., "it spreads like a plague, and your finger can't pull the trigger and your eyes don't see straight and you run like the wind. And you think of the terrible stories the Arab notables tell about what the Jews do to the Arabs who fall into their hands, and you run still faster."

"But you know the Jews so well," N. pressed him. "Why did *you* flee?"

"I thought maybe I know them only 90 per cent. Perhaps the leaders are right about the other ten per cent.," he said. "So I also fled."

We gave a lift at Rosh Pina to a husky young American. We asked what brought him here. He replied:

"Well, I thought Palestine was full of Jews with long beards wanting to pray at the Wailing Wall, and I wasn't going to let any Goddam Arabs stop them. . . . Now I find it plenty tough to keep up with these Jews."

8 July

THE LAST DAY OF the truce. To-morrow, by all the signs, it will be war again. The Arabs refused Bernadotte's request for a 30-day truce extension. Earlier, the Jews accepted it. Bernadotte is arranging to withdraw the U.N.O. observers to-morrow, but will continue his efforts for a solution. His immediate concern is to try to obtain the demilitarization of Jerusalem.

In their hearts, most people, I think, are resigned, as I am, to a resumption of the battle. We speculate about how we will take it. Has the truce refreshed us or sapped our resistance? I think it has stiffened us. The feeling seems to be: this time they must be taught a lesson. But the other half of my mind keeps remembering the crying of the shells, the horror of the bodies at Hadassah.

The Arabs haven't been idle in the truce. The Legion has brought up masses of armed Bedouins from the desert and entrenched them along the Jerusalem highway. They have built themselves new roads. The Egyptians have linked up with Arab villages in a tight quarter-circle to the south-west of the city. They and the Legion have brought up more heavy guns.

But for our part, we are also far better off than we were. Arms have come in by yet another hush-hush route through the mountains. About 8,000 trucks of food entered the city, besides the tens of thousands of food parcels that poured in from all over the world for people in Jerusalem. If the battle breaks out again, we shall be able to face it very differently from the last time.

Whatever happens, I don't think we shall ever again feel as isolated as we did. The letters that came to us during the truce, some of them three or four months old, echoes of the prayers, greetings and gifts from friends we know and from far more whom we don't, all the precious little bonds with the millions of ordinary people outside who deeply feel with us, that is another link in our armour. I don't think we felt the strength of it before these days.

Something more: Jerusalem has never been so united. Once you felt that it was in truth the most international city in the world, a kind of window looking out on the vast universe; peoples, cultures, communities, sub-communities, religions, sectaries, races, colours, languages. Even among the Jews, diversities that span the whole globe in space, and thousands of years in time. And now they are all one. No less the Gentiles who have remained, the Christian priests, the Greeks, Armenians, the handful of retired Englishmen, all feeling the same crash of shells and getting the same rations, all for this once are united with us. I wonder if Jerusalem has ever been so undivided before; and if over there in the Old City the same unity prevails. Our reports are that most civilian Arabs of the Old City have left.

We collected three more food parcels to-day: one each from Haifa, America and South Africa. Urchins with prams or home-made wheel-barrows stood offering their transport for hire. Prams are the commonest form of civilian transport these days. . . .

New wave of spy rumours; but this time it is more than idle talk. Just heard the strange story of T.,[1] a Russian-born Jew who lived here for 25 years, held an important senior post in the Haganah, then in the Israel Army, and was convicted last week by a military court and shot as a spy. Was said to have passed on information about our arms and the location of workshops and factories. The story is that he got mixed up financially with some Englishmen while serving as Chief Engineer of the Electric Corporation, and through them got involved.

---

[1] An Israel Court of Justice in November, 1949, found that Meyer Tobiansky had been innocent. Lieut.-Colonel Isser Beray, former Intelligence Chief of Haganah, later of the Israel Army, was found guilty of manslaughter and given a token sentence of one day's imprisonment. The Court ruled that Beray's negligence in setting up a field general court-martial of three junior and judiciary inexperienced officers and in ordering an immediate execution without awaiting confirmation by the Jerusalem Commander was unjustifiable and was responsible for this tragedy. Lieut.-Colonel Beray indicated that he would appeal against this conviction.

The T. case may be connected with to-day's further sensation: Etzel's seizure of five British officials of the Electric Corporation as alleged spies. Y. tells me that the Army has been keeping some of them under observation, but Etzel decided, apparently, to get in first. They will certainly be forced out of Etzel's hands for proper trial or release.[1]

Another spy report: Stern Group posters on the hoardings announce the execution of Mrs. Rosa B. "after trial on charges of revealing Jewish military positions to the enemy, and of acting as informer against their Group during the British Administration." We are supposed to have an Israel Military Governor in Jerusalem and administration under the authority of the Israel Government. But the Dissidents go their own way, a law unto themselves. That's what comes from the uncertain political status of Jerusalem. As long as that persists, the Dissidents will go on setting themselves up as the only real champions of the city.

Surprised and delighted last week to have a wire from the Bs. in Haifa that they were staying on, after all. Waited for further word, hoping they would return to Jerusalem, but heard to-day that at the last minute they sailed.

I am writing these lines by lamplight, thanks to the three rations of kerosene we got during this truce. Ruth is preparing supper, a real supper, and cooking it on a real stove in the kitchen. In spite of our little hoard, we have decided to go slow on food. Who knows how long it may have to last? And the memories of hunger are still too fresh.

Sounds of mortaring and sniping from the Old City. Just the usual infractions of the truce, or is the truce finally melting away? To-morrow we shall know.

[1] Subsequently tried by the Israeli Courts and acquitted.

9 July

AT 9.35 THIS MORNING, twenty-five minutes before cease-fire formally ended, the battle broke out again. Arab guns opened from the Old City, and from Bethlehem and other outskirts soon after. Confess I didn't like it, especially the roar of the hundred-pounders, which sound so overwhelming in their power. For a few minutes I felt my heart beat faster; but it passed.

Most people appear calm, as though the shelling were a usual thing. Some jokes about it, most of them a little hollow. I vividly remember the crashes of the first shells. Nothing is so effective a second time, not even shelling. Although I half-expected it to be so, am still surprised by the calmness people show. Many must be afraid, but hide it. Only at Dr. B.'s I saw an elderly spinster, with features drawn, who couldn't hide her fear.

"I keep on remembering," she said, "the man who was killed near me the day before the truce started."

Dr. B., dispensing calm:

"But we've got big guns now ourselves. We'll teach them this time. And don't you remember how our buildings took the shells? Why, every house is a fortress! I can laugh when I think that an Englishman forced us to build our houses of thick stone. Sir Ronald Storrs it was, when he was Governor of the city. He said you had to build in stone to preserve the character of Jerusalem. That's why even British shells can't flatten our houses."

The spinster felt better.

Again the Arabs are bombarding every part of the city, switching back and forth, as they did before. Our office building had a direct hit in the first hour. The alarm bell rang, people went down to the shelter, and the first-aid girls explained again the procedure in this eventuality and that.

The streets are almost empty again; shops closed; children out

of sight. Continuous movement of Army traffic. I watched a unit
drive out towards the west: brown-skinned, confident-looking,
but rather quiet. I wondered what makes one unit sing when it
goes out into action and another keep silent.

There's fighting in the city. We attacked Sheikh Jarrah, and
the Legion counter-attacked. They are using their tanks now.

First news from the rest of the country: our forces advancing in
Galilee, Jordan Valley, Lydda. In the Negev the Egyptians, who
renewed the fighting yesterday, recaptured an Arab village, but
took some heavy blows to-day; 300 of their men killed, including
200 Sudanese. Egyptian Spitfires bombed Tel-Aviv; Syrian
raiders over Galilee.

9 a.m. A pitch-dark night. The guns are racketing all over. On
the city's south-western outskirts, towards Ain Karem, incessant
mortar and machine-gun fire; from the direction, sounds as
though the attack is ours, and Ain Karem the objective. I think
of the handful of friendly Russian monks and nuns, and Miss
Carey's rest-house, now become a geographical name even on the
maps. Muffled echoes of more fighting north-west of Bethlehem;
are we out to turn the Egyptians' flank? From Nebi Samwil, the
multiple roar of hundred-pounders sweeping towards us like a
broken echo.

Try to guess what lies ahead. . . . Tons of iron, and mangled
bodies. But I am confident. We shall win. I think of seething
Tel-Aviv, bursting with assurance, of the Emek and Galilee, of
the men who conquered those swamps and rock and desert, and
their sons now facing the invaders.

The Ks. have invited us again to sleep in their passage, but
we shall sleep in our own room.

12 July

BERTIE CAME IN THIS evening to tell us: Tamara is dead. I thought I was hardened to death. Is one ever hardened to it? The thought of Tamara and Don stands like a weight between my eyes, all my thoughts keep stumbling against it.

She was killed early this morning by a sniper's shot or stray bullet while on duty in Mea Shearim. They couldn't reach Don until after she died.

It seems so incongruous, and so doubly cruel. She, who survived Etzion, and had so much for which to live. I hardly knew her; yet I seemed to know her well, through Don's laughing eyes and warm voice, and the embarrassed, awkward way he first spoke of her; as though he were offering into the bright light something which was still too big for his own grasp. . . .

All over the country the fighting is going remarkably well, both in attack against the Legion and Iraqis, and in defence against the Egyptians. In Jerusalem there is stiff fighting inside the city and on the outskirts, and all of it in our favour. The shelling here goes on, frightful and implacable.

15 July

OUR MILITARY SUCCESSES grow more striking every day. On every front, except the little wedge held by the Syrians in Galilee, Israel's advance gains momentum. And with it, a new sense of urgency seems to invade U.N.O. The Security Council has ordered a cease-fire, of indefinite duration, to start three days from to-day. For the first time in U.N.O.'s history it is invoking Chapter VII of its Charter: drastic sanctions. Now it is claimed that hostilities in the Holy Land constitute a threat to world peace. Now, apparently, that the Arabs are coming to grief.

The most extraordinary success is on the central front. Lydda and Ramleh and all the territory up to the edge of Latrun fell in 48 hours! A catastrophe for the Arabs. The battle was amazing; it started with a Palmach column in armoured cars and jeeps bearing machine-guns blazing its way through the main street of Lydda. Up the street they swept, then swung round and came back the same way. Nothing survived that came in their path. That blitz knocked the fighting spirit out of Lydda. The Legion tried to mount a counter-attack. Heavily reinforced, they advanced with tanks on the single Israel battalion. But the Palmach didn't wait; they swept out to meet the Legion in another hurricane attack. Only pockets of Arab resistance were left after that. Next morning all Ramleh, too, was captured. This conquest not only drives the Legion from the coastal plain, but also threatens their position around Jerusalem. Now we can close in on Latrun from three sides. . . .

Similar swift enveloping movements are pushing back Kaukji's forces in Galilee and threatening his rear. We are driving on Nazareth, the key road junction controlling Central Galilee. In the south, the siege of Negba broken, an Egyptian battalion routed. At least 1,000 Egyptian casualties inflicted and prisoners taken in five days. Cairo bombed.

In Jerusalem, the main fighting, on our initiative, is on the outskirts. Seems designed to isolate Latrun from its bases at this end. The Arab shelling keeps up, on the same endlessly grim level. But now our own heavy artillery is replying. For the first time, the Legion's main supply route from Transjordan, via Jericho, is under Israel fire.

Politically, the Arab states aren't happy either: the Arab League is torn by dissension. But the Hebrew Press warns the Jews not to be led into a too easy optimism; the war has still to be won, militarily and politically, and Bevin is still trying to squeeze Israel into boundaries "the size of a coffin."

16 July

WE'VE HAD AN AIR-RAID, first in Jerusalem's history. Even the Nazis avoided that, but the Arabs couldn't resist. Fortunately, little damage.

It started about an hour after midnight. I woke up feeling Ruth gaze into the darkness with a fixed look. Then I heard the plane flying round and round in the sky. "Must be ours," I said. But the way in which it just circled steadily, like a dentist's drill spinning round in your tooth, gave us the creeps. Then the siren cleared its throat, but its thin wail was drowned by the crash of the first bomb. It fell very near us and Ruth grew worried, Foolishly, I wouldn't go down to the shelter, but at the second bomb we compromised, and went into the passage. And still the plane went round and round with impunity, knowing that we have no defences. It was like some malignant giant leisurely hunting down its prey with an exactly calculating eye. Then the third bomb. When the raid was over, the shelling started up again, more viciously than ever. Woke up this morning, bleary-eyed and unrested, to learn that the bombs all fell in our street. They tried so hard, and accomplished so little.

Fighting all over the country is growing, dominated by a sense of urgency, a race against time before the new cease-fire. Our successes continue. Only a week ago they would have seemed unbelievable, but now we expect them. Those 28 days of truce made Haganah into an Army, and seem to have given it even greater speed and mobility. Here in Jerusalem we have captured more commanding heights beyond the city.

The great battle for the Old City, predicted and expected for several days, has not yet taken place. The Arab League agreed in principle on the demilitarization of Jerusalem, but on its own terms and only for the Old City!

The Arab flight is assuming massive proportions. The bulk

are not being evacuated; they evacuate themselves, fleeing before the fighting reaches them. And nobody seems to be giving much thought to them, not even the Arab states that got them into this tragic plight. Most Arabs have no heart for the war, and never had. Now they run, most of them without even a notion of where they are going. Some have never been 20 miles from their own village. Yet they get up, collect their wives, children, belongings and flee. To our eyes most of their villages are pretty miserable: primitive, backward, filthy; mud walls and grimy floors. But they have their own easy life, their cluster of traditions, customs, beliefs. Doesn't the *fellah* see any significance in his abandonment of his home, in the destruction of his life? Isn't it worth making a stand for? Does he know why he flees?

L. was telling about the refugees he saw fleeing to Transjordan. An inert mass, sunk in a frustrated despair. He asked some of them why they were fleeing.

"The Jews!" they said.

L. asked them:

"What did the Jews do to you?"

"They didn't do anything to us. We didn't see them. But we heard . . ."

'Do you know what you will do in Transjordan?"

"No; but the great King Abdullah will look after us until the Jews are driven out."

So they tramp towards a phantom heaven. The same is happening all over. And as the tide flows past, other villages become panicky and fearful in turn, and join the stream.

Once L. saw a Jerusalem effendi and his family hooting his way through the shuffling mass. He leaned back on the upholstery with the distinction of a ruler, put his head through the window to shout at someone for not moving quickly enough out of the way. L. saw him again in Jericho, dividing his wrath between "the Jewish criminals," Britain, U.N.O., and "our braggarts who call themselves soldiers."

Electricity came on last night for a few hours, and the shelling came on at the same time. So we had Beethoven and shells together. The kids below woke up and kept singing out for all the world to hear, "*Lanu yesh or! Lanu yesh or!*" ("We've got lights! We've got lights!") The way the electricians keep repairing the essential lines (which get cut again every day by the shelling) for hospitals, bakeries, printing presses is splendid. They go out by day in an armoured car, observe the damage through a peephole, memorize it, and return during a lull in the shelling at night to make the repairs in the dark.

11 a.m. now, and the war seems to have gone to sleep for the morning. The birds are chirping outside, the green leaves of the carob and fig trees in the garden are fluttering faintly against the soft blue sky, the street is perfectly quiet, and all seems as peaceful as a parsonage garden.

18 July

THE SECOND CEASE-FIRE has begun. From 7 this evening the guns are silent. This morning's newspaper headlines tell the news: "Nazareth Occupied by Israel Army without Bombardment"; "Arab Refugees Choke Galilee Roads"; "Old City Walls Pierced"; "Israel Planes Raid Damascus"; "Fierce Attack on Arab Triangle."

Without the wireless-set it has been hard to keep pace with the news of growing victory from day to day.

The Israel Army Staff vigorously opposed acceptance of the truce. For it robbed Israel of the victory at Latrun that was within its grasp; leaves the Egyptians holding most of the Negev, the Legion still masters of the Old City, and Kaukji in a stretch of Galilee.

But the success is fantastic. Alone, Israel has implemented the partition decision of U.N.O. And more. Beyond the proposed frontiers, it holds 550 square miles allotted to the unborn Arab State, 6 towns and 112 of its villages; from Jerusalem it holds a clear five-mile corridor to the coast. In the last 9 days of fighting it inflicted over 5,000 casualties on the Arab armies.

For its part, Israel lost 33 square miles of the Jewish State, most of it, however, unoccupied desert around Beersheba, and 12 Jewish settlements (11 of them in the Arab area). Against the whole Arab world and its 30 millions, the tiny new-born State and its 700,000 people have held their own. What a lesson in the power of faith and the insubstantiality of mere numbers!

Last night, the most shell-shattered night we have known, we sat in the shelter for the last time. The attack on the Old City was on, and this morning we learnt that a 1,000-shell barrage from our guns and mortars preceded it. They called it Operation *Kedem* (Antiquity), for it took place on the anniversary of the day, 2,500 years ago, when the walls were pierced by Nebuchadnezzer's Babylonian Army.

The clock moved slowly in the shelter, yet we sat indifferent to the shells. Somebody was saying he still wakes up early every morning with a feeling of hunger. Reuvy told of a unit coming in from Ain Karem with a captured Arab flag at its head and a captured black umbrella at the rear. A little girl said she had long stopped counting the small bullet and shrapnel holes in the outside walls. Next to me, the old evacuee from Beth Israel sat poring in the dim light over his book of Psalms. He read aloud to himself:

> *As for man, his days are as grass;*
> *As a flower of the field. . . .*
> *For the wind passeth over it and it is gone;*
> *And the place thereof shall know it no more.*"

R. was saying, in explanation of the Arab defeat, that Arabs never had stamina; like the Arab horse, which runs magnificently, but stops dead after a short distance; like their literature, which shines best in gem-like verses and epigrams.

The shelling lasted till dawn. We went back to bed long before the end of the shelling and our restless sleep was nibbled at by a thousand sounds and bursts from the Old City. . . .

And now it is truce. This evening Ruth and I went walking in the *wadi* at Mer Salabe. The old man who lives next door to us was there, too; we recalled how he used to take his walks back and forth, back and forth, in the tiny space between the entrance gate of his house and the street corner, so as to slip in as soon as the shelling started; we smiled again at the memory of the way he would peer around the corner, as though a shell might be coming down the street.

Another man sat motionless on a rock overlooking the valley. His body slouched, his head hung down, and the cigarette between his fingers was guttering out. My mind flicked back to Don as I saw him last a few days ago, his face gone quite small.

There was not a light anywhere in the world, it seemed,

except the stars. Everything was black. From the distance came the ghostly call of jackals. Suddenly in the far hillside a lamp lit up. I remembered such a single light on a hillside in Spain when I sailed once in a little vessel up the coast; a dark night, it was, like this, and we saw the lamp still shining out, an unmoving sentinel, long after we passed the spot.

"Soon the lights will be coming back."

Ruth broke the silence; then paused:

"And we are alive, perhaps for a long time!"

Behind us, the shadowy skyline of Jerusalem rose up, dimly, in the dark.

GLOSSARY

Agudat Yisrael (Heb.). The organization of ultra-Orthodox Jews in Israel and abroad.

Ashkenazi (Heb.). Literally: German. Jews hailing from Northern, Central and Eastern Europe.

Baruch Hashem (Heb.). "Praised be the Lord."

Bezalel (Heb.). School of arts and crafts in Jerusalem.

Cali (Ara.). Dish of roasted young corn.

Chasid (pl., *Chassidim*) (Heb.). Pious man, "saint."

Chassidim (Heb.). Members of a mystic sect, particularly followers of Rabbi *Baal Shem*.

Diaspora. Literally: "Dispersion"; Jewry outside of Israel.

Doar (Heb.). Post, mail.

Emda (Heb.). Position, stand; post (in military sense).

Emek (Heb.). "Valley"; commonly used to refer to the Valley of Jezreel.

Esther. See *Purim.* Heroine of the *Book of Esther.*

Etzel (Heb.). See *Irgun Zvai Leumi.*

Fantaseeya (Ara.). Form of Arab celebration, characterized by horse-galloping and shooting in the air.

Fellah (pl., *fellaheen*) (Ara.). Arab peasant.

Gadna (Heb.). Haganah auxiliary unit of boys and girls under seventeen.

Hablan (pl., *Hablanim*) (Heb.). Saboteur; sapper.

Hacham (Heb.). Title for a Rabbi of a Sephardic congregation.

Haggadah (pl., *Haggadoth*) (Heb.). Prayer-book for family services on Passover Eve, consisting largely of the narrative of the Jewish Exodus from Egypt.

Haganah (Heb.). Literally: Defence. The Jewish Defence Organization of the Jews of Palestine.

Hamsin (Ara.). Sirocco; hot wind from the desert.

Hashomer (Heb.). Literally: "The Watchman." The Jewish watchmen's organization founded in Palestine in the early years of the century; out of it grew the Haganah.

Hatikvah (Heb.). Literally: "The Hope." Hebrew National Anthem.

Hazak v'ematz (pl., *Hizku v'imtzu*) (Heb.). "Be strong and of good courage!"

Hora (Heb.). Popular Israel folk dance.

Irgun Zvai Leumi (I.Z.L—Etzel) (Heb.). Literally: "National military organization." One of the two resistance groups advocating a policy of terror; grew up in the latter years of the Mandatory régime.

Jihad (Ara.). Moslem holy war.

Jewish Agency for Palestine. The authoritative body established by the Jewish people during the period of the British Mandate to represent Zionists and non-Zionists in all matters affecting the establishment of a Jewish National Home in Palestine.

Jewish National Fund (Hebrew name: *Keren Kayemeth Leisrael*). Central Zionist instrument for the purchase and development of land as the national possession of the Jewish people. Established in 1901.

Kabbalah (Heb.). The system of mystical, esoteric knowledge that arose in opposition to the rationalism of the Talmud in the thirteenth century.

Kaddish (Heb.). Prayer for mourners.

Kaffiya (Ara.). Arab headgear.

Kaftan (Heb.). Type of cloak worn by ultra-Orthodox Jews.

Kasher (Heb.). Food prepared according to Jewish dietary laws.

Kevutzah (pl., *Kevutzoth*) (Heb.). Similar basically to *Kibbutz.*

Kfar (Heb.). Village.

Kibbutz (pl., *Kibbutzim*) (Heb.). Literally: "Collective." Type of communal village of workers, owned and administered on a collective basis.

Kol Hamegen Haivri (Heb.). "Voice of the Hebrew Defender." Broadcast service of the Haganah.

Kol Yerushalayim (Heb.). "Voice of Jerusalem." Jewish broadcast service in Jerusalem after the establishment of the State of Israel.

Lebben (Ara.). Curdled milk.

Lehi. See Stern Group.

£P. Palestine pound, equal to pound sterling; divided into 1,000 mils.

Magen David Adom (Heb.). Literally: "Red Star of David." Jewish first-aid organization.

Mas Lehaganatenu (Heb.). Literally: "Tax for our Defence." Imposed in Jerusalem before the Siege.

Mateh (Heb.). Haganah H.Q.

Matzah (pl., *Matzoth*) (Heb.). Unleavened bread served on Passover to recall the Jewish Exodus from Egypt.

Mazal Tov (Heb.). "Good Luck!"

Mishmar Haam (Heb.). Civic Guard.

Mitzva (Heb.). A pious or righteous act.

Moshav Ovdim (pl., *Moshavei Ovdim*) (Heb.). Type of workers co-operative small-holders' village.

Mukhtar (Ara.). Village headman.

Palmach (Heb.). Abbreviation for *Plugot Machatz*. Mobile detachment of the Jewish Defence Organization.

Pegaz (Heb.). A shell.

Pesach (Heb.). Passover. The festival commemorating the liberation of the Jews from their bondage in Egypt.

Peula (Heb.). Activity, operation (military).

P.B.S. Palesting Broadcasting Service under the Mandatory régime.

Peyot (Heb.). Side curls as worn by ultra-Orthodox Jews.

Portzim (Heb.). Literally: "The Stormers." A unit of Palmach.

Purim (Heb.). The Festival of Lots, celebrating the deliverance of the Jews from Haman's plot to exterminate them, as narrated in the Book of Esther.

Seder (Heb.). The home service performed on the first night of Passover (in the Diaspora: on the first two nights).

Sephardi (Heb.). Literally: Spanish. A Jew from Southern Europe and Turkey whose language was originally Spanish or Portuguese. Applied now to all Oriental Jews from Arabic countries.

Shabbath (Heb.). Sabbath (Saturday).

Shalom (Heb.). "Peace." Hebrew greeting.

Shehehiyanu (Heb.). Literally: "He who has kept us alive." Benediction on joyous occasions.

Shevuoth (Heb.). Pentecost, or Feast of Weeks—originally a harvest festival, celebrated several weeks after Passover.

Shofar (Heb.). Ram's horn blown in the synagogue at the most solemn seasons in the Jewish calendar, at the services on the New Year and Day of Atonement.

Slik (Heb.) (from *sallek*, Hebrew: to dispose of or hide). Hiding places for Haganah arms.

Stern Group. A resistance group advocating a policy of terror; adopted the name of "Fighters for Israel's Freedom," whence the shortened name, *Lehi.*

Streimel (Yiddish). Type of felt hat worn by ultra-Orthodox Jews.

Tafkid (Heb.). Duty, task.

Talit (Heb.). Jewish prayer shawl.

Talmud (Heb.), The Corpus Juris of the Jews; a compilation of religious, ethical and legal teachings and decisions interpreting the Bible. Completed about 500 C.E.

Tigboret (Heb.). Reinforcement.

Wadi (Ara.). Dry river bed.

Yahrzeit (Yiddish). Death anniversary.

Yerushalayim (Heb.). Jerusalem.

Yeshiva (pl., *Yeshivoth*) (Heb.). A Talmudic college.

Yishuv (Heb.). Literally: "Settlement." The name of the Jewish community of Palestine before the establishment of Israel.